Employment Protection (Consolidation) Act 1978

CHAPTER 44

ARRANGEMENT OF SECTIONS

PART I

PARTICULARS OF TERMS OF EMPLOYMENT

Written particulars of terms of employment

Section
1. Written particulars of terms of employment.
2. Supplementary provisions relating to statements under s. 1.
3. Certain hours of employment to be disregarded.
4. Changes in terms of employment.
5. Exclusion of certain contracts in writing.
6. Power of Secretary of State to require further particulars.
7. Power to vary number of weekly hours of employment necessary to qualify for rights.

Itemised pay statements

8. Right to itemised pay statement.
9. Standing statement of fixed deductions.
10. Power to amend ss. 8 and 9.

Enforcement of rights under Part I

11. References to industrial tribunals.

PART II

RIGHTS ARISING IN COURSE OF EMPLOYMENT

Guarantee payments

12. Right to guarantee payment.
13. General exclusions from right under s. 12.
14. Calculation of guarantee payment.
15. Limits on amount of and entitlement to guarantee payment.
16. Supplementary provisions relating to guarantee payments.
17. Complaint to industrial tribunal.
18. Exemption orders.

A

Suspension from work on medical grounds

Section
19. Right to remuneration on suspension on medical grounds.
20. General exclusions from right under s. 19.
21. Calculation of remuneration.
22. Complaint to industrial tribunal.

Trade union membership and activities

23. Trade union membership and activities.
24. Complaint to industrial tribunal.
25. Supplementary provisions relating to complaints under s. 24.
26. Assessment of compensation on a complaint under s. 24.

Time off work

27. Time off for carrying out trade union duties.
28. Time off for trade union activities.
29. Time off for public duties.
30. Provisions as to industrial tribunals.
31. Time off to look for work or make arrangements for training.
32. Provisions supplementary to ss. 27 to 31.

Part III

Maternity

General provisions

33. Rights of employee in connection with pregnancy and confinement.

Maternity pay

34. Maternity pay.
35. Calculation of maternity pay.
36. Complaint to industrial tribunal.
37. Maternity Pay Fund.
38. Advances out of National Loans Fund.
39. Maternity pay rebate.
40. Payments to employees out of Maternity Pay Fund.
41. Unreasonable default by employer.
42. Supplementary provisions relating to employer's insolvency.
43. Complaints and appeals to industrial tribunal.
44. Provisions as to information.

Right to return to work

45. Right to return to work.
46. Enforcement of rights under s. 45.
47. Exercise of right to return to work.
48. Contractual right to return to work.

Part IV

Termination of Employment

Section
49. Rights of employer and employee to a minimum period of notice.
50. Rights of employee in period of notice.
51. Measure of damages in proceedings against employers.
52. Statutory contracts.
53. Written statement of reasons for dismissal.

Part V

Unfair Dismissal

Right not to be unfairly dismissed

54. Right of employee not to be unfairly dismissed.

Meaning of unfair dismissal

55. Meaning of "dismissal".
56. Failure to permit woman to return to work after confinement treated as dismissal.
57. General provisions relating to fairness of dismissal.
58. Dismissal relating to trade union membership.
59. Dismissal on ground of redundancy.
60. Dismissal on ground of pregnancy.
61. Dismissal of replacement.
62. Dismissal in connection with a lock-out, strike or other industrial action.
63. Pressure on employer to dismiss unfairly.

Exclusion of section 54

64. Qualifying period and upper age limit.
65. Exclusion in respect of dismissal procedures agreement.
66. Revocation of exclusion order under s. 65.

Remedies for unfair dismissal

67. Complaint to industrial tribunal.
68. Remedies for unfair dismissal.
69. Order for reinstatement or re-engagement.
70. Supplementary provisions relating to s. 69.
71. Enforcement of s. 69 order and compensation.

Amount of compensation

72. Compensation for unfair dismissal.
73. Calculation of basic award.
74. Calculation of compensatory award.
75. Limit on compensation.
76. Compensation for act which is both sex or racial discrimination (or both) and unfair dismissal.

Interim relief

Section
77. Interim relief pending determination of complaint of unfair dismissal.
78. Orders for continuation of contract of employment.
79. Supplementary provisions relating to interim relief.

Teachers in aided schools

80. Teacher in aided school dismissed on requirement of local education authority.

PART VI

REDUNDANCY PAYMENTS

Right to redundancy payment

81. General provisions as to right to redundancy payment.
82. General exclusions from right to redundancy payment.
83. Dismissal by employer.
84. Renewal of contract or re-engagement.
85. Employee anticipating expiry of employer's notice.
86. Failure to permit woman to return to work after confinement treated as dismissal.
87. Lay-off and short-time.
88. Right to redundancy payment by reason of lay-off or short-time.
89. Supplementary provisions relating to redundancy payments in respect of lay-off or short-time.
90. The relevant date.
91. Reference of questions to tribunal.
92. Special provisions as to termination of contract in cases of misconduct or industrial dispute.
93. Implied or constructive termination of contract.
94. Change of ownership of business.
95. Transfer to Crown employment.
96. Exemption orders.
97. Claims as to extension of terms and conditions.
98. Exclusion or reduction of redundancy payment on account of pension rights.
99. Public offices, etc.
100. Domestic servants.
101. Claims for redundancy payments.
102. Written particulars of redundancy payment.

Redundancy Fund

103. Establishment and maintenance of fund.
104. Redundancy rebates.

Section
105. Payments out of fund to employers in other cases.
106. Payments out of fund to employees.
107. Supplementary provisions relating to applications under s. 106.
108. References and appeals to tribunal relating to payments out of fund.
109. Financial provisions relating to the fund.

Miscellaneous and supplemental

110. Strike during currency of employer's notice to terminate contract.
111. Payments equivalent to redundancy rebates in respect of civil servants, etc.
112. References to tribunal relating to equivalent payments.
113. Employment under Government of overseas territory.
114. Meaning of " Government of overseas territory ".
115. Application of Part VI to employment not under contract of employment.
116. Provision for treating termination of certain employments by statute as equivalent to dismissal.
117. Employees paid by person other than employer.
118. Statutory compensation schemes.
119. Provisions as to notices.
120. Offences.

PART VII
INSOLVENCY OF EMPLOYER

121. Priority of certain debts on insolvency.
122. Employee's rights on insolvency of employer.
123. Payment of unpaid contributions to occupational pension scheme.
124. Complaint to industrial tribunal.
125. Transfer to Secretary of State of rights and remedies.
126. Power of Secretary of State to obtain information in connection with applications.
127. Interpretation of ss. 122 to 126.

PART VIII
RESOLUTION OF DISPUTES RELATING TO EMPLOYMENT
Industrial tribunals

128. Industrial tribunals.
129. Remedy for infringement of certain rights under this Act.
130. Jurisdiction of referees to be exercised by tribunals.
131. Power to confer jurisdiction on industrial tribunals in respect of damages, etc., for breach of contract of employment.

Recoupment of certain benefits

Section
132. Recoupment of unemployment benefit and supplementary benefit.

Conciliation officers

133. General provisions as to conciliation officers.
134. Functions of conciliation officers on complaint under s. 67.

Employment Appeal Tribunal

135. Employment Appeal Tribunal.
136. Appeals to Tribunal from industrial tribunals and Certification Officer.

PART IX

MISCELLANEOUS AND SUPPLEMENTAL

Extension of employment protection legislation

137. Power to extend employment protection legislation.

Crown employment

138. Application of Act to Crown employment.

House of Commons staff

139. Provisions as to House of Commons staff.

Contracting out of provisions of Act

140. Restrictions on contracting out.

Excluded classes of employment

141. Employment outside Great Britain.
142. Contracts for a fixed term.
143. Minimum periods of employment.
144. Mariners.
145. Dock workers.
146. Miscellaneous classes of employment.
147. Application of ss. 1 to 4 to excluded employment.

Supplementary provisions

148. Review of limits.
149. General power to amend Act.
150. Death of employee or employer.
151. Continuous employment.
152. Calculation of normal working hours and a week's pay.

Section
153. Interpretation.
154. Orders, rules and regulations.
155. Offences by bodies corporate.
156. Payments into the Consolidated Fund.
157. Northern Ireland.
158. The Isle of Man.
159. Transitional provisions, savings, consequential amendments and repeals.
160. Citation, commencement and extent.

SCHEDULES:
Schedule 1—Provisions leading to suspension on medical grounds.
Schedule 2—Supplementary provisions relating to maternity.
Schedule 3—Rights of employee in period of notice.
Schedule 4—Calculation of redundancy payments.
Schedule 5—National health service employers.
Schedule 6—Calculation of redundancy rebates.
Schedule 7—Calculation of payments to employees out of Redundancy Fund.
Schedule 8—Employees paid by virtue of statutory provision by person other than employer.
Schedule 9—Industrial tribunals.
Schedule 10—Statutory provisions relating to referees and boards of referees.
Schedule 11—Employment Appeal Tribunal.
Schedule 12—Death of employee or employer.
Schedule 13—Computation of period of employment.
Schedule 14—Calculation of normal working hours and a week's pay.
Schedule 15—Transitional provisions and savings.
Schedule 16—Consequential amendments.
Schedule 17—Repeals.

ELIZABETH II

Employment Protection (Consolidation) Act 1978

1978 CHAPTER 44

An Act to consolidate certain enactments relating to rights of employees arising out of their employment; and certain enactments relating to the insolvency of employers; to industrial tribunals; to recoupment of certain benefits; to conciliation officers; and to the Employment Appeal Tribunal. [31st July 1978]

BE IT ENACTED by the Queen's most Excellent Majesty, by and with the advice and consent of the Lords Spiritual and Temporal, and Commons, in this present Parliament assembled, and by the authority of the same, as follows:—

PART I

PARTICULARS OF TERMS OF EMPLOYMENT

Written particulars of terms of employment

1.—(1) Not later than thirteen weeks after the beginning of an employee's period of employment with an employer, the employer shall give to the employee a written statement in accordance with the following provisions of this section. [Written particulars of terms of employment.]

(2) An employer shall in a statement under this section—

(a) identify the parties;

(b) specify the date when the employment began;

(c) state whether any employment with a previous employer counts as part of the employee's continuous period of employment, and, if so, specify the date when the continuous period of employment began.

(3) A statement under this section shall contain the following particulars of the terms of employment as at a specified date

PART I not more than one week before the statement is given, that is to say—

    (a) the scale or rate of remuneration, or the method of calculating remuneration,

    (b) the intervals at which remuneration is paid (that is, whether weekly or monthly or by some other period),

    (c) any terms and conditions relating to hours of work (including any terms and conditions relating to normal working hours),

    (d) any terms and conditions relating to—

        (i) entitlement to holidays, including public holidays, and holiday pay (the particulars given being sufficient to enable the employee's entitlement, including any entitlement to accrued holiday pay on the termination of employment, to be precisely calculated),

        (ii) incapacity for work due to sickness or injury, including any provision for sick pay,

        (iii) pensions and pension schemes,

    (e) the length of notice which the employee is obliged to give and entitled to receive to determine his contract of employment, and

    (f) the title of the job which the employee is employed to do:

Provided that paragraph (d)(iii) shall not apply to the employees of any body or authority if the employees' pension rights depend on the terms of a pension scheme established under any provision contained in or having effect under an Act of Parliament and the body or authority are required by any such provision to give to new employees information concerning their pension rights, or concerning the determination of questions affecting their pension rights.

(4) Subject to subsection (5), every statement given to an employee under this section shall include a note—

    (a) specifying any disciplinary rules applicable to the employee, or referring to a document which is reasonably accessible to the employee and which specifies such rules;

    (b) specifying, by description or otherwise—

        (i) a person to whom the employee can apply if he is dissatisfied with any disciplinary decision relating to him; and

        (ii) a person to whom the employee can apply for the purpose of seeking redress of any grievance relating to his employment,

and the manner in which any such application should be made;

(c) where there are further steps consequent upon any such application, explaining those steps or referring to a document which is reasonably accessible to the employee and which explains them; and

(d) stating whether a contracting-out certificate is in force for the employment in respect of which the statement is given.

(5) The provisions of paragraphs (a) to (c) of subsection (4) shall not apply to rules, disciplinary decisions, grievances or procedures relating to health or safety at work.

(6) The definition of week given by section 153(1) does not apply for the purposes of this section.

2.—(1) If there are no particulars to be entered under any of the heads of paragraph (d) of subsection (3) of section 1, or under any of the other provisions of section 1(2) and (3), that fact shall be stated.

Supplementary provisions relating to statements under s 1.

(2) If the contract is for a fixed term, the statement given under section 1 shall state the date when the contract expires.

(3) A statement given under section 1 may, for all or any of the particulars to be given by the statement, refer the employee to some document which the employee has reasonable opportunities of reading in the course of his employment or which is made reasonably accessible to him in some other way.

(4) If not more than six months after the termination of an employee's period of employment, a further period of employment is begun with the same employer, and the terms of employment are the same, no statement need be given under section 1 in respect of the second period of employment, but without prejudice to the operation of subsection (1) of section 4 if there is a change in the terms of employment.

3.—(1) Subject to the following provisions of this section, no account shall be taken under section 1 of employment during any period when the hours of employment are normally less than sixteen hours weekly.

Certain hours of employment to be disregarded.

(2) If the employee's relations with his employer cease to be governed by a contract which normally involves work for sixteen hours or more weekly and become governed by a contract which normally involves employment for eight hours or more, but less than sixteen hours, weekly, the employee shall nevertheless for a period of twenty-six weeks (computed in accordance with subsection (3)) be treated for the purposes of subsection (1) as if his contract normally involved employment for sixteen hours or more weekly.

PART I

(3) In computing the said period of twenty-six weeks no account shall be taken of any week—

(a) during which the employee is in fact employed for sixteen hours or more;

(b) during which the employee takes part in a strike (as defined in paragraph 24 of Schedule 13) or is absent from work because of a lock-out (as so defined) by his employer; or

(c) during which there is no contract of employment but which, by virtue of paragraph 9(1) of Schedule 13, counts in computing a period of continuous employment.

(4) An employee whose relations with his employer are governed by a contract of employment which normally involves employment for eight hours or more, but less than sixteen hours, weekly shall nevertheless, if he has been continuously employed for a period of five years or more, be treated for the purposes of subsection (1) as if his contract normally involved employment for sixteen hours or more weekly.

Changes in terms of employment.

4.—(1) If after the date to which a statement given under section 1 relates there is a change in the terms of employment to be included, or referred to, in that statement the employer shall, not more than one month after the change, inform the employee of the nature of the change by a written statement and, if he does not leave a copy of the statement with the employee, shall preserve the statement and ensure that the employee has reasonable opportunities of reading it in the course of his employment, or that it is made reasonably accessible to him in some other way.

(2) A statement given under subsection (1) may, for all or any of the particulars to be given by the statement, refer the employee to some document which the employee has reasonable opportunities of reading in the course of his employment, or which is made reasonably accessible to him in some other way.

(3) If, in referring in the statement given under section 1 or under subsection (1) of this section to any such document, the employer indicates to the employee that future changes in the terms of which the particulars are given in the document will be entered up in the document (or recorded by some other means for the information of persons referring to the document), the employer need not under subsection (1) inform the employee of any such change if it is duly entered up or recorded not later than one month after the change is made.

(4) Where, after an employer has given to an employee a written statement in accordance with section 1—

    (a) the name of the employer (whether an individual or a body corporate or partnership) is changed, without any change in the identity of the employer, or

    (b) the identity of the employer is changed, in such circumstances that, in accordance with section 139(7) or paragraph 17 or paragraph 18 of Schedule 13, the continuity of the employee's period of employment is not broken,

and (in either case) the change does not involve any change in the terms (other than the names of the parties) included or referred to in the statement, then, the person who, immediately after the change, is the employer shall not be required to give to the employee a statement in accordance with section 1, but, subject to subsection (5), the change shall be treated as a change falling within subsection (1) of this section.

(5) A written statement under this section which informs an employee of such a change in his terms of employment as is referred to in subsection (4)(b) shall specify the date on which the employee's continuous period of employment began.

5. Sections 1 and 4 shall not apply to an employee if and so long as the following conditions are fulfilled in relation to him, that is to say—

    (a) the employee's contract of employment is a contract which has been reduced to writing in one or more documents and which contains express terms affording the particulars to be given under each of the paragraphs in subsection (3) of section 1, and under each head of paragraph (d) of that subsection;

    (b) there has been given to the employee a copy of the contract (with any variations made from time to time), or he has reasonable opportunities of reading such a copy in the course of his employment, or such a copy is made reasonably accessible to him in some other way; and

    (c) such a note as is mentioned in section 1(4) has been given to the employee or he has reasonable opportunities of reading such a note in the course of his employment or such a note is made reasonably accessible to him in some other way:

Provided that if at any time after the beginning of an employee's period of employment these conditions cease to be fulfilled in relation to him, the employer shall give the employee a written statement under section 1 not more than one month after that time.

Exclusion of certain contracts in writing.

PART I

Power of Secretary of State to require further particulars.

6. The Secretary of State may by order provide that section 1 shall have effect as if such further particulars as may be specified in the order were included in the particulars to be included in a statement under that section, and, for that purpose, the order may include such provisions amending section 1(1), (2) and (3) as appear to the Secretary of State to be expedient.

Power to vary number of weekly hours of employment necessary to qualify for rights.

7.—(1) The Secretary of State may by order provide that this Part and Schedule 13 shall have effect as if—

(a) for each of the references to sixteen hours in section 3 and in paragraphs 3 to 7 of Schedule 13 there were substituted a reference to such other number of hours less than sixteen as may be specified in the order; and

(b) as if for each of the references to eight hours in section 3 and in paragraphs 6 and 7 of Schedule 13 there were substituted a reference to such other number of hours less than eight as may be specified in the order.

(2) An order under subsection (1) shall not be made unless a draft of the order has been laid before Parliament and approved by resolution of each House.

Itemised pay statements

Right to itemised pay statement.

8. Every employee shall have the right to be given by his employer at or before the time at which any payment of wages or salary is made to him an itemised pay statement, in writing, containing the following particulars, that is to say,—

(a) the gross amount of the wages or salary;

(b) the amounts of any variable and, subject to section 9, any fixed deductions from that gross amount and the purposes for which they are made;

(c) the net amount of wages or salary payable; and

(d) where different parts of the net amount are paid in different ways, the amount and method of payment of each part-payment.

Standing statement of fixed deductions.

9.—(1) A pay statement given in accordance with section 8 need not contain separate particulars of a fixed deduction if it contains instead an aggregate amount of fixed deductions, including that deduction, and the employer has given to the employee, at or before the time at which that pay statement is given, a standing statement of fixed deductions, in writing, which contains the following particulars of each deduction comprised in that aggregate amount, that is to say,—

(a) the amount of the deduction;

(b) the intervals at which the deduction is to be made; and

(c) the purpose for which it is made,

and which, in accordance with subsection (4), is effective at the date on which the pay statement is given.

(2) A standing statement of fixed deductions may be amended, whether by addition of a new deduction or by a change in the particulars or cancellation of an existing deduction, by notice in writing, containing particulars of the amendment, given by the employer to the employee.

(3) An employer who has given to an employee a standing statement of fixed deductions shall, within the period of twelve months beginning with the date on which the first standing statement was given and at intervals of not more than twelve months thereafter, re-issue it in a consolidated form incorporating any amendments notified in accordance with subsection (2).

(4) A standing statement of fixed deductions shall become effective, for the purposes of subsection (1), on the date on which it is given to the employee and shall cease to have effect on the expiration of the period of twelve months beginning with that date, or, where it is re-issued in accordance with subsection (3), the expiration of the period of twelve months beginning with the date on which it was last re-issued.

10. The Secretary of State may by order— *Power to amend ss. 8 and 9.*

(a) vary the provisions of sections 8 and 9 as to the particulars which must be included in a pay statement or a standing statement of fixed deductions by adding items to or removing items from the particulars listed in those sections or by amending any such particulars; and

(b) vary the provisions of section 9(3) and (4) so as to shorten or extend the periods of twelve months referred to in those subsections, or those periods as varied from time to time under this section.

Enforcement of rights under Part I

11.—(1) Where an employer does not give an employee a statement as required by section 1 or 4(1) or 8, the employee may require a reference to be made to an industrial tribunal to determine what particulars ought to have been included or referred to in a statement so as to comply with the requirements of the relevant section. *References to industrial tribunals.*

(2) Where—

(a) a statement purporting to be a statement under section 1 or 4(1), or

(b) a pay statement, or a standing statement of fixed deductions, purporting to comply with section 8 or 9(1),

has been given to an employee, and a question arises as to the particulars which ought to have been included or referred to in the statement so as to comply with the requirements of this Part, either the employer or the employee may require that question to be referred to and determined by an industrial tribunal.

(3) Where a statement under section 1 or 4(1) given by an employer to an employee contains such an indication as is mentioned in section 4(3), and

(a) any particulars purporting to be particulars of a change to which that indication relates are entered up or recorded in accordance with that indication, and

(b) a question arises as to the particulars which ought to have been so entered up or recorded,

either the employer or the employee may require that question to be referred to and determined by an industrial tribunal.

(4) In this section, a question as to the particulars which ought to have been included—

(a) in a pay statement, or in a standing statement of fixed deductions, does not include a question solely as to the accuracy of an amount stated in any such particulars;

(b) in a note under section 1(4), does not include any question whether the employment is, has been or will be contracted-out employment for the purposes of Part III of the Social Security Pensions Act 1975.

(5) Where, on a reference under subsection (1), an industrial tribunal determines particulars as being those which ought to have been included or referred to in a statement given under section 1 or 4(1) the employer shall be deemed to have given to the employee a statement in which those particulars were included, or referred to, as specified in the decision of the tribunal.

(6) On determining a reference under subsection (2)(a), an industrial tribunal may either confirm the particulars as included or referred to in the statement given by the employer, or may amend those particulars, or may substitute other particulars for them, as the tribunal may determine to be appropriate; and the statement shall be deemed to have been given by the employer to the employee in accordance with the decision of the tribunal.

(7) On determining a reference under subsection (3), an industrial tribunal may either confirm the particulars to which the reference relates, or may amend those particulars or may substitute other particulars for them, as the tribunal may determine to be appropriate; and particulars of the change to which the reference relates shall be deemed to have been entered up or recorded in accordance with the decision of the tribunal.

(8) Where on a reference under this section an industrial tribunal finds that an employer has failed to give an employee any pay statement in accordance with section 8 or that a pay statement or standing statement of fixed deductions does not, in relation to a deduction, contain the particulars required to be included in that statement by that section or section 9(1)—

(a) the tribunal shall make a declaration to that effect; and

(b) where the tribunal further finds that any unnotified deductions have been made from the pay of the employee during the period of thirteen weeks immediately preceding the date of the application for the reference (whether or not the deductions were made in breach of the contract of employment), the tribunal may order the employer to pay the employee a sum not exceeding the aggregate of the unnotified deductions so made.

In this subsection "unnotified deduction" means a deduction made without the employer giving the employee, in any pay statement or standing statement of fixed deductions, the particulars of that deduction required by section 8 or 9(1).

(9) An industrial tribunal shall not entertain a reference under this section in a case where the employment to which the reference relates has ceased unless an application requiring the reference to be made was made before the end of the period of three months beginning with the date on which the employment ceased.

PART II

RIGHTS ARISING IN COURSE OF EMPLOYMENT

Guarantee payments

12.—(1) Where an employee throughout a day during any part of which he would normally be required to work in accordance with his contract of employment is not provided with work by his employer by reason of—

(a) a diminution in the requirements of the employer's business for work of the kind which the employee is employed to do, or

Right to guarantee payment.

PART II
    (b) any other occurrence affecting the normal working of the employer's business in relation to work of the kind which the employee is employed to do,

he shall, subject to the following provisions of this Act, be entitled to be paid by his employer a payment, referred to in this Act as a guarantee payment, in respect of that day, and in this section and sections 13 and 16—

    (i) such a day is referred to as a " workless day ", and

    (ii) " workless period " has a corresponding meaning.

(2) In this section and sections 13 to 17, " day " means the period of twenty-four hours from midnight to midnight, and where a period of employment begun on any day extends over midnight into the following day, or would normally so extend, then—

    (a) if the employment before midnight is, or would normally be, of longer duration than that after midnight, that period of employment shall be treated as falling wholly on the first day ; and

    (b) in any other case, that period of employment shall be treated as falling wholly on the second day.

General exclusions from right under s. 12.

13.—(1) An employee shall not be entitled to a guarantee payment in respect of a workless day if the failure to provide him with work occurs in consequence of a trade dispute involving any employee of his employer or of an associated employer.

(2) An employee shall not be entitled to a guarantee payment in respect of a workless day if—

    (a) his employer has offered to provide alternative work for that day which is suitable in all the circumstances whether or not work which the employee is under his contract employed to perform, and the employee has unreasonably refused that offer ; or

    (b) he does not comply with reasonable requirements imposed by his employer with a view to ensuring that his services are available.

Calculation of guarantee payment.

14.—(1) Subject to the limits set by section 15, the amount of a guarantee payment payable to an employee in respect of any day shall be the sum produced by multiplying the number of normal working hours on that day by the guaranteed hourly rate, and, accordingly, no guarantee payment shall be payable to an employee in whose case there are no normal working hours on the day in question.

(2) Subject to subsection (3), the guaranteed hourly rate in relation to an employee shall be the amount of one week's pay divided by—

(a) the number of normal working hours in a week for that employee when employed under the contract of employment in force on the day in respect of which the guarantee payment is payable; or

(b) where the number of such normal working hours differs from week to week or over a longer period, the average number of such hours calculated by dividing by twelve the total number of the employee's normal working hours during the period of twelve weeks ending with the last complete week before the day in respect of which the guarantee payment is payable; or

(c) in a case falling within paragraph (b) but where the employee has not been employed for a sufficient period to enable the calculation to be made under that paragraph, a number which fairly represents the number of normal working hours in a week having regard to such of the following considerations as are appropriate in the circumstances, that is to say,—

(i) the average number of normal working hours in a week which the employee could expect in accordance with the terms of his contract;

(ii) the average number of such hours of other employees engaged in relevant comparable employment with the same employer.

(3) If in any case an employee's contract has been varied, or a new contract has been entered into, in connection with a period of short-time working, subsection (2) shall have effect as if for the reference to the day in respect of which the guarantee payment is payable there was substituted a reference to the last day on which the original contract was in force.

15.—(1) The amount of a guarantee payment payable to an employee in respect of any day shall not exceed £6·60.

(2) An employee shall not be entitled to guarantee payments in respect of more than the specified number of days in any one of the relevant periods, that is to say, the periods of three months commencing on 1st February, 1st May, 1st August and 1st November in each year.

(3) The specified number of days for the purposes of subsection (2) shall be, subject to subsection (4),—

(a) the number of days, not exceeding five, on which the employee normally works in a week under the contract of employment in force on the day in respect of which the guarantee payment is claimed; or

PART II

(b) where that number of days varies from week to week or over a longer period, the average number of such days, not exceeding five, calculated by dividing by twelve the total number of such days during the period of twelve weeks ending with the last complete week before the day in respect of which the guarantee payment is claimed, and rounding up the resulting figure to the next whole number; or

(c) in a case falling within paragraph (b) but where the employee has not been employed for a sufficient period to enable the calculation to be made under that paragraph, a number which fairly represents the number of the employee's normal working days in a week, not exceeding five, having regard to such of the following considerations as are appropriate in the circumstances, that is to say,—

(i) the average number of normal working days in a week which the employee could expect in accordance with the terms of his contract;

(ii) the average number of such days of other employees engaged in relevant comparable employment with the same employer.

(4) If in any case an employee's contract has been varied, or a new contract has been entered into, in connection with a period of short-time working, subsection (3) shall have effect as if for the references to the day in respect of which the guarantee payment is claimed there were substituted references to the last day on which the original contract was in force.

(5) The Secretary of State may vary any of the limits referred to in this section, and may in particular vary the relevant periods referred to in subsection (2), after a review under section 148, by order made in accordance with that section.

Supplementary provisions relating to guarantee payments.

16.—(1) Subject to subsection (2), a right to a guarantee payment shall not affect any right of an employee in relation to remuneration under his contract of employment (in this section referred to as "contractual remuneration").

(2) Any contractual remuneration paid to an employee in respect of a workless day shall go towards discharging any liability of the employer to pay a guarantee payment in respect of that day, and conversely any guarantee payment paid in respect of a day shall go towards discharging any liability of the employer to pay contractual remuneration in respect of that day.

(3) For the purposes of subsection (2), contractual remuneration shall be treated as paid in respect of a workless day—

(a) where it is expressed to be calculated or payable by reference to that day or any part of that day, to the extent that it is so expressed; and

(b) in any other case, to the extent that it represents guaranteed remuneration, rather than remuneration for work actually done, and is referable to that day when apportioned rateably between that day and any other workless period falling within the period in respect of which the remuneration is paid.

(4) The Secretary of State may by order provide that in relation to any description of employees the provisions of sections 12(2), 14 and 15(3) (as originally enacted or as varied under section 15(5)) and of subsections (1) to (3), and, so far as they apply for the purposes of those provisions, the provisions of Schedule 14 shall have effect subject to such modifications and adaptations as may be prescribed by the order.

17.—(1) An employee may present a complaint to an industrial tribunal that his employer has failed to pay the whole or any part of a guarantee payment to which the employee is entitled.

Complaint to industrial tribunal.

(2) An industrial tribunal shall not entertain a complaint relating to a guarantee payment in respect of any day unless the complaint is presented to the tribunal before the end of the period of three months beginning with that day or within such further period as the tribunal considers reasonable in a case where it is satisfied that it was not reasonably practicable for the complaint to be presented within the period of three months.

(3) Where an industrial tribunal finds a complaint under subsection (1) well-founded, the tribunal shall order the employer to pay the complainant the amount of guarantee payment which it finds is due to him.

18.—(1) If at any time there is in force a collective agreement, or a wages order, whereby employees to whom the agreement or order relates have a right to guaranteed remuneration and on the application of all the parties to the agreement or, as the case may be, of the council or Board making the order, the appropriate Minister, having regard to the provisions of the agreement or order, is satisfied that section 12 should not apply to those employees, he may make an order under this section excluding those employees from the operation of that section.

Exemption orders.

(2) In subsection (1), a wages order means an order made under any of the following provisions, that is to say—
    (a) section 11 of the Wages Councils Act 1959; 1959 c. 69.
    (b) section 3 of the Agricultural Wages Act 1948; 1948 c. 47.
    (c) section 3 of the Agricultural Wages (Scotland) Act 1949. 1949 c. 30.

(3) In subsection (1), "the appropriate Minister" means—

(a) as respects a collective agreement or such an order as is referred to in subsection (2)(a) or (c), the Secretary of State;

(b) as respects such an order as is referred to in subsection (2)(b), the Minister of Agriculture, Fisheries and Food.

(4) The Secretary of State shall not make an order under this section in respect of an agreement unless—

(a) the agreement provides for procedures to be followed (whether by arbitration or otherwise) in cases where an employee claims that his employer has failed to pay the whole or any part of any guaranteed remuneration to which the employee is entitled under the agreement, and that those procedures include a right to arbitration or adjudication by an independent referee or body in cases where (by reason of an equality of votes or otherwise) a decision cannot otherwise be reached; or

(b) the agreement indicates that an employee to whom the agreement relates may present a complaint to an industrial tribunal that his employer has failed to pay the whole or any part of any guaranteed remuneration to which the employee is entitled under the agreement;

and where an order under this section is in force in respect of such an agreement as is described in paragraph (b) an industrial tribunal shall have jurisdiction over such a complaint as if it were a complaint falling within section 17.

(5) Without prejudice to section 154(4), an order under this section may be varied or revoked by a subsequent order thereunder, whether in pursuance of an application made by all or any of the parties to the agreement in question, or, as the case may be, by the council or Board which made the order in question, or without any such application.

Suspension from work on medical grounds

Right to remuneration on suspension on medical grounds.

19.—(1) An employee who is suspended from work by his employer on medical grounds in consequence of—

(a) any requirement imposed by or under any provision of any enactment or of any instrument made under any enactment, or

(b) any recommendation in any provision of a code of practice issued or approved under section 16 of the Health and Safety at Work etc. Act 1974,

1974 c. 37.

which is a provision for the time being specified in Schedule 1 shall, subject to the following provisions of this Act, be entitled to be paid by his employer remuneration while he is so suspended for a period not exceeding twenty-six weeks.

PART II

(2) For the purposes of this section and sections 20 to 22 and 61, an employee shall be regarded as suspended from work only if, and so long as, he continues to be employed by his employer, but is not provided with work or does not perform the work he normally performed before the suspension.

(3) The Secretary of State may by order add provisions to or remove provisions from the list of specified provisions in Schedule 1.

20.—(1) An employee shall not be entitled to remuneration under section 19 in respect of any period during which he is incapable of work by reason of disease or bodily or mental disablement.

General exclusions from right under s. 19.

(2) An employee shall not be entitled to remuneration under section 19 in respect of any period during which—

(a) his employer has offered to provide him with suitable alternative work, whether or not work which the employee is under his contract, or was under the contract in force before the suspension, employed to perform, and the employee has unreasonably refused to perform that work; or

(b) he does not comply with reasonable requirements imposed by his employer with a view to ensuring that his services are available.

21.—(1) The amount of remuneration payable by an employer to an employee under section 19 shall be a week's pay in respect of each week of the period of suspension referred to in subsection (1) of that section, and if in any week remuneration is payable in respect only of part of that week the amount of a week's pay shall be reduced proportionately.

Calculation of remuneration.

(2) Subject to subsection (3), a right to remuneration under section 19 shall not affect any right of an employee in relation to remuneration under his contract of employment (in this section referred to as " contractual remuneration ").

(3) Any contractual remuneration paid by an employer to an employee in respect of any period shall go towards discharging the employer's liability under section 19 in respect of that period, and conversely any payment of remuneration in discharge

PART II of an employer's liability under section 19 in respect of any period shall go towards discharging any obligation of the employer to pay contractual remuneration in respect of that period.

Complaint to industrial tribunal.

22.—(1) An employee may present a complaint to an industrial tribunal that his employer has failed to pay the whole or any part of remuneration to which the employee is entitled under section 19.

(2) An industrial tribunal shall not entertain a complaint relating to remuneration under section 19 in respect of any day unless the complaint is presented to the tribunal before the end of the period of three months beginning with that day, or within such further period as the tribunal considers reasonable in a case where it is satisfied that it was not reasonably practicable for the complaint to be presented within the period of three months.

(3) Where an industrial tribunal finds a complaint under subsection (1) well-founded the tribunal shall order the employer to pay the complainant the amount of remuneration which it finds is due to him.

Trade union membership and activities

Trade union membership and activities.

23.—(1) Subject to the following provisions of this section, every employee shall have the right not to have action (short of dismissal) taken against him as an individual by his employer for the purpose of—

(a) preventing or deterring him from being or seeking to become a member of an independent trade union, or penalising him for doing so ; or

(b) preventing or deterring him from taking part in the activities of an independent trade union at any appropriate time, or penalising him for doing so ; or

(c) compelling him to be or become a member of a trade union which is not independent.

(2) In this section " appropriate time ", in relation to an employee taking part in any activities of a trade union, means time which either—

(a) is outside his working hours, or

(b) is a time within his working hours at which, in accordance with arrangements agreed with, or consent given by his employer, it is permissible for him to take part in those activities ;

and in this subsection " working hours ", in relation to an employee, means any time when, in accordance with his contract of employment, he is required to be at work.

(3) The provisions of subsection (4) shall have effect in relation to an employee—

    (*a*) of the same class as employees for whom it is the practice in accordance with a union membership agreement to belong to a specified independent trade union or to one of a number of specified independent trade unions; or

    (*b*) not of the same class as described in paragraph (*a*) but of the same grade or category as such employees as are referred to in that paragraph.

(4) In relation to such an employee the right conferred by subsection (1)(*b*) in relation to the activities of an independent trade union shall extend to activities on the employer's premises only if that union is a specified union.

(5) For the purposes of this section a trade union—

    (*a*) shall be taken to be specified for the purposes of, or in relation to, a union membership agreement if it is specified in the agreement or is accepted by the parties to the agreement as being the equivalent of a union so specified; and

    (*b*) shall also be treated as so specified if—

        (i) the Advisory, Conciliation and Arbitration Service has made a recommendation for recognition of that union covering the employee in question which is operative within the meaning of section 15 of the Employment Protection Act 1975; or

        (ii) the union has referred a recognition issue covering that employee to the Advisory, Conciliation and Arbitration Service under section 11 of the said Act of 1975 and the Service has not declined to proceed on the reference under section 12 of that Act, the union has not withdrawn the reference, or from the reference, and the issue has not been settled or reported on under that section.

(6) An employee who genuinely objects on grounds of religious belief to being a member of any trade union whatsoever shall have the right not to have action (short of dismissal) taken against him by his employer for the purpose of compelling him to belong to a trade union.

(7) In this section, unless the context otherwise requires, references to a trade union include references to a branch or section of a trade union.

PART II
Complaint to industrial tribunal.

24.—(1) An employee may present a complaint to an industrial tribunal on the ground that action has been taken against him by his employer in contravention of section 23.

(2) An industrial tribunal shall not entertain a complaint under subsection (1) unless it is presented to the tribunal before the end of the period of three months beginning with the date on which there occurred the action complained of, or where that action is part of a series of similar actions, the last of those actions, or within such further period as the tribunal considers reasonable in a case where it is satisfied that it was not reasonably practicable for the complaint to be presented within the period of three months.

(3) Where the tribunal finds the complaint well-founded it shall make a declaration to that effect and may make an award of compensation, calculated in accordance with section 26, to be paid by the employer to the employee in respect of the action complained of.

Supplementary provisions relating to complaints under s. 24.

25.—(1) On a complaint under section 24 it shall be for the employer to show—

(a) the purpose for which action was taken against the complainant; and

(b) that the purpose was not such a purpose as is referred to in section 23(1)(a) to (c) or (6).

(2) In determining on a complaint under section 24, any question as to whether action was taken by the complainant's employer or the purpose for which it was taken, no account shall be taken of any pressure which, by calling, organising, procuring or financing a strike or other industrial action, or threatening to do so, was exercised on the employer to take the action complained of, and that question shall be determined as if no such pressure had been exercised.

Assessment of compensation on a complaint under s. 24.

26.—(1) The amount of the compensation awarded by a tribunal on a complaint under section 24 shall be such amount as the tribunal considers just and equitable in all the circumstances having regard to the infringement of the complainant's right under section 23 by the employer's action complained of and to any loss sustained by the complainant which is attributable to that action.

(2) The said loss shall be taken to include—

(a) any expenses reasonably incurred by the complainant in consequence of the action complained of, and

(b) loss of any benefit which he might reasonably be expected to have had but for that action.

(3) In ascertaining the said loss the tribunal shall apply the same rule concerning the duty of a person to mitigate his loss as applies to damages recoverable under the common law of England and Wales or of Scotland, as the case may be.

(4) In determining the amount of compensation to be awarded under subsection (1), no account shall be taken of any pressure as is referred to in section 25(2), and that question shall be determined as if no such pressure had been exercised.

(5) Where the tribunal finds that the action complained of was to any extent caused or contributed to by any action of the complainant it shall reduce the amount of the compensation by such proportion as it considers just and equitable having regard to that finding.

Time off work

27.—(1) An employer shall permit an employee of his who is an official of an independent trade union recognised by him to take time off, subject to and in accordance with subsection (2), during the employee's working hours for the purpose of enabling him—

- (a) to carry out those duties of his as such an official which are concerned with industrial relations between his employer and any associated employer, and their employees; or
- (b) to undergo training in aspects of industrial relations which is—
    - (i) relevant to the carrying out of those duties; and
    - (ii) approved by the Trades Union Congress or by the independent trade union of which he is an official.

(2) The amount of time off which an employee is to be permitted to take under this section and the purposes for which, the occasions on which and any conditions subject to which time off may be so taken are those that are reasonable in all the circumstances having regard to any relevant provisions of a Code of Practice issued by the Advisory, Conciliation and Arbitration Service under section 6 of the Employment Protection Act 1975.

(3) An employer who permits an employee to take time off under this section for any purpose shall, subject to the following provisions of this section, pay him for the time taken off for that purpose in accordance with the permission—

- (a) where the employee's remuneration for the work he would ordinarily have been doing during that time

PART II

does not vary with the amount of work done, as if he had worked at that work for the whole of that time;

(b) where the employee's remuneration for that work varies with the amount of work done, an amount calculated by reference to the average hourly earnings for that work.

(4) The average hourly earnings referred to in subsection (3)(b) shall be the average hourly earnings of the employee concerned or, if no fair estimate can be made of those earnings, the average hourly earnings for work of that description of persons in comparable employment with the same employer or, if there are no such persons, a figure of average hourly earnings which is reasonable in the circumstances.

(5) Subject to subsection (6), a right to be paid any amount under subsection (3) shall not affect any right of an employee in relation to remuneration under his contract of employment (in this section referred to as " contractual remuneration ").

(6) Any contractual remuneration paid to an employee in respect of a period of time off to which subsection (1) applies shall go towards discharging any liability of the employer under subsection (3) in respect of that period, and conversely any payment of any amount under subsection (3) in respect of a period shall go towards discharging any liability of the employer to pay contractual remuneration in respect of that period.

(7) An employee who is an official of an independent trade union recognised by his employer may present a complaint to an industrial tribunal that his employer has failed to permit him to take time off as required by this section or to pay him the whole or part of any amount so required to be paid.

Time off for trade union activities.

28.—(1) An employer shall permit an employee of his who is a member of an appropriate trade union to take time off, subject to and in accordance with subsection (3), during the employee's working hours for the purpose of taking part in any trade union activity to which this section applies.

(2) In this section " appropriate trade union ", in relation to an employee of any description, means an independent trade union which is recognised by his employer in respect of that description of employee, and the trade union activities to which this section applies are—

(a) any activities of an appropriate trade union of which the employee is a member; and

(b) any activities, whether or not falling within paragraph (a), in relation to which the employee is acting as a representative of such a union,

excluding activities which themselves consist of industrial action whether or not in contemplation or furtherance of a trade dispute.

(3) The amount of time off which an employee is to be permitted to take under this section and the purposes for which, the occasions on which and any conditions subject to which time off may be so taken are those that are reasonable in all the circumstances having regard to any relevant provisions of a Code of Practice issued by the Advisory, Conciliation and Arbitration Service under section 6 of the Employment Protection Act 1975.

1975 c. 71.

(4) An employee who is a member of an independent trade union recognised by his employer may present a complaint to an industrial tribunal that his employer has failed to permit him to take time off as required by this section.

29.—(1) An employer shall permit an employee of his who is—

(a) a justice of the peace;

(b) a member of a local authority;

(c) a member of any statutory tribunal;

(d) a member of, in England and Wales, a Regional Health Authority or Area Health Authority or, in Scotland, a Health Board;

(e) a member of, in England and Wales, the managing or governing body of an educational establishment maintained by a local education authority, or, in Scotland, a school or college council or the governing body of a central institution or a college of education; or

(f) a member of, in England and Wales, a water authority or, in Scotland, river purification board,

to take time off, subject to and in accordance with subsection (4), during the employee's working hours for the purposes of performing any of the duties of his office or, as the case may be, his duties as such a member.

Time off for public duties.

(2) In subsection (1)—

(a) " local authority " in relation to England and Wales includes the Common Council of the City of London but otherwise has the same meaning as in the Local Government Act 1972, and in relation to Scotland has the same meaning as in the Local Government (Scotland) Act 1973;

1972 c. 70.

1973 c. 65.

(b) " Regional Health Authority " and " Area Health Authority " have the same meaning as in the National

1977 c. 49.

PART II
1972 c. 58.

1972 c. 70.

1973 c. 65.

1962 c. 47.

Health Service Act 1977, and "Health Board" has the same meaning as in the National Health Service (Scotland) Act 1972;

(c) "local education authority" means the authority designated by section 192(1) of the Local Government Act 1972, "school or college council" means a body appointed under section 125(1) of the Local Government (Scotland) Act 1973, and "central institution" and "college of education" have the meanings assigned to them by section 145(10) and (14) respectively of the Education (Scotland) Act 1962; and

(d) "river purification board" means a board established under section 135 of the Local Government (Scotland) Act 1973.

(3) For the purposes of subsection (1) the duties of a member of a body referred to in paragraphs (b) to (f) of that subsection are:—

(a) attendance at a meeting of the body or any of its committees or sub-committees;

(b) the doing of any other thing approved by the body, or anything of a class so approved, for the purpose of the discharge of the functions of the body or of any of its committees or sub-committees.

(4) The amount of time off which an employee is to be permitted to take under this section and the occasions on which and any conditions subject to which time off may be so taken are those that are reasonable in all the circumstances having regard, in particular, to the following:—

(a) how much time off is required for the performance of the duties of the office or as a member of the body in question, and how much time off is required for the performance of the particular duty;

(b) how much time off the employee has already been permitted under this section or sections 27 and 28;

(c) the circumstances of the employer's business and the effect of the employee's absence on the running of that business.

(5) The Secretary of State may by order—

(a) modify the provisions of subsection (1) by adding any office or body to, or removing any office or body from, that subsection or by altering the description of any office or body in that subsection; and

(b) modify the provisions of subsection (3).

(6) An employee may present a complaint to an industrial tribunal that his employer has failed to permit him to take time off as required by this section.

30.—(1) An industrial tribunal shall not consider—

(a) a complaint under section 27, 28 or 29 that an employer has failed to permit an employee to take time off ; or

(b) a complaint under section 27 that an employer has failed to pay an employee the whole or part of any amount required to be paid under that section ;

unless it is presented within three months of the date when the failure occurred or within such further period as the tribunal considers reasonable in a case where it is satisfied that it was not reasonably practicable for the complaint to be presented within the period of three months.

(2) Where an industrial tribunal finds any complaint mentioned in subsection (1)(a) well-founded, the tribunal shall make a declaration to that effect and may make an award of compensation to be paid by the employer to the employee which shall be of such amount as the tribunal considers just and equitable in all the circumstances having regard to the employer's default in failing to permit time off to be taken by the employee and to any loss sustained by the employee which is attributable to the matters complained of.

(3) Where on a complaint under section 27 an industrial tribunal finds that the employer has failed to pay the employee the whole or part of the amount required to be paid under that section, the tribunal shall order the employer to pay the employee the amount which it finds due to him.

PART II
Provisions as to industrial tribunals.

31.—(1) An employee who is given notice of dismissal by reason of redundancy shall, subject to the following provisions of this section, be entitled before the expiration of his notice to be allowed by his employer reasonable time off during the employee's working hours in order to look for new employment or make arrangements for training for future employment.

Time off to look for work or make arrangements for training.

(2) An employee shall not be entitled to time off under this section unless, on whichever is the later of the following dates, that is to say,—

(a) the date on which the notice is due to expire ; or

(b) the date on which it would expire were it the notice required to be given by section 49(1),

he will have been or, as the case may be, would have been continuously employed for a period of two years or more.

(3) An employee who is allowed time off during his working hours under subsection (1) shall, subject to the following provisions of this section, be entitled to be paid remuneration by his employer for the period of absence at the appropriate hourly rate.

PART II
(4) The appropriate hourly rate in relation to an employee shall be the amount of one week's pay divided by—

(a) the number of normal working hours in a week for that employee when employed under the contract of employment in force on the day when notice was given; or

(b) where the number of such normal working hours differs from week to week or over a longer period, the average number of such hours calculated by dividing by twelve the total number of the employee's normal working hours during the period of twelve weeks ending with the last complete week before the day on which notice was given.

(5) If an employer unreasonably refuses to allow an employee time off from work under this section, the employee shall, subject to subsection (9), be entitled to be paid an amount equal to the remuneration to which he would have been entitled under subsection (3) if he had been allowed the time off.

(6) An employee may present a complaint to an industrial tribunal on the ground that his employer has unreasonably refused to allow him time off under this section or has failed to pay the whole or any part of any amount to which the employee is entitled under subsection (3) or (5).

(7) An industrial tribunal shall not entertain a complaint under subsection (6) unless it is presented to the tribunal within the period of three months beginning with the day on which it is alleged that the time off should have been allowed, or within such further period as the tribunal considers reasonable in a case where it is satisfied that it was not reasonably practicable for the complaint to be presented within the period of three months.

(8) If on a complaint under subsection (6) the tribunal finds the grounds of the complaint well-founded it shall make a declaration to that effect and shall order the employer to pay to the employee the amount which it finds due to him.

(9) The amount—

(a) of an employer's liability to pay remuneration under subsection (3); or

(b) which may be ordered by a tribunal to be paid by an employer under subsection (8),

or, where both paragraphs (a) and (b) are applicable, the aggregate amount of the liabilities referred to in those paragraphs, shall not exceed, in respect of the notice period of any employee, two-fifths of a week's pay of that employee.

(10) Subject to subsection (11), a right to any amount under subsection (3) or (5) shall not affect any right of an employee in relation to remuneration under the contract of employment (in this section referred to as " contractual remuneration ").

(11) Any contractual remuneration paid to an employee in respect of a period when he takes time off for the purposes referred to in subsection (1) shall go towards discharging any liability of the employer to pay remuneration under subsection (3) in respect of that period, and conversely any payment of remuneration under subsection (3) in respect of a period shall go towards discharging any liability of the employer to pay contractual remuneration in respect of that period.

32.—(1) For the purposes of sections 27 to 31— Provisions supplementary to ss. 27 to 31.

(a) a trade union shall be treated as recognised not only if it is recognised for the purposes of collective bargaining, but also if the Advisory, Conciliation and Arbitration Service has made a recommendation for recognition which is operative within the meaning of section 15 of the Employment Protection Act 1975 ; and 1975 c. 71.

(b) the working hours of an employee shall be taken to be any time when, in accordance with his contract of employment, he is required to be at work.

(2) In subsection (1)—

" collective bargaining " means negotiations related to or connected with one or more of the matters specified in section 29(1) of the Trade Union and Labour Relations Act 1974 ; 1974 c. 52.

" recognised " means recognised by an employer, or two or more associated employers, to any extent for the purposes of collective bargaining.

Part III

Maternity

General provisions

33.—(1) An employee who is absent from work wholly or partly because of pregnancy or confinement shall, subject to the following provisions of this Act,— Rights of employee in connection with pregnancy and confinement.

(a) be entitled to be paid by her employer a sum to be known as maternity pay ; and

(b) be entitled to return to work.

B

(2) Schedule 2 shall have effect for the purpose of supplementing the following provisions of this Act in relation to an employee's right to return to work.

(3) An employee shall be entitled to the rights referred to in subsection (1) whether or not a contract of employment subsists during the period of her absence but, subject to subsection (4), she shall not be so entitled unless—

(a) she continues to be employed by her employer (whether or not she is at work) until immediately before the beginning of the eleventh week before the expected week of confinement;

(b) she has at the beginning of that eleventh week been continuously employed for a period of not less than two years; and

(c) she informs her employer (in writing if he so requests) at least twenty-one days before her absence begins or, if that is not reasonably practicable, as soon as reasonably practicable,—

(i) that she will be (or is) absent from work wholly or partly because of pregnancy or confinement, and

(ii) in the case of the right to return, that she intends to return to work with her employer.

(4) An employee who has been dismissed by her employer for a reason falling within section 60(1)(a) or (b) and has not been re-engaged in accordance with that section, shall be entitled to the rights referred to in subsection (1) of this section notwithstanding that she has thereby ceased to be employed before the beginning of the eleventh week before the expected week of confinement if, but for that dismissal, she would at the beginning of that eleventh week have been continuously employed for a period of not less than two years, but she shall not be entitled to the right to return unless she informs her employer (in writing if he so requests), before or as soon as reasonably practicable after the dismissal takes effect, that she intends to return to work with him.

In this subsection "dismiss" and "dismissal" have the same meaning as they have for the purposes of Part V.

(5) An employee shall not be entitled to either of the rights referred to in subsection (1) unless, if requested to do so by her employer, she produces for his inspection a certificate from a registered medical practitioner or a certified midwife stating the expected week of her confinement.

(6) The Secretary of State may by order vary the periods of two years referred to in subsections (3) and (4), or those periods

as varied from time to time under this subsection, but no such order shall be made unless a draft of the order has been laid before Parliament and approved by resolution of each House of Parliament.

PART III

Maternity pay

34.—(1) Maternity pay shall be paid in respect of a period not exceeding, or periods not exceeding in the aggregate, six weeks during which the employee is absent from work wholly or partly because of pregnancy or confinement (in this section and sections 35 and 36 referred to as the payment period or payment periods).

Maternity pay.

(2) An employee shall not be entitled to maternity pay for any absence before the beginning of the eleventh week before the expected week of confinement, and her payment period or payment periods shall be the first six weeks of absence starting on or falling after the beginning of that eleventh week.

(3) The Secretary of State may by order vary the periods of six weeks referred to in subsections (1) and (2), or those periods as varied from time to time under this subsection, but no such order shall be made unless a draft of the order has been laid before Parliament and approved by resolution of each House of Parliament.

(4) Where an employee gives her employer the information required by section 33(3)(*c*) or produces any certificate requested under section 33(5) after the beginning of the payment period or the first of the payments periods, she shall not be entitled to maternity pay for any part of that period until she gives him that information or certificate, but on giving him the information or, as the case may be, producing the certificate, she shall be entitled to be paid in respect of that part of the period or periods which fell before the giving of the information or the production of the certificate.

35.—(1) The amount of maternity pay to which an employee is entitled as respects any week shall be nine-tenths of a week's pay reduced by the amount of maternity allowance payable for the week under Part I of Schedule 4 to the Social Security Act 1975, whether or not the employee in question is entitled to the whole or any part of that allowance.

Calculation of maternity pay.

1975 c. 14.

(2) Maternity pay shall accrue due to an employee from day to day and in calculating the amount of maternity pay payable for any day—

(*a*) there shall be disregarded Sunday or such other day in each week as may be prescribed in relation to that

PART III
1975 c. 14.

employee under section 22(10) of the Social Security Act 1975 for the purpose of calculating the daily rate of maternity allowance under that Act; and

(b) the amount payable for any other day shall be taken as one-sixth of the amount of the maternity pay for the week in which the day falls.

(3) Subject to subsection (4), a right to maternity pay shall not affect any right of an employee in relation to remuneration under any contract of employment (in this section referred to as " contractual remuneration ").

(4) Any contractual remuneration paid to an employee in respect of a day within a payment period shall go towards discharging any liability of the employer to pay maternity pay in respect of that day, and conversely any maternity pay paid in respect of a day shall go towards discharging any liability of the employer to pay contractual remuneration in respect of that day.

Complaint to industrial tribunal.

36.—(1) A complaint may be presented to an industrial tribunal by an employee against her employer that he has failed to pay her the whole or any part of the maternity pay to which she is entitled.

(2) An industrial tribunal shall not entertain a complaint under subsection (1) unless it is presented to the tribunal before the end of the period of three months beginning with the last day of the payment period or, as the case may be, the last of the payment periods, or within such further period as the tribunal considers reasonable in a case where it is satisfied that it was not reasonably practicable for the complaint to be presented within the period of three months.

(3) Where an industrial tribunal finds a complaint under subsection (1) well-founded, the tribunal shall order the employer to pay the complainant the amount of maternity pay which it finds is due to her.

Maternity Pay Fund.
1975 c. 71.

37.—(1) The Secretary of State shall continue to have the control and management of the Maternity Pay Fund established under section 39 of the Employment Protection Act 1975, and payments shall be made out of that fund in accordance with the following provisions of this Part and section 156(1).

(2) The Secretary of State shall prepare accounts of the Maternity Pay Fund in such form as the Treasury may direct and shall send them to the Comptroller and Auditor General not later than the end of the month of November following the end of the

financial year to which the accounts relate; and the Comptroller and Auditor General shall examine and certify every such account and shall lay copies thereof, together with his report thereon, before Parliament.

PART III

(3) Any money in the Maternity Pay Fund may from time to time be paid over to the National Debt Commissioners and invested by them, in accordance with such directions as may be given by the Treasury, in any such manner as may be specified by an order of the Treasury for the time being in force under section 22(1) of the National Savings Bank Act 1971.

1971 c. 29.

38.—(1) Subject to the provisions of subsections (2) to (4), the Treasury may from time to time advance out of the National Loans Fund to the Secretary of State for the purposes of the Maternity Pay Fund such sums as the Secretary of State may request; and any sums advanced to the Secretary of State under this section shall be paid into the Maternity Pay Fund.

Advances out of National Loans Fund.

(2) The aggregate amount outstanding by way of principal in respect of sums advanced to the Secretary of State under subsection (1) shall not at any time exceed £4 million, or such larger sum, not exceeding £10 million, as the Secretary of State may by order made with the consent of the Treasury determine.

(3) No order under subsection (2) shall be made unless a draft of the order has been laid before Parliament and approved by resolution of each House of Parliament.

(4) Any sums advanced to the Secretary of State under subsection (1) shall be re-paid by the Secretary of State out of the Maternity Pay Fund into the National Loans Fund in such manner and at such times, and with interest thereon at such rate, as the Treasury may direct.

39.—(1) Subject to any regulations made under this section, the Secretary of State shall pay out of the Maternity Pay Fund to every employer who makes a claim under this section and who, being liable to pay, has paid maternity pay to an employee, an amount equal to the full amount of maternity pay so paid (in this section and sections 42 and 43 referred to as a " maternity pay rebate ").

Maternity pay rebate.

(2) The Secretary of State may if he thinks fit, and if he is satisfied that it would be just and equitable to do so having regard to all the relevant circumstances, pay such a rebate to an employer who makes a claim under this section and who has paid maternity pay to an employee in circumstances in which, by reason of the time limit provided for in section 36(2) a complaint by the employee has been dismissed, or would not be entertained, by an industrial tribunal.

PART III

(3) For the purposes of subsections (1) and (2), a payment of contractual remuneration by an employer shall be treated as a payment of maternity pay to the extent that, by virtue of section 35(4),—

    (a) it extinguishes the employer's liability to pay maternity pay; or

    (b) in a case falling within subsection (2), it would extinguish that liability if a complaint by the employee were not time-barred as described in that subsection.

(4) The Secretary of State shall make provision by regulations as to the making of claims for maternity pay rebates under this section and such regulations may in particular—

    (a) require a claim to be made within such time limit as may be prescribed; and

    (b) require a claim to be supported by such evidence as may be prescribed.

Payments to employees out of Maternity Pay Fund.

40.—(1) Where an employee claims that her employer is liable to pay her maternity pay and—

    (a) that she has taken all reasonable steps (other than proceedings to enforce a tribunal award) to recover payment from the employer; or

    (b) that her employer is insolvent (as defined in section 127 for the purposes of sections 122 to 126);

and that the whole or part of the maternity pay remains unpaid, the employee may apply to the Secretary of State under this section.

(2) If the Secretary of State is satisfied that the claim is well-founded the Secretary of State shall pay the employee out of the Maternity Pay Fund the amount of the maternity pay which appears to the Secretary of State to be unpaid.

(3) A payment made by the Secretary of State to an employee under this section shall, for the purpose of discharging any liability of the employer to the employee, be treated as if it had been made by the employer.

Unreasonable default by employer.

41.—(1) Where the Secretary of State makes a payment to an employee in respect of unpaid maternity pay in a case falling within section 40(1)(a) and it appears to the Secretary of State that the employer's default in payment was without reasonable excuse, the Secretary of State may recover from the employer such amount as the Secretary of State considers appropriate, not exceeding the amount of maternity pay which the employer failed to pay.

(2) Where a sum is recovered by the Secretary of State by virtue of this section that sum shall be paid into the Maternity Pay Fund.

42.—(1) Where the Secretary of State makes a payment to an employee under section 122 (which provides for payments out of the Redundancy Fund in respect of certain debts where an employer is insolvent) and that payment, in whole or in part, represents arrears of pay, then, in ascertaining for the purpose of section 40 the amount of any unpaid maternity pay, section 35(4) shall apply as if the arrears of pay in question had been duly paid by the employer to the employee in accordance with the contract of employment.

PART III
Supplementary provisions relating to employer's insolvency.

(2) Where the Secretary of State makes a payment to an employee out of the Redundancy Fund under section 122 which, if it had been made by the employer to the employee, would have attracted a maternity pay rebate from the Maternity Pay Fund in accordance with section 39, then, the Secretary of State shall make a payment out of the Maternity Pay Fund into the Redundancy Fund of an amount corresponding to the amount of rebate which would have been so payable.

43.—(1) A person who has—

(a) made a claim for a maternity pay rebate under section 39, in a case to which subsection (1) of that section applies; or

(b) applied for a payment under section 40,

may, subject to subsection (5), present a complaint to an industrial tribunal that—

(i) the Secretary of State has failed to make any such payment; or

(ii) any such payment made by the Secretary of State is less than the amount which should have been paid.

Complaints and appeals to industrial tribunal.

(2) Where an industrial tribunal finds that the Secretary of State ought to make any such payment or further payment, it shall make a declaration to that effect and shall also declare the amount of any such payment which it finds the Secretary of State ought to make.

(3) An employer who has made a claim for a maternity pay rebate under section 39, in a case to which subsection (2) of that section applies, may, subject to subsection (5), appeal to an industrial tribunal on the ground that—

(a) the Secretary of State has refused to pay a maternity pay rebate; or

(b) any rebate paid by the Secretary of State is less than the amount which should have been paid,

and if on any such appeal the tribunal is satisfied that it is just and equitable having regard to all the relevant circumstances

PART III that a maternity pay rebate should be paid or, as the case may be, finds that a further payment by way of rebate should be made, the tribunal shall determine accordingly, and the Secretary of State shall comply with the determination.

(4) Where the Secretary of State determines that an amount is recoverable from an employer under section 41, the employer may, subject to subsection (5), appeal to an industrial tribunal; and if on any such appeal the tribunal is satisfied that no amount should be recovered from the employer, or that a lesser or greater amount should be recovered (but in any case not exceeding the amount of maternity pay which the employer failed to pay) the tribunal shall determine accordingly and the amount, if any, so determined shall be the amount recoverable from the employer by the Secretary of State.

(5) An industrial tribunal shall not entertain a complaint or appeal under this section unless it is presented to the tribunal within the period of three months beginning with the date on which the relevant decision of the Secretary of State was communicated to the complainant or appellant or within such further period as the tribunal considers reasonable in a case where it is satisfied that it was not reasonably practicable for the complaint or appeal to be presented within the period of three months.

Provisions as to information.

44.—(1) Where an application is made to the Secretary of State by an employee under section 40, the Secretary of State may require—

(a) the employer to provide him with such information as the Secretary of State may reasonably require for the purpose of determining whether the employee's application is well-founded; and

(b) any person having the custody or control of any relevant records or other documents to produce for examination on behalf of the Secretary of State any such document in that person's custody or under his control which is of such a description as the Secretary of State may require.

(2) Any such requirement shall be made by a notice in writing given to the person on whom the requirement is imposed and may be varied or revoked by a subsequent notice so given.

(3) If a person refuses or wilfully neglects to furnish any information or produce any document which he has been required to furnish or produce by a notice under this section he shall be liable on summary conviction to a fine not exceeding £100.

(4) If any person in making a claim under section 39 or an application under section 40 or in purporting to comply with a

requirement of a notice under this section knowingly or recklessly makes any false statement he shall be liable on summary conviction to a fine not exceeding £400.

Right to return to work

45.—(1) The right to return to work of an employee who has been absent from work wholly or partly because of pregnancy or confinement is, subject to the following provisions of this Act, a right to return to work with her original employer, or, where appropriate, his successor, at any time before the end of the period of twenty-nine weeks beginning with the week in which the date of confinement falls, in the job in which she was employed under the original contract of employment and on terms and conditions not less favourable than those which would have been applicable to her if she had not been so absent.

(2) In subsection (1) " terms and conditions not less favourable than those which would have been applicable to her if she had not been so absent " means, as regards seniority, pension rights and other similar rights, that the period or periods of employment prior to the employee's absence shall be regarded as continuous with her employment following that absence.

(3) If an employee is entitled to return to work in accordance with subsection (1), but it is not practicable by reason of redundancy for the employer to permit her so to return to work she shall be entitled, where there is a suitable available vacancy, to be offered alternative employment with her employer (or his successor), or an associated employer, under a new contract of employment complying with subsection (4).

(4) The new contract of employment must be such that—

(a) the work to be done under the contract is of a kind which is both suitable in relation to the employee and appropriate for her to do in the circumstances; and

(b) the provisions of the new contract as to the capacity and place in which she is to be employed and as to the other terms and conditions of her employment are not substantially less favourable to her than if she had returned to work in accordance with subsection (1).

46. The remedies of an employee for infringement of either of the rights mentioned in section 45 are those conferred by or by virtue of the provisions of sections 47, 56 and 86 and Schedule 2.

Part III
Exercise of right to return to work.

47.—(1) An employee shall exercise her right to return to work by notifying the employer (who may be her original employer or a successor of that employer) at least seven days before the day on which she proposes to return of her proposal to return on that day (in this section referred to as the "notified day of return").

(2) An employer may postpone an employee's return to work until a date not more than four weeks after the notified day of return if he notifies her before that day that for specified reasons he is postponing her return until that date, and accordingly she will be entitled to return to work with him on that date.

(3) Subject to subsection (4), an employee may—

(a) postpone her return to work until a date not exceeding four weeks from the notified day of return, notwithstanding that that date falls after the end of the period of twenty-nine weeks mentioned in section 45(1); and

(b) where no day of return has been notified to the employer, extend the time during which she may exercise her right to return in accordance with subsection (1), so that she returns to work not later than four weeks from the expiration of the said period of twenty-nine weeks;

if before the notified day of return or, as the case may be, the expiration of the period of twenty-nine weeks she gives the employer a certificate from a registered medical practitioner stating that by reason of disease or bodily or mental disablement she will be incapable of work on the notified day of return or the expiration of that period, as the case may be.

(4) Where an employee has once exercised a right of postponement or extension under subsection (3)(a) or (b), she shall not again be entitled to exercise a right of postponement or extension under that subsection in connection with the same return to work.

(5) If an employee has notified a day of return but there is an interruption of work (whether due to industrial action or some other reason) which renders it unreasonable to expect the employee to return to work on the notified day of return, she may instead return to work when work resumes after the interruption or as soon as reasonably practicable thereafter.

(6) If no day of return has been notified and there is an interruption of work (whether due to industrial action or some other reason) which renders it unreasonable to expect the

PART III

employee to return to work before the expiration of the period of twenty-nine weeks referred to in section 45(1), or which appears likely to have that effect, and in consequence the employee does not notify a day of return, the employee may exercise her right to return in accordance with subsection (1) so that she returns to work at any time before the end of the period of fourteen days from the end of the interruption notwithstanding that she returns to work outside the said period of twenty-nine weeks.

(7) Where the employee has either—

(a) exercised the right under subsection (3)(b) to extend the period during which she may exercise her right to return; or

(b) refrained from notifying the day of return in the circumstances described in subsection (6),

the other of those subsections shall apply as if for the reference to the expiration of the period of twenty-nine weeks there were substituted a reference to the expiration of the further period of four weeks or, as the case may be, of the period of fourteen days from the end of the interruption of work.

(8) Where—

(a) an employee's return is postponed under subsection (2) or (3)(a), or

(b) the employee returns to work on a day later than the notified day of return in the circumstances described in subsection (5),

then, subject to subsection (4), references in those subsections and in sections 56 and 86 and Schedule 2 to the notified day of return shall be construed as references to the day to which the return is postponed or, as the case may be, that later day.

Contractual right to return to work.

48.—(1) An employee who has a right both under this Act and under a contract of employment, or otherwise, to return to work, may not exercise the two rights separately but may in returning to work take advantage of whichever right is, in any particular respect, the more favourable.

(2) The provisions of sections 45, 46, 47, 56 and 86 and paragraphs 1 to 4 and 6 of Schedule 2 shall apply, subject to any modifications necessary to give effect to any more favourable contractual terms, to the exercise of the composite right described in subsection (1) as they apply to the exercise of the right to return conferred solely by this Part.

Part IV

Termination of Employment

Rights of employer and employee to a minimum period of notice.

49.—(1) The notice required to be given by an employer to terminate the contract of employment of a person who has been continuously employed for four weeks or more—

(a) shall be not less than one week's notice if his period of continuous employment is less than two years;

(b) shall be not less than one week's notice for each year of continuous employment if his period of continuous employment is two years or more but less than twelve years; and

(c) shall be not less than twelve weeks' notice if his period of continuous employment is twelve years or more.

(2) The notice required to be given by an employee who has been continuously employed for four weeks or more to terminate his contract of employment shall be not less than one week.

(3) Any provision for shorter notice in any contract of employment with a person who has been continuously employed for four weeks or more shall have effect subject to the foregoing subsections, but this section shall not be taken to prevent either party from waiving his right to notice on any occasion, or from accepting a payment in lieu of notice.

(4) Any contract of employment of a person who has been continuously employed for twelve weeks or more which is a contract for a term certain of four weeks or less shall have effect as if it were for an indefinite period and, accordingly, subsections (1) and (2) shall apply to the contract.

(5) It is hereby declared that this section does not affect any right of either party to treat the contract as terminable without notice by reason of such conduct by the other party as would have enabled him so to treat it before the passing of this Act.

(6) The definition of week given by section 153(1) does not apply for the purposes of this section.

Rights of employee in period of notice.

50.—(1) If an employer gives notice to terminate the contract of employment of a person who has been continuously employed for four weeks or more, the provisions of Schedule 3 shall have effect as respects the liability of the employer for the period of notice required by section 49(1).

(2) If an employee who has been continuously employed for four weeks or more gives notice to terminate his contract of employment, the provisions of Schedule 3 shall have effect as respects the liability of the employer for the period of notice required by section 49(2).

(3) This section shall not apply in relation to a notice given by the employer or the employee if the notice to be given by the employer to terminate the contract must be at least one week more than the notice required by section 49(1).

51. If an employer fails to give the notice required by section 49, the rights conferred by section 50 (with Schedule 3) shall be taken into account in assessing his liability for breach of the contract.

PART IV
Measure of damages in proceedings against employers.

52. Sections 49 and 50 shall apply in relation to a contract all or any of the terms of which are terms which take effect by virtue of any provision contained in or having effect under an Act of Parliament, whether public or local, as they apply in relation to any other contract; and the reference in this section to an Act of Parliament includes, subject to any express provision to the contrary, an Act passed after this Act.

Statutory contracts.

53.—(1) An employee shall be entitled—

(a) if he is given by his employer notice of termination of his contract of employment;

(b) if his contract of employment is terminated by his employer without notice; or

(c) if, where he is employed under a contract for a fixed term, that term expires without being renewed under the same contract,

to be provided by his employer, on request, within fourteen days of that request, with a written statement giving particulars of the reasons for his dismissal.

Written statement of reasons for dismissal.

(2) An employee shall not be entitled to a written statement under subsection (1) unless on the effective date of termination he has been, or will have been, continuously employed for a period of twenty-six weeks ending with the last complete week before that date.

(3) A written statement provided under this section shall be admissible in evidence in any proceedings.

(4) A complaint may be presented to an industrial tribunal by an employee against his employer on the ground that the employer unreasonably refused to provide a written statement under subsection (1) or that the particulars of reasons given in purported compliance with that subsection are inadequate or untrue, and if the tribunal finds the complaint well-founded—

(a) it may make a declaration as to what it finds the employer's reasons were for dismissing the employee; and

(b) it shall make an award that the employer pay to the employee a sum equal to the amount of two weeks' pay.

PART IV

(5) An industrial tribunal shall not entertain a complaint under this section relating to the reasons for a dismissal unless it is presented to the tribunal at such a time that the tribunal would, in accordance with section 67(2) or (4), entertain a complaint of unfair dismissal in respect of that dismissal presented at the same time.

PART V

UNFAIR DISMISSAL

Right not to be unfairly dismissed

Right of employee not to be unfairly dismissed.

54.—(1) In every employment to which this section applies every employee shall have the right not to be unfairly dismissed by his employer.

(2) This section applies to every employment except in so far as its application is excluded by or under any provision of this Part or by section 141 to 149.

Meaning of unfair dismissal

Meaning of " dismissal ".

55.—(1) In this Part, except as respects a case to which section 56 applies, " dismissal " and " dismiss " shall be construed in accordance with the following provisions of this section.

(2) Subject to subsection (3), an employee shall be treated as dismissed by his employer if, but only if,—

(a) the contract under which he is employed by the employer is terminated by the employer, whether it is so terminated by notice or without notice, or

(b) where under that contract he is employed for a fixed term, that term expires without being renewed under the same contract, or

(c) the employee terminates that contract, with or without notice, in circumstances such that he is entitled to terminate it without notice by reason of the employer's conduct.

(3) Where an employer gives notice to an employee to terminate his contract of employment and, at a time within the period of that notice, the employee gives notice to the employer to terminate the contract of employment on a date earlier than the date on which the employer's notice is due to expire, the employee shall for the purposes of this Part be taken to be dismissed by his employer, and the reasons for the dismissal shall be taken to be the reasons for which the employer's notice is given.

(4) In this Part " the effective date of termination "—

(a) in relation to an employee whose contract of employment is terminated by notice, whether given by his employer or by the employee, means the date on which that notice expires;

(b) in relation to an employee whose contract of employment is terminated without notice, means the date on which the termination takes effect; and

(c) in relation to an employee who is employed under a contract for a fixed term, where that term expires without being renewed under the same contract, means the date on which that term expires.

(5) Where the notice required to be given by an employer by section 49 would, if duly given when notice of termination was given by the employer, or (where no notice was given) when the contract of employment was terminated by the employer, expire on a date later than the effective date of termination as defined by subsection (4), that later date shall be treated as the effective date of termination in relation to the dismissal for the purposes of sections 53(2), 64(1)(a) and 73(3) and paragraph 8(3) of Schedule 14.

56. Where an employee is entitled to return to work and has exercised her right to return in accordance with section 47 but is not permitted to return to work, then she shall be treated for the purposes of this Part as if she had been employed until the notified day of return, and, if she would not otherwise be so treated, as having been continuously employed until that day, and as if she had been dismissed with effect from that day for the reason for which she was not permitted to return.

Failure to permit woman to return to work after confinement treated as dismissal.

57.—(1) In determining for the purposes of this Part whether the dismissal of an employee was fair or unfair, it shall be for the employer to show—

General provisions relating to fairness of dismissal.

(a) what was the reason (or, if there was more than one, the principal reason) for the dismissal, and

(b) that it was a reason falling within subsection (2) or some other substantial reason of a kind such as to justify the dismissal of an employee holding the position which that employee held.

(2) In subsection (1)(b) the reference to a reason falling within this subsection is a reference to a reason which—

(a) related to the capability or qualifications of the employee for performing work of the kind which he was employed by the employer to do, or

(b) related to the conduct of the employee, or

PART V

(c) was that the employee was redundant, or

(d) was that the employee could not continue to work in the position which he held without contravention (either on his part or on that of his employer) of a duty or restriction imposed by or under an enactment.

(3) Where the employer has fulfilled the requirements of subsection (1), then, subject to sections 58 to 62, the determination of the question whether the dismissal was fair or unfair, having regard to the reason shown by the employer, shall depend on whether the employer can satisfy the tribunal that in the circumstances (having regard to equity and the substantial merits of the case) he acted reasonably in treating it as a sufficient reason for dismissing the employee.

(4) In this section, in relation to an employee,—

(a) " capability " means capability assessed by reference to skill, aptitude, health or any other physical or mental quality;

(b) " qualifications " means any degree, diploma or other academic, technical or professional qualification relevant to the position which the employee held.

Dismissal relating to trade union membership.

58.—(1) For the purposes of this Part, the dismissal of an employee by an employer shall be regarded as having been unfair if the reason for it (or, if more than one, the principal reason) was that the employee—

(a) was, or proposed to become, a member of an independent trade union;

(b) had taken, or proposed to take, part at any appropriate time in the activities of an independent trade union; or

(c) had refused, or proposed to refuse, to become or remain a member of a trade union which was not an independent trade union.

(2) In subsection (1), " appropriate time " in relation to an employee taking part in the activities of a trade union, means time which either—

(a) is outside his working hours, or

(b) is a time within his working hours at which, in accordance with arrangements agreed with or consent given by his employer, it is permissible for him to take part in those activities;

and in this subsection " working hours ", in relation to an employee, means any time when, in accordance with his contract of employment, he is required to be at work.

(3) Dismissal of an employee by an employer shall be regarded as fair for the purposes of this Part if—

    (a) it is the practice, in accordance with a union membership agreement, for employees for the time being of the same class as the dismissed employee to belong to a specified independent trade union, or to one of a number of specified independent trade unions; and

    (b) the reason for the dismissal was that the employee was not a member of the specified union or one of the specified unions, or had refused or proposed to refuse to become or remain a member of that union or one of those unions;

unless the employee genuinely objects on grounds of religious belief to being a member of any trade union whatsoever, in which case the dismissal shall be regarded as unfair.

(4) For the purposes of subsection (3), a union shall be treated as specified for the purposes of or in relation to a union membership agreement (in a case where it would not otherwise be so treated) if—

    (a) the Advisory, Conciliation and Arbitration Service has made a recommendation for recognition covering the employee in question which is operative within the meaning of section 15 of the Employment Protection Act 1975; or

    (b) the union has referred a recognition issue (within the meaning of that Act) covering that employee to the Advisory, Conciliation and Arbitration Service under section 11 of that Act and the Service has not declined to proceed on the reference under section 12 of that Act, the union has not withdrawn the reference, or from the reference, and the issue has not been settled or reported on under that section.

(5) Any reason by virtue of which a dismissal is to be regarded as unfair in consequence of subsection (1) or (3) is in this Part referred to as an inadmissible reason.

(6) In this section, unless the context otherwise requires, references to a trade union include references to a branch or section of a trade union.

59. Where the reason or principal reason for the dismissal of an employee was that he was redundant, but it is shown that the circumstances constituting the redundancy applied equally to one or more other employees in the same undertaking who

PART V held positions similar to that held by him and who have not been dismissed by the employer, and either—

(a) that the reason (or, if more than one, the principal reason) for which he was selected for dismissal was an inadmissible reason; or

(b) that he was selected for dismissal in contravention of a customary arrangement or agreed procedure relating to redundancy and there were no special reasons justifying a departure from that arrangement or procedure in his case,

then, for the purposes of this Part, the dismissal shall be regarded as unfair.

Dismissal on ground of pregnancy.

60.—(1) An employee shall be treated for the purposes of this Part as unfairly dismissed if the reason or principal reason for her dismissal is that she is pregnant or is any other reason connected with her pregnancy, except one of the following reasons—

(a) that at the effective date of termination she is or will have become, because of her pregnancy, incapable of adequately doing the work which she is employed to do;

(b) that, because of her pregnancy, she cannot or will not be able to continue after that date to do that work without contravention (either by her or her employer) of a duty or restriction imposed by or under any enactment.

(2) An employee shall be treated for the purposes of this Part as unfairly dismissed if her employer dismisses her for a reason mentioned in subsection (1)(a) or (b), but neither he nor any successor of his, where there is a suitable available vacancy, makes her an offer before or on the effective date of termination to engage her under a new contract of employment complying with subsection (3).

(3) The new contract of employment must—

(a) take effect immediately on the ending of employment under the previous contract, or, where that employment ends on a Friday, Saturday or Sunday, on or before the next Monday after that Friday, Saturday or Sunday;

(b) be such that the work to be done under the contract is of a kind which is both suitable in relation to the employee and appropriate for her to do in the circumstances; and

(c) be such that the provisions of the new contract as to the capacity and place in which she is to be employed and as to the other terms and conditions of her employment are not substantially less favourable to her than the corresponding provisions of the previous contract.

(4) On a complaint of unfair dismissal on the ground of failure to offer to engage an employee as mentioned in subsection (2), it shall be for the employer to show that he or a successor made an offer to engage her in compliance with subsections (2) and (3) or, as the case may be, that there was no suitable available vacancy for her.

(5) Section 55(3) shall not apply in a case where an employer gives notice to an employee to terminate her contract of employment for a reason mentioned in subsection (1)(a) or (b).

61.—(1) Where an employer—

(a) on engaging an employee informs the employee in writing that his employment will be terminated on the return to work of another employee who is, or will be, absent wholly or partly because of pregnancy or confinement; and

(b) dismisses the first-mentioned employee in order to make it possible to give work to the other employee;

then, for the purposes of section 57(1)(b), but without prejudice to the application of section 57(3), the dismissal shall be regarded as having been for a substantial reason of a kind such as to justify the dismissal of an employee holding the position which that employee held.

(2) Where an employer—

(a) on engaging an employee informs the employee in writing that his employment will be terminated on the end of a suspension such as is referred to in section 19 of another employee; and

(b) dismisses the first-mentioned employee in order to make it possible to allow the other employee to resume his original work;

then, for the purposes of section 57(1)(b), but without prejudice to the application of section 57(3), the dismissal shall be regarded as having been for a substantial reason of a kind such as to justify the dismissal of an employee holding the position which that employee held.

Dismissal of replacement.

PART V

Dismissal in connection with a lock-out, strike or other industrial action.

62.—(1) The provisions of this section shall have effect in relation to an employee who claims that he has been unfairly dismissed by his employer where at the date of dismissal—

(a) the employer was conducting or instituting a lock-out, or

(b) the employee was taking part in a strike or other industrial action.

(2) In such a case an industrial tribunal shall not determine whether the dismissal was fair or unfair unless it is shown—

(a) that one or more relevant employees of the same employer have not been dismissed, or

(b) that one or more such employees have been offered re-engagement, and that the employee concerned has not been offered re-engagement.

(3) Where it is shown that the condition referred to in paragraph (b) of subsection (2) is fulfilled, the provisions of sections 57 to 60 shall have effect as if in those sections for any reference to the reason or principal reason for which the employee was dismissed there were substituted a reference to the reason or principal reason for which he has not been offered re-engagement.

(4) In this section—

(a) " date of dismissal " means—

(i) where the employee's contract of employment was terminated by notice, the date on which the employer's notice was given, and

(ii) in any other case, the effective date of termination;

(b) " relevant employees " means—

(i) in relation to a lock-out, employees who were directly interested in the trade dispute in contemplation or furtherance of which the lock-out occurred, and

(ii) in relation to a strike or other industrial action, employees who took part in it; and

(c) any reference to an offer of re-engagement is a reference to an offer (made either by the original employer or by a successor of that employer or an associated employer) to re-engage an employee, either in the job which he held immediately before the date of dismissal or in a different job which would be reasonably suitable in his case.

63. In determining, for the purposes of this Part any question as to the reason, or principal reason, for which an employee was dismissed or any question whether the reason or principal reason for which an employee was dismissed was a reason fulfilling the requirements of section 57(1)(b) or whether the employer acted reasonably in treating it as a sufficient reason for dismissing him,—

PART V
Pressure on employer to dismiss unfairly.

(a) no account shall be taken of any pressure which, by calling, organising, procuring or financing a strike or other industrial action, or threatening to do so, was exercised on the employer to dismiss the employee, and

(b) any such question shall be determined as if no such pressure had been exercised.

Exclusion of section 54

64.—(1) Subject to subsection (3), section 54 does not apply to the dismissal of an employee from any employment if the employee—

Qualifying period and upper age limit.

(a) was not continuously employed for a period of not less than twenty-six weeks ending with the effective date of termination, or

(b) on or before the effective date of termination attained the age which, in the undertaking in which he was employed, was the normal retiring age for an employee holding the position which he held, or, if a man, attained the age of sixty-five, or, if a woman, attained the age of sixty.

(2) If an employee is dismissed by reason of any such requirement or recommendation as is referred to in section 19(1), subsection (1)(a) shall have effect in relation to that dismissal as if for the words " twenty-six weeks " there were substituted the words " four weeks ".

(3) Subsection (1) shall not apply to the dismissal of an employee if it is shown that the reason (or, if more than one, the principal reason) for the dismissal was an inadmissible reason.

65.—(1) An application may be made jointly to the Secretary of State by all the parties to a dismissal procedures agreement to make an order designating that agreement for the purposes of this section.

Exclusion in respect of dismissal procedures agreement.

(2) On any such application the Secretary of State may make such an order if he is satisfied—

(a) that every trade union which is a party to the dismissal procedures agreement is an independent trade union;

(b) that the agreement provides for procedures to be followed in cases where an employee claims that he has been, or is in the course of being, unfairly dismissed;

PART V

(c) that those procedures are available without discrimination to all employees falling within any description to which the agreement applies;

(d) that the remedies provided by the agreement in respect of unfair dismissal are on the whole as beneficial as (but not necessarily identical with) those provided in respect of unfair dismissal by this Part;

(e) that the procedures provided by the agreement include a right to arbitration or adjudication by an independent referee, or by a tribunal or other independent body, in cases where (by reason of an equality of votes or for any other reason) a decision cannot otherwise be reached; and

(f) that the provisions of the agreement are such that it can be determined with reasonable certainty whether a particular employee is one to whom the agreement applies or not.

(3) Where a dismissal procedures agreement is designated by an order under this section which is for the time being in force, the provisions of that agreement relating to dismissal shall have effect in substitution for any rights under section 54; and accordingly that section shall not apply to the dismissal of an employee from any employment if it is employment to which, and he is an employee to whom, those provisions of the agreement apply.

(4) Subsection (3) shall not apply to the right not to be unfairly dismissed for any reason mentioned in subsection (1) or (2) of section 60.

Revocation of exclusion order under s. 65.

66.—(1) At any time when an order under section 65 is in force, any of the parties to the dismissal procedures agreement to which the order relates may apply to the Secretary of State for the order to be revoked.

(2) If on any such application the Secretary of State is satisfied either—

(a) that it is the desire of all the parties to the dismissal procedures agreement that the order should be revoked, or

(b) that the agreement has ceased to fulfil all the conditions specified in section 65(2),

the Secretary of State shall revoke the order by a further order made under this section.

(3) Any order made under this section may contain such transitional provisions as appear to the Secretary of State to be

appropriate in the circumstances, and, in particular, may direct—

(a) that, notwithstanding section 65(3), an employee shall not be excluded from his rights under section 54 where the effective date of termination falls within a transitional period which is specified in the order and is a period ending with the date on which the order under this section takes effect and shall have an extended time for presenting a complaint under section 67 in respect of a dismissal where the effective date of termination falls within that period, and

(b) that in determining any complaint of unfair dismissal presented by an employee to whom the dismissal procedures agreement applies, where the effective date of termination falls within that transitional period, an industrial tribunal shall have regard to such considerations (in addition to those specified in this Part and paragraph 2 of Schedule 9) as may be specified in the order.

Remedies for unfair dismissal

67.—(1) A complaint may be presented to an industrial tribunal against an employer by any person (in this Part referred to as the complainant) that he was unfairly dismissed by the employer.

(2) Subject to subsection (4), an industrial tribunal shall not consider a complaint under this section unless it is presented to the tribunal before the end of the period of three months beginning with the effective date of termination or within such further period as the tribunal considers reasonable in a case where it is satisfied that it was not reasonably practicable for the complaint to be presented before the end of the period of three months.

(3) Subsection (2) shall apply in relation to a complaint to which section 62(3) applies as if for the reference to the effective date of termination there were substituted a reference to the first date on which any relevant employee was offered re-engagement (within the meaning of section 62(4)).

(4) An industrial tribunal shall consider a complaint under this section if, where the dismissal is with notice, the complaint is presented after the notice is given notwithstanding that it is presented before the effective date of termination and in relation to such a complaint the provisions of this Act, so far as they relate to unfair dismissal, shall have effect—

(a) as if references to a complaint by a person that he was unfairly dismissed by his employer included references

PART V

to a complaint by a person that his employer has given him notice in such circumstances that he will be unfairly dismissed when the notice expires;

(b) as if references to reinstatement included references to the withdrawal of the notice by the employer;

(c) as if references to the effective date of termination included references to the date which would be the effective date of termination on the expiry of the notice; and

(d) as if references to an employee ceasing to be employed included references to an employee having been given notice of dismissal.

Remedies for unfair dismissal.

68.—(1) Where on a complaint under section 67 an industrial tribunal finds that the grounds of the complaint are well-founded, it shall explain to the complainant what orders for reinstatement or re-engagement may be made under section 69 and in what circumstances they may be made, and shall ask him whether he wishes the tribunal to make such an order, and if he does express such a wish the tribunal may make an order under section 69.

(2) If on a complaint under section 67 the tribunal finds that the grounds of the complaint are well-founded and no order is made under section 69, the tribunal shall make an award of compensation for unfair dismissal, calculated in accordance with sections 72 to 74, to be paid by the employer to the employee.

Order for reinstatement or re-engagement.

69.—(1) An order under this section may be an order for reinstatement (in accordance with subsections (2) and (3)) or an order for re-engagement (in accordance with subsection (4)), as the industrial tribunal may decide, and in the latter case may be on such terms as the tribunal may decide.

(2) An order for reinstatement is an order that the employer shall treat the complainant in all respects as if he had not been dismissed, and on making such an order the tribunal shall specify—

(a) any amount payable by the employer in respect of any benefit which the complainant might reasonably be expected to have had but for the dismissal, including arrears of pay, for the period between the date of termination of employment and the date of reinstatement;

(b) any rights and privileges, including seniority and pension rights, which must be restored to the employee; and

(c) the date by which the order must be complied with.

(3) Without prejudice to the generality of subsection (2), if the complainant would have benefited from an improvement in his terms and conditions of employment had he not been dismissed, an order for reinstatement shall require him to be treated as if he had benefited from that improvement from the date on which he would have done so but for being dismissed.

(4) An order for re-engagement is an order that the complainant be engaged by the employer, or by a successor of the employer or by an associated employer, in employment comparable to that from which he was dismissed or other suitable employment, and on making such an order the tribunal shall specify the terms on which re-engagement is to take place including—
- (a) the identity of the employer;
- (b) the nature of the employment;
- (c) the remuneration for the employment;
- (d) any amount payable by the employer in respect of any benefit which the complainant might reasonably be expected to have had but for the dismissal, including arrears of pay, for the period between the date of termination of employment and the date of re-engagement;
- (e) any rights and privileges, including seniority and pension rights, which must be restored to the employee; and
- (f) the date by which the order must be complied with.

(5) In exercising its discretion under this section the tribunal shall first consider whether to make an order for reinstatement and in so doing shall take into account the following considerations, that is to say—
- (a) whether the complainant wishes to be reinstated;
- (b) whether it is practicable for the employer to comply with an order for reinstatement;
- (c) where the complainant caused or contributed to some extent to the dismissal, whether it would be just to order his reinstatement.

(6) If the tribunal decides not to make an order for reinstatement it shall then consider whether to make an order for re-engagement and if so on what terms; and in so doing the tribunal shall take into account the following considerations, that is to say—
- (a) any wish expressed by the complainant as to the nature of the order to be made;
- (b) whether it is practicable for the employer or, as the case may be, a successor or associated employer to comply with an order for re-engagement;

PART V

(c) where the complainant caused or contributed to some extent to the dismissal, whether it would be just to order his re-engagement and if so on what terms;

and except in a case where the tribunal takes into account contributory fault under paragraph (c) it shall, if it orders re-engagement, do so on terms which are, so far as is reasonably practicable, as favourable as an order for reinstatement.

Supplementary provisions relating to s.69.

70.—(1) Where in any case an employer has engaged a permanent replacement for a dismissed employee, the tribunal shall not take that fact into account in determining, for the purposes of subsection (5)(b) or (6)(b) of section 69, whether it is practicable to comply with an order for reinstatement or re-engagement unless the employer shows—

(a) that it was not practicable for him to arrange for the dismissed employee's work to be done without engaging a permanent replacement; or

(b) that he engaged the replacement after the lapse of a reasonable period, without having heard from the dismissed employee that he wished to be reinstated or re-engaged, and that when the employer engaged the replacement it was no longer reasonable for him to arrange for the dismissed employee's work to be done except by a permanent replacement.

(2) In calculating for the purpose of subsection (2)(a) or (4)(d) of section 69 any amount payable by the employer, the tribunal shall take into account, so as to reduce the employer's liability, any sums received by the complainant in respect of the period between the date of termination of employment and the date of reinstatement or re-engagement by way of—

(a) wages in lieu of notice or ex gratia payments paid by the employer;

(b) remuneration paid in respect of employment with another employer;

and such other benefits as the tribunal thinks appropriate in the circumstances.

Enforcement of s. 69 order and compensation.

71.—(1) If an order under section 69 is made and the complainant is reinstated or, as the case may be, re-engaged but the terms of the order are not fully complied with, then, subject to section 75, an industrial tribunal shall make an award of compensation, to be paid by the employer to the employee, of such amount as the tribunal thinks fit having regard to the loss sustained by the complainant in consequence of the failure to comply fully with the terms of the order.

(2) Subject to subsection (1), if an order under section 69 is made but the complainant is not reinstated or, as the case may be, re-engaged in accordance with the order—

> (a) the tribunal shall make an award of compensation for unfair dismissal, calculated in accordance with sections 72 to 74, to be paid by the employer to the employee; and
>
> (b) unless the employer satisfies the tribunal that it was not practicable to comply with the order, the tribunal shall make an additional award of compensation to be paid by the employer to the employee of an amount—
>
>> (i) where the dismissal is of a description referred to in subsection (3), not less than twenty-six nor more than fifty-two weeks' pay, or
>>
>> (ii) in any other case, not less than thirteen nor more than twenty-six weeks' pay.

(3) The descriptions of dismissal in respect of which an employer may incur a higher additional award in accordance with subsection (2)(b)(i) are the following, that is to say,—

> (a) a dismissal which is unfair by virtue of section 58(1) or (3);
>
> (b) a dismissal which is an act of discrimination within the meaning of the Sex Discrimination Act 1975 which is unlawful by virtue of that Act;
>
> (c) a dismissal which is an act of discrimination within the meaning of the Race Relations Act 1976 which is unlawful by virtue of that Act.

(4) Where in any case an employer has engaged a permanent replacement for a dismissed employee the tribunal shall not take that fact into account in determining, for the purposes of subsection (2)(b) whether it was practicable to comply with the order for reinstatement or re-engagement unless the employer shows that it was not practicable for him to arrange for the dismissed employee's work to be done without engaging a permanent replacement.

(5) Where in any case an industrial tribunal makes an award of compensation for unfair dismissal, calculated in accordance with sections 72 to 74, and the tribunal finds that the complainant has unreasonably prevented an order under section 69 from being complied with, it shall, without prejudice to the generality of section 74(4), take that conduct into account as a failure on the part of the complainant to mitigate his loss.

PART V

Compensation for unfair dismissal.

Amount of compensation

72. Where a tribunal makes an award of compensation for unfair dismissal under section 68(2) or 71(2)(*a*) the award shall consist of a basic award (calculated in accordance with section 73) and a compensatory award (calculated in accordance with section 74).

Calculation of basic award.

73.—(1) The amount of the basic award shall be the amount calculated in accordance with subsections (3) to (6), subject to—

(*a*) subsection (2) of this section (which provides for an award of two weeks' pay in certain redundancy cases);

(*b*) subsection (7) (which provides for the amount of the award to be reduced where the employee contributed to the dismissal);

(*c*) subsection (8) (which provides for a minimum award of two weeks' pay in certain cases);

(*d*) subsection (9) (which provides for the amount of the award to be reduced where the employee received a payment in respect of redundancy); and

1975 c. 65.
1976 c. 74.

(*e*) section 76 (which prohibits compensation being awarded under this Part and under the Sex Discrimination Act 1975 or the Race Relations Act 1976 in respect of the same matter).

(2) The amount of the basic award shall be two weeks' pay where the tribunal finds that the reason or principal reason for the dismissal of the employee was that he was redundant and the employee—

(*a*) by virtue of section 82(5) or (6) is not, or if he were otherwise entitled would not be, entitled to a redundancy payment; or

(*b*) by virtue of the operation of section 84(1) is not treated as dismissed for the purposes of Part VI.

(3) The amount of the basic award shall be calculated by reference to the period, ending with the effective date of termination, during which the employee has been continuously employed, by starting at the end of that period and reckoning backwards the numbers of years of employment falling within that period, and allowing—

(*a*) one and a half weeks' pay for each such year of employment which consists wholly of weeks in which the employee was not below the age of forty-one;

(b) one week's pay for each such year of employment which consists wholly of weeks in which the employee was below the age of forty-one and was not below the age of twenty-two; and

(c) half a week's pay for each such year of employment which consists wholly of weeks in which the employee was below the age of twenty-two and was not below the age of eighteen.

(4) Where, in reckoning the number of years of employment in accordance with subsection (3), twenty years of employment have been reckoned no account shall be taken of any year of employment earlier than those twenty years.

(5) Where in the case of an employee the effective date of termination is after the specified anniversary the amount of the basic award calculated in accordance with subsections (3) and (4) shall be reduced by the appropriate fraction.

(6) In subsection (5) " the specified anniversary " in relation to a man means the sixty-fourth anniversary of the day of his birth, and in relation to a woman means the fifty-ninth anniversary of the day of her birth, and " the appropriate fraction " means the fraction of which—

(a) the numerator is the number of whole months reckoned from the specified anniversary in the period beginning with that anniversary and ending with the effective date of termination; and

(b) the denominator is twelve.

(7) Where the tribunal finds that the dismissal was to any extent caused or contributed to by any action of the complainant it shall, except in a case where the dismissal was by reason of redundancy, reduce the amount of the basic award by such proportion as it considers just and equitable having regard to that finding.

(8) Where the amount calculated in accordance with subsections (3) to (7) is less than the amount of two weeks' pay, the amount of the basic award shall be two weeks' pay.

(9) The amount of the basic award shall be reduced or, as the case may be, be further reduced, by the amount of any redundancy payment awarded by the tribunal under Part VI in respect of the same dismissal or of any payment made by the employer to the employee on the ground that the dismissal was by reason of redundancy, whether in pursuance of Part VI or otherwise.

74.—(1) Subject to sections 75 and 76, the amount of the compensatory award shall be such amount as the tribunal considers just and equitable in all the circumstances having regard to the loss sustained by the complainant in consequence of the dismissal in so far as that loss is attributable to action taken by the employer.

PART V

(2) The said loss shall be taken to include—

(a) any expenses reasonably incurred by the complainant in consequence of the dismissal, and

(b) subject to subsection (3), loss of any benefit which he might reasonably be expected to have had but for the dismissal.

(3) The said loss, in respect of any loss of any entitlement or potential entitlement to, or expectation of, a payment on account of dismissal by reason of redundancy, whether in pursuance of Part VI or otherwise, shall include only the loss referable to the amount, if any, by which the amount of that payment would have exceeded the amount of a basic award (apart from any reduction under section 73(7) or (9)) in respect of the same dismissal.

(4) In ascertaining the said loss the tribunal shall apply the same rule concerning the duty of a person to mitigate his loss as applies to damages recoverable under the common law of England and Wales or of Scotland, as the case may be.

(5) In determining, for the purposes of subsection (1), how far any loss sustained by the complainant was attributable to action taken by the employer no account shall be taken of any pressure which, by calling, organising, procuring or financing a strike or other industrial action, or threatening to do so, was exercised on the employer to dismiss the employee, and that question shall be determined as if no such pressure had been exercised.

(6) Where the tribunal finds that the dismissal was to any extent caused or contributed to by any action of the complainant it shall reduce the amount of the compensatory award by such proportion as it considers just and equitable having regard to that finding.

(7) If the amount of any payment made by the employer to the employee on the ground that the dismissal was by reason of redundancy, whether in pursuance of Part VI or otherwise, exceeds the amount of the basic award which would be payable but for section 73(9) that excess shall go to reduce the amount of the compensatory award.

Limit on compensation.

75.—(1) The amount of compensation awarded to a person under section 71(1) or of a compensatory award to a person calculated in accordance with section 74 shall not exceed £5,200.

(2) The Secretary of State may by order increase the said limit of £5,200 or that limit as from time to time increased under this subsection, but no such order shall be made unless a draft of the order has been laid before Parliament and approved by a resolution of each House of Parliament.

(3) It is hereby declared for the avoidance of doubt that the limit imposed by this section applies to the amount which the industrial tribunal would, apart from this section, otherwise award in respect of the subject matter of the complaint after taking into account any payment made by the respondent to the complainant in respect of that matter and any reduction in the amount of the award required by any enactment or rule of law.

76.—(1) Where compensation falls to be awarded in respect of any act both under the provisions of this Act relating to unfair dismissal and under one or both of the following Acts, namely the Sex Discrimination Act 1975 and the Race Relations Act 1976, an industrial tribunal shall not award compensation under any one of those two or, as the case may be, three Acts in respect of any loss or other matter which is or has been taken into account under the other or any other of them by the tribunal or another industrial tribunal in awarding compensation on the same or another complaint in respect of that act.

Compensation for act which is both sex or racial discrimination (or both) and unfair dismissal.
1975 c. 65.
1976 c. 74.

(2) Without prejudice to section 75 (whether as enacted or as applied by section 65 of the Sex Discrimination Act 1975 or section 56 of the Race Relations Act 1976) in a case to which subsection (1) applies, the aggregate of the following amounts of compensation awarded by an industrial tribunal, that is to say—

(a) any compensation awarded under the said Act of 1975; and

(b) any compensation awarded under the said Act of 1976; and

(c) any compensation awarded under section 71(1) or, as the case may be, which is calculated in accordance with section 74,

shall not exceed the limit for the time being imposed by section 75.

Interim relief

77.—(1) An employee who presents a complaint to an industrial tribunal that he has been unfairly dismissed by his employer and that the reason for the dismissal (or, if more than one, the principal reason) was that the employee—

(a) was, or proposed to become, a member of a particular independent trade union; or

(b) had taken, or proposed to take, part at any appropriate time in the activities of a particular independent trade union of which he was or proposed to become a member;

may, subject to the following provisions of this section, apply to the tribunal for an order under the following provisions of this section.

Interim relief pending determination of complaint of unfair dismissal.

PART V

(2) An industrial tribunal shall not entertain an application under this section unless—

(a) it is presented to the tribunal before the end of the period of seven days immediately following the effective date of termination (whether before, on or after that date); and

(b) before the end of that period there is also so presented a certificate in writing signed by an authorised official of the independent trade union of which the employee was or had proposed to become a member stating that on the date of the dismissal the employee was or had proposed to become a member of the union and that there appear to be reasonable grounds for supposing that the reason for his dismissal (or, if more than one, the principal reason) was one alleged in the complaint.

(3) An industrial tribunal shall determine an application under this section as soon as practicable after receiving the application and the relevant certificate, but shall, at least seven days before the date of the hearing, give the employer a copy of the application and certificate, together with notice of the date, time and place of the hearing.

(4) An industrial tribunal shall not exercise any power it has of postponing the hearing in the case of an application under this section except where the tribunal is satisfied that special circumstances exist which justify it in doing so.

(5) If on hearing an application under this section it appears to an industrial tribunal that it is likely that on determining the complaint to which the application relates the tribunal will find that the complainant was unfairly dismissed and that the reason for the dismissal (or if more than one, the principal reason) was a reason mentioned in subsection (1), the tribunal shall announce its findings and explain to both parties (if present) what powers the tribunal may exercise on an application under this section and in what circumstances it may exercise them, and shall ask the employer (if present) whether he is willing, pending the determination or settlement of the complaint—

(a) to reinstate the employee, that is to say, to treat the employee in all respects as if he had not been dismissed; or

(b) if not, to re-engage him in another job on terms and conditions not less favourable than those which would have been applicable to him if he had not been dismissed.

(6) In subsection (5) " terms and conditions not less favourable than those which would have been applicable to him if he had not been dismissed " means, as regards seniority, pension

rights and other similar rights, that the period prior to the dismissal shall be regarded as continuous with his employment following the dismissal.

(7) If the employer states that he is willing to reinstate the employee, the tribunal shall make an order to that effect.

(8) If the employer states that he is willing to re-engage the employee in another job and specifies the terms and conditions on which he is willing to do so, the tribunal shall ask the employee whether he is willing to accept the job on those terms and conditions, and—

(a) if the employee is willing to accept the job on those terms and conditions, the tribunal shall make an order to that effect; and

(b) if the employee is unwilling to accept the job on those terms and conditions, then, if the tribunal is of the opinion that the refusal is reasonable, the tribunal shall make an order for the continuation of his contract of employment, but otherwise the tribunal shall make no order under this section.

(9) If, on the hearing of an application under this section, the employer fails to attend before the tribunal or he states that he is unwilling either to reinstate the employee or re-engage him as mentioned in subsection (5), the tribunal shall make an order for the continuation of the employee's contract of employment.

(10) In this section—

"appropriate time" has the same meaning as in section 23;

"authorised official", in relation to a trade union, means an official of the union authorised by the union to act for the purposes of this section;

and any reference to the date of dismissal is a reference—

(a) where the employee's contract of employment was terminated by notice (whether given by his employer or by him), to the date on which the employer's notice was given; and

(b) in any other case, to the effective date of termination.

(11) A document purporting to be an authorisation of an official by a trade union to act for the purposes of this section and to be signed on behalf of the union shall be taken to be such an authorisation unless the contrary is proved, and a document purporting to be a certificate signed by such an official shall be taken to be signed by him unless the contrary is proved.

PART V
Orders for continuation of contract of employment.

78.—(1) An order for the continuation of a contract of employment under section 77 shall be an order that the contract of employment, if it has been terminated, shall continue in force as if it had not been terminated and if not, shall on its termination, continue in force, in either case until the determination or settlement of the complaint and only for the purposes of pay or any other benefit derived from the employment, seniority, pension rights and other similar matters and for the purpose of determining for any purpose the period for which the employee has been continuously employed.

(2) Where the tribunal makes any such order it shall specify in the order the amount which is to be paid by the employer to the employee by way of pay in respect of each normal pay period or part of any such period falling between the date of the dismissal and the determination or settlement of the complaint and, subject to subsection (5), the amount so specified shall be that which the employee could reasonably have been expected to earn during that period or part, and shall be paid, in the case of a payment for any such period falling wholly or partly after the order, on the normal pay day for that period and, in the case of a payment for any past period, within a time so specified.

(3) If an amount is payable by way of pay in pursuance of any such order in respect only of part of a normal pay period the amount shall be calculated by reference to the whole period and be reduced proportionately.

(4) Any payment made to an employee by an employer under his contract of employment, or by way of damages for breach of that contract, in respect of any normal pay period or part of any such period shall go towards discharging the employer's liability in respect of that period under subsection (2), and conversely any payment under subsection (2) in respect of any period shall go towards discharging any liability of the employer under, or in respect of breach of, the contract of employment in respect of that period.

(5) If an employee, on or after being dismissed by his employer, receives a lump sum which, or part of which, is in lieu of wages but is not referable to any normal pay period, the tribunal shall take the payment into account in determining the amount of pay to be payable in pursuance of any such order.

(6) For the purposes of this section the amount which an employee could reasonably have been expected to earn, his normal pay period and the normal pay day for each such period shall be determined as if he had not been dismissed.

79.—(1) At any time between the making of an order by an industrial tribunal under section 77 and the determination or settlement of the complaint to which it relates, the employer or the employee may apply to the tribunal for the revocation or variation of the order on the ground of a relevant change of circumstances since the making of the order, and that section shall apply to the application as it applies to an application for an order under that section except that—

> (a) no certificate need be presented to the tribunal under subsection (2)(b), and no copy of the certificate need be given to the employer under subsection (3), of that section; and
>
> (b) in the case of an application by an employer, for the reference in the said subsection (3) to the employer there shall be substituted a reference to the employee.

PART V
Supplementary provisions relating to interim relief.

(2) If on the application of an employee an industrial tribunal is satisfied that the employer has not complied with the terms of an order for the reinstatement or re-engagement of the employee under section 77(7) or (8),—

> (a) the tribunal shall make an order for the continuation of the employee's contract of employment and section 78 shall apply to an order under this subsection as it applies to an order for the continuation of a contract of employment under section 77; and
>
> (b) the tribunal shall also order the employer to pay the employee such compensation as the tribunal considers just and equitable in all the circumstances having regard to the infringement of the employee's right to be reinstated or re-engaged in pursuance of the order under section 77(7) or (8) and to any loss suffered by the employee in consequence of the non-compliance.

(3) If on the application of an employee an industrial tribunal is satisfied that the employer has not complied with the terms of an order for the continuation of a contract of employment, then—

> (a) if the non-compliance consists of a failure to pay an amount by way of pay specified in the order, the tribunal shall determine the amount of pay owed by the employer to the employee on the date of the determination, and, if on that date the tribunal also determines the employee's complaint that he has been unfairly dismissed by his employer, the tribunal shall specify that amount separately from any other sum awarded to the employee; and
>
> (b) in any other case, the tribunal shall order the employer to pay the employee such compensation as the tribunal

PART V

Teacher in aided school dismissed on requirement of local education authority.
1944 c. 31.

considers just and equitable in all the circumstances having regard to any loss suffered by the employee in consequence of the non-compliance.

Teachers in aided schools

80.—(1) Where a teacher in an aided school is dismissed by the governors or managers of the school in pursuance of a requirement of the local education authority under paragraph (*a*) of the proviso to section 24(2) of the Education Act 1944, this Part shall have effect in relation to the dismissal as if—

(*a*) the local education authority had at all material times been the teacher's employer, and

(*b*) the local education authority had dismissed him, and the reason or principal reason for which they did so had been the reason or principal reason for which they required his dismissal.

(2) For the purposes of a complaint under section 67 as applied by this section—

(*a*) section 71(2)(*b*) shall have effect as if for the words "not practicable to comply" there were substituted the words "not practicable for the local education authority to permit compliance"; and

(*b*) section 74(5) shall have effect as if any reference to the employer were a reference to the local education authority.

PART VI

REDUNDANCY PAYMENTS

Right to redundancy payment

General provisions as to right to redundancy payment.

81.—(1) Where an employee who has been continuously employed for the requisite period—

(*a*) is dismissed by his employer by reason of redundancy, or

(*b*) is laid off or kept on short-time to the extent specified in subsection (1) of section 88 and complies with the requirements of that section,

then, subject to the following provisions of this Act, the employer shall be liable to pay to him a sum (in this Act referred to as a "redundancy payment") calculated in accordance with Schedules 4, 13 and 14.

(2) For the purposes of this Act an employee who is dismissed shall be taken to be dismissed by reason of redundancy if the dismissal is attributable wholly or mainly to—

(*a*) the fact that his employer has ceased, or intends to cease, to carry on the business for the purposes of which the employee was employed by him, or has ceased, or intends to cease, to carry on that business in the place where the employee was so employed, or

(b) the fact that the requirements of that business for employees to carry out work of a particular kind, or for employees to carry out work of a particular kind in the place where he was so employed, have ceased or diminished or are expected to cease or diminish.

For the purposes of this subsection, the business of the employer together with the business or businesses of his associated employers shall be treated as one unless either of the conditions specified in this subsection would be satisfied without so treating those businesses.

(3) In subsection (2), "cease" means cease either permanently or temporarily and from whatsoever cause, and "diminish" has a corresponding meaning.

(4) For the purposes of subsection (1), the requisite period is the period of two years ending with the relevant date, excluding any week which began before the employee attained the age of eighteen.

82.—(1) An employee shall not be entitled to a redundancy payment if immediately before the relevant date the employee—

(a) if a man, has attained the age of sixty-five, or

(b) if a woman, has attained the age of sixty.

(2) Except as provided by section 92, an employee shall not be entitled to a redundancy payment by reason of dismissal where his employer, being entitled to terminate his contract of employment without notice by reason of the employee's conduct, terminates it either—

(a) without notice, or

(b) by giving shorter notice than that which, in the absence of such conduct, the employer would be required to give to terminate the contract, or

(c) by giving notice (not being such shorter notice as is mentioned in paragraph (b)) which includes, or is accompanied by, a statement in writing that the employer would, by reason of the employee's conduct, be entitled to terminate the contract without notice.

(3) If an employer makes an employee an offer (whether in writing or not) before the ending of his employment under the previous contract to renew his contract of employment, or to re-engage him under a new contract of employment, so that the

PART VI

General exclusions from right to redundancy payment.

Part VI renewal or re-engagement would take effect either immediately on the ending of his employment under the previous contract or after an interval of not more than four weeks thereafter, the provisions of subsections (5) and (6) shall have effect.

(4) For the purposes of the application of subsection (3) to a contract under which the employment ends on a Friday, Saturday or Sunday—

   (a) the renewal or re-engagement shall be treated as taking effect immediately on the ending of the employment under the previous contract if it takes effect on or before the next Monday after that Friday, Saturday or Sunday ; and

   (b) the interval of four weeks shall be calculated as if the employment had ended on that Monday.

(5) If an employer makes an employee such an offer as is referred to in subsection (3) and either—

   (a) the provisions of the contract as renewed, or of the new contract, as to the capacity and place in which he would be employed, and as to the other terms and conditions of his employment, would not differ from the corresponding provisions of the previous contract; or

   (b) the first-mentioned provisions would differ (wholly or in part) from those corresponding provisions, but the offer constitutes an offer of suitable employment in relation to the employee ;

and in either case the employee unreasonably refuses that offer, he shall not be entitled to a redundancy payment by reason of his dismissal.

(6) If an employee's contract of employment is renewed, or he is re-engaged under a new contract of employment, in pursuance of such an offer as is referred to in subsection (3), and the provisions of the contract as renewed, or of the new contract, as to the capacity and place in which he is employed, and as to the other terms and conditions of his employment, differ (wholly or in part) from the corresponding provisions of the previous contract but the employment is suitable in relation to the employee, and during the trial period referred to in section 84 the employee unreasonably terminates the contract, or unreasonably gives notice to terminate it and the contract is thereafter, in consequence, terminated, he shall not be entitled to a redundancy payment by reason of his dismissal from employment under the previous contract.

(7) Any reference in this section to re-engagement by the employer shall be construed as including a reference to re-engagement by the employer or by any associated employer, and any reference in this section to an offer made by the employer shall be construed as including a reference to an offer made by an associated employer.

83.—(1) In this Part, except as respects a case to which section 86 applies, "dismiss" and "dismissal" shall, subject to sections 84, 85 and 93, be construed in accordance with subsection (2).

(2) An employee shall be treated as dismissed by his employer if, but only if,—

(a) the contract under which he is employed by the employer is terminated by the employer, whether it is so terminated by notice or without notice, or

(b) where under that contract he is employed for a fixed term, that term expires without being renewed under the same contract, or

(c) the employee terminates that contract with or without notice, in circumstances (not falling within section 92(4)) such that he is entitled to terminate it without notice by reason of the employer's conduct.

84.—(1) If an employee's contract of employment is renewed, or he is re-engaged under a new contract of employment in pursuance of an offer (whether in writing or not) made by his employer before the ending of his employment under the previous contract, and the renewal or re-engagement takes effect either immediately on the ending of that employment or after an interval of not more than four weeks thereafter, then, subject to subsections (3) to (6), the employee shall not be regarded as having been dismissed by his employer by reason of the ending of his employment under the previous contract.

(2) For the purposes of the application of subsection (1) to a contract under which the employment ends on a Friday, Saturday or Sunday—

(a) the renewal or re-engagement shall be treated as taking effect immediately on the ending of the employment if it takes effect on or before the Monday after that Friday, Saturday or Sunday, and

(b) the interval of four weeks referred to in that subsection shall be calculated as if the employment had ended on that Monday.

PART VI

(3) If, in a case to which subsection (1) applies, the provisions of the contract as renewed, or of the new contract, as to the capacity and place in which the employee is employed, and as to the other terms and conditions of his employment, differ (wholly or in part) from the corresponding provisions of the previous contract, there shall be a trial period in relation to the contract as renewed, or the new contract (whether or not there has been a previous trial period under this section).

(4) The trial period shall begin with the ending of the employee's employment under the previous contract and end with the expiration of the period of four weeks beginning with the date on which the employee starts work under the contract as renewed, or the new contract, or such longer period as may be agreed in accordance with the next following subsection for the purpose of retraining the employee for employment under that contract.

(5) Any such agreement shall—
   (a) be made between the employer and the employee or his representative before the employee starts work under the contract as renewed or, as the case may be, the new contract;
   (b) be in writing;
   (c) specify the date of the end of the trial period; and
   (d) specify the terms and conditions of employment which will apply in the employee's case after the end of that period.

(6) If during the trial period—
   (a) the employee, for whatever reason, terminates the contract, or gives notice to terminate it and the contract is thereafter, in consequence, terminated; or
   (b) the employer, for a reason connected with or arising out of the change to the renewed, or new, employment, terminates the contract, or gives notice to terminate it and the contract is thereafter, in consequence, terminated,

then, unless the employee's contract of employment is again renewed, or he is again re-engaged under a new contract of employment, in circumstances such that subsection (1) again applies, he shall be treated as having been dismissed on the date on which his employment under the previous contract or, if there has been more than one trial period, the original contract ended for the reason for which he was then dismissed or would have been dismissed had the offer (or original offer) of renewed, or new, employment not been made, or, as the case may be, for the reason which resulted in that offer being made.

(7) Any reference in this section to re-engagement by the employer shall be construed as including a reference to re-engagement by the employer or by any associated employer, and any reference in this section to an offer made by the employer shall be construed as including a reference to an offer made by an associated employer.

85.—(1) The provisions of this section shall have effect where—

(a) an employer gives notice to an employee to terminate his contract of employment, and

(b) at a time within the obligatory period of that notice, the employee gives notice in writing to the employer to terminate the contract of employment on a date earlier than the date on which the employer's notice is due to expire.

(2) Subject to the following provisions of this section, in the circumstances specified in subsection (1) the employee shall, for the purposes of this Part, be taken to be dismissed by his employer.

(3) If, before the employee's notice is due to expire, the employer gives him notice in writing—

(a) requiring him to withdraw his notice terminating the contract of employment as mentioned in subsection (1)(b) and to continue in the employment until the date on which the employer's notice expires, and

(b) stating that, unless he does so, the employer will contest any liability to pay to him a redundancy payment in respect of the termination of his contract of employment,

but the employee does not comply with the requirements of that notice, the employee shall not be entitled to a redundancy payment by virtue of subsection (2) except as provided by subsection (4).

(4) Where, in the circumstances specified in subsection (1), the employer has given notice to the employee under subsection (3), and on a reference to a tribunal it appears to the tribunal, having regard both to the reasons for which the employee seeks to leave the employment and those for which the employer requires him to continue in it, to be just and equitable that the employee should receive the whole or part of any redundancy payment to which he would have been entitled apart from subsection (3), the tribunal may determine that the employer shall be liable to pay to the employee—

(a) the whole of the redundancy payment to which the employee would have been so entitled, or

PART VI

      (*b*) such part of that redundancy payment as the tribunal thinks fit.

  (5) In this section—

      (*a*) if the actual period of the employer's notice (that is to say, the period beginning at the time when the notice is given and ending at the time when it expires) is equal to the minimum period which (whether by virtue of any enactment or otherwise) is required to be given by the employer to terminate the contract of employment, " the obligatory period ", in relation to that notice, means the actual period of the notice;

      (*b*) in any other case, " the obligatory period ", in relation to an employer's notice, means that period which, being equal to the minimum period referred to in paragraph (*a*), expires at the time when the employer's notice expires.

Failure to permit woman to return to work after confinement treated as dismissal.

86. Where an employee is entitled to return to work and has exercised her right to return in accordance with section 47 but is not permitted to return to work, then she shall be treated for the purposes of the provisions of this Part as if she had been employed until the notified day of return, and, if she would not otherwise be so treated, as having been continuously employed until that day, and as if she had been dismissed with effect from that day for the reason for which she was not permitted to return.

Lay-off and short-time.

87.—(1) Where an employee is employed under a contract on such terms and conditions that his remuneration thereunder depends on his being provided by the employer with work of the kind which he is employed to do, he shall, for the purposes of this Part, be taken to be laid off for any week in respect of which, by reason that the employer does not provide such work for him, he is not entitled to any remuneration under the contract.

(2) Where by reason of a diminution in the work provided for an employee by his employer (being work of a kind which under his contract the employee is employed to do) the employee's remuneration for any week is less than half a week's pay, he shall for the purposes of this Part be taken to be kept on short-time for that week.

Right to redundancy payment by reason of lay-off or short-time.

88.—(1) An employee shall not be entitled to a redundancy payment by reason of being laid off or kept on short-time unless he gives notice in writing to his employer indicating (in whatsoever terms) his intention to claim a redundancy payment in respect of lay-off or short-time (in this Act referred to as a " notice of intention to claim ") and, before the service of that notice, either—

(a) he has been laid off or kept on short-time for four or more consecutive weeks of which the last before the service of the notice ended on the date of service thereof or ended not more than four weeks before that date, or

(b) he has been laid off or kept on short-time for a series of six or more weeks (of which not more than three were consecutive) within a period of thirteen weeks, where the last week of the series before the service of the notice ended on the date of service thereof or ended not more than four weeks before that date.

(2) Where an employee has given notice of intention to claim,—

(a) he shall not be entitled to a redundancy payment in pursuance of that notice unless he terminates his contract of employment by a week's notice which (whether given before or after or at the same time as the notice of intention to claim) is given before the end of the period allowed for the purposes of this paragraph (as specified in subsection (5) of section 89), and

(b) he shall not be entitled to a redundancy payment in pursuance of the notice of intention to claim if he is dismissed by his employer (but without prejudice to any right to a redundancy payment by reason of the dismissal):

Provided that, if the employee is required by his contract of employment to give more than a week's notice to terminate the contract, the reference in paragraph (a) to a week's notice shall be construed as a reference to the minimum notice which he is so required to give.

(3) Subject to subsection (4), an employee shall not be entitled to a redundancy payment in pursuance of a notice of intention to claim if, on the date of service of that notice, it was reasonably to be expected that the employee (if he continued to be employed by the same employer) would, not later than four weeks after that date, enter upon a period of employment of not less than thirteen weeks during which he would not be laid off or kept on short-time for any week.

(4) Subsection (3) shall not apply unless, within seven days after the service of the notice of intention to claim, the employer gives to the employee notice in writing that he will contest any liability to pay to him a redundancy payment in pursuance of the notice of intention to claim.

PART VI
Supplementary provisions relating to redundancy payments in respect of lay-off or short-time.

89.—(1) If, in a case where an employee gives notice of intention to claim and the employer gives notice under section 88(4) (in this section referred to as a "counter-notice"), the employee continues or has continued, during the next four weeks after the date of service of the notice of intention to claim, to be employed by the same employer, and he is or has been laid off or kept on short-time for each of those weeks, it shall be conclusively presumed that the condition specified in subsection (3) of section 88 was not fulfilled.

(2) For the purposes of both subsection (1) of section 88 and subsection (1) of this section, it is immaterial whether a series of weeks (whether it is four weeks, or four or more weeks, or six or more weeks) consists wholly of weeks for which the employee is laid off or wholly of weeks for which he is kept on short-time or partly of the one and partly of the other.

(3) For the purposes mentioned in subsection (2), no account shall be taken of any week for which an employee is laid off or kept on short-time where the lay-off or short-time is wholly or mainly attributable to a strike or a lock-out (within the meaning of paragraph 24 of Schedule 13) whether the strike or lock-out is in the trade or industry in which the employee is employed or not and whether it is in Great Britain or elsewhere.

(4) Where the employer gives a counter-notice within seven days after the service of a notice of intention to claim, and does not withdraw the counter-notice by a subsequent notice in writing, the employee shall not be entitled to a redundancy payment in pursuance of the notice of intention to claim except in accordance with a decision of an industrial tribunal.

(5) The period allowed for the purposes of subsection (2)(a) of section 88 is as follows, that is to say,—

(a) if the employer does not give a counter-notice within seven days after the service of the notice of intention to claim, that period is three weeks after the end of those seven days;

(b) if the employer gives a counter-notice within those seven days, but withdraws it by a subsequent notice in writing, that period is three weeks after the service of the notice of withdrawal;

(c) if the employer gives a counter-notice within those seven days and does not so withdraw it, and a question as to the right of the employee to a redundancy payment in pursuance of the notice of intention to claim is referred to a tribunal, that period is three weeks after the tribunal has notified to the employee its decision on that reference.

(6) For the purposes of paragraph (c) of subsection (5) no account shall be taken of any appeal against the decision of the tribunal, or of any requirement to the tribunal to state a case for the opinion of the High Court or the Court of Session, or of any proceedings or decision in consequence of such an appeal or requirement.

PART VI

90.—(1) Subject to the following provisions of this section, for the purposes of the provisions of this Act so far as they relate to redundancy payments, " the relevant date ", in relation to the dismissal of an employee—

The relevant date.

- (a) where his contract of employment is terminated by notice, whether given by his employer or by the employee, means the date on which that notice expires;
- (b) where his contract of employment is terminated without notice, means the date on which the termination takes effect;
- (c) where he is employed under a contract for a fixed term and that term expires as mentioned in subsection (2)(b) of section 83, means the date on which that term expires;
- (d) where he is treated, by virtue of subsection (6) of section 84, as having been dismissed on the termination of his employment under a previous contract, means—
    - (i) for the purposes of section 101, the date which is the relevant date as defined by paragraph (a), (b) or (c) in relation to the renewed, or new, contract, or, where there has been more than one trial period under section 84, the last such contract; and
    - (ii) for the purposes of any other provision, the date which is the relevant date as defined by paragraph (a), (b) or (c) in relation to the previous contract, or, where there has been more than one trial period under section 84, the original contract; and
- (e) where he is taken to be dismissed by virtue of section 85(2), means the date on which the employee's notice to terminate his contract of employment expires.

(2) " The relevant date ", in relation to a notice of intention to claim or a right to a redundancy payment in pursuance of such a notice,—

- (a) in a case falling within paragraph (a) of subsection (1) of section 88, means the date on which the last of the four or more consecutive weeks before the service of the notice came to an end, and

PART VI

(b) in a case falling within paragraph (b) of that subsection means the date on which the last of the series of six or more weeks before the service of the notice came to an end.

(3) Where the notice required to be given by an employer to terminate a contract of employment by section 49(1) would, if duly given when notice of termination was given by the employer, or (where no notice was given) when the contract of employment was terminated by the employer, expire on a date later than the relevant date as defined by subsection (1), then for the purposes of section 81(4) and paragraph 1 of Schedule 4 and paragraph 8(4) of Schedule 14, that later date shall be treated as the relevant date in relation to the dismissal.

Reference of questions to tribunal.

91.—(1) Any question arising under this Part as to the right of an employee to a redundancy payment, or as to the amount of a redundancy payment, shall be referred to and determined by an industrial tribunal.

(2) For the purposes of any such reference, an employee who has been dismissed by his employer shall, unless the contrary is proved, be presumed to have been so dismissed by reason of redundancy.

(3) In relation to lay-off or short-time, the questions which may be referred to and determined by an industrial tribunal, as mentioned in subsection (1), shall include any question whether an employee will become entitled to a redundancy payment if he is not dismissed by his employer and he terminates his contract of employment as mentioned in subsection (2)(a) of section 88; and any such question shall for the purposes of this Part be taken to be a question as to the right of the employee to a redundancy payment.

Special provisions as to termination of contract in cases of misconduct or industrial dispute.

92.—(1) Where at any such time as is mentioned in subsection (2), an employee who—

(a) has been given notice by his employer to terminate his contract of employment, or

(b) has given notice to his employer under subsection (1) of section 88,

takes part in a strike, in such circumstances that the employer is entitled, by reason of his taking part in the strike, to treat the contract of employment as terminable without notice, and the employer for that reason terminates the contract as mentioned in subsection (2) of section 82, that subsection shall not apply to that termination of the contract.

(2) The times referred to in subsection (1) are—
- (a) in a case falling within paragraph (a) of that subsection any time within the obligatory period of the employer's notice (as defined by section 85(5)), and
- (b) in a case falling within paragraph (b) of subsection (1), any time after the service of the notice mentioned in that paragraph.

(3) Where at any such time as is mentioned in subsection (2) an employee's contract of employment, otherwise than by reason of his taking part in a strike, is terminated by his employer in the circumstances specified in subsection (2) of section 82, and is so terminated as mentioned therein, and on a reference to an industrial tribunal it appears to the tribunal, in the circumstances of the case, to be just and equitable that the employee should receive the whole or part of any redundancy payment to which he would have been entitled apart from section 82(2), the tribunal may determine that the employer shall be liable to pay to the employee—

- (a) the whole of the redundancy payment to which the employee would have been so entitled, or
- (b) such part of that redundancy payment as the tribunal thinks fit.

(4) Where an employee terminates his contract of employment without notice, being entitled to do so by reason of a lock-out by his employer, section 83(2)(c) shall not apply to that termination of the contract.

(5) In this section "strike" and "lock-out" each has the meaning given by paragraph 24 of Schedule 13.

93.—(1) Where in accordance with any enactment or rule of law—

- (a) any act on the part of an employer, or
- (b) any event affecting an employer (including, in the case of an individual, his death),

operates so as to terminate a contract under which an employee is employed by him, that act or event shall for the purposes of this Part be treated as a termination of the contract by the employer, if apart from this subsection it would not constitute a termination of the contract by him and, in particular, the provisions of sections 83, 84 and 90 shall apply accordingly.

(2) Where subsection (1) applies, and the employee's contract of employment is not renewed, and he is not re-engaged under a new contract of employment, so as to be treated, by virtue of section 84(1), as not having been dismissed, he shall, without prejudice to section 84(6), be taken for the purposes of this

PART VI

Part to be dismissed by reason of redundancy if the circumstances in which his contract is not so renewed and he is not so re-engaged are wholly or mainly attributable to one or other of the facts specified in paragraphs (a) and (b) of section 81(2)

(3) For the purposes of subsection (2), section 81(2)(a), in so far as it relates to the employer ceasing or intending to cease to carry on the business, shall be construed as if the reference to the employer included a reference to any person to whom, in consequence of the act or event in question, power to dispose of the business has passed.

(4) In this section, any reference to section 84(1) includes a reference to that subsection as applied by section 94(2) or as so applied and (where appropriate) modified by section 95(2), and where section 84(1) applies as so modified the references in subsection (2) of this section to renewal of or re-engagement under a contract of employment shall be construed as including references to renewal of or re-engagement in employment otherwise than under a contract of employment.

Change of ownership of business.

94.—(1) The provisions of this section shall have effect where—

(a) a change occurs (whether by virtue of a sale or other disposition or by operation of law) in the ownership of a business for the purposes of which a person is employed, or of a part of such a business, and

(b) in connection with that change the person by whom the employee is employed immediately before the change occurs (in this section referred to as " the previous owner ") terminates the employee's contract of employment, whether by notice or without notice.

(2) If, by agreement with the employee, the person who immediately after the change occurs is the owner of the business, or of the part of the business in question, as the case may be (in this section referred to as " the new owner "), renews the employee's contract of employment (with the substitution of the new owner for the previous owner) or re-engages him under a new contract of employment, sections 84 and 90 shall have effect as if the renewal or re-engagement had been a renewal or re-engagement by the previous owner (without any substitution of the new owner for the previous owner).

(3) If the new owner offers to renew the employee's contract of employment (with the substitution of the new owner for the previous owner) or to re-engage him under a new contract of employment, subsections (3) to (6) of section 82 shall have effect, subject to subsection (4), in relation to that offer as they would have had effect in relation to the like offer made by the previous owner.

(4) For the purposes of the operation, in accordance with subsection (3), of subsections (3) to (6) of section 82 in relation to an offer made by the new owner—

- (a) the offer shall not be treated as one whereby the provisions of the contract as renewed, or of the new contract, as the case may be, would differ from the corresponding provisions of the contract as in force immediately before the dismissal by reason only that the new owner would be substituted for the previous owner as the employer, and
- (b) no account shall be taken of that substitution in determining whether the refusal of the offer was unreasonable or, as the case may be, whether the employee acted reasonably in terminating the renewed, or new, employment during the trial period referred to in section 84.

(5) The preceding provisions of this section shall have effect (subject to the necessary modifications) in relation to a case where—

- (a) the person by whom a business, or part of a business, is owned immediately before a change is one of the persons by whom (whether as partners, trustees or otherwise) it is owned immediately after the change, or
- (b) the persons by whom a business, or part of a business, is owned immediately before a change (whether as partners, trustees or otherwise) include the person by whom, or include one or more of the persons by whom, it is owned immediately after the change,

as those provisions have effect where the previous owner and the new owner are wholly different persons.

(6) Sections 82(7) and 84(7) shall not apply in any case to which this section applies.

(7) Nothing in this section shall be construed as requiring any variation of a contract of employment by agreement between the parties to be treated as constituting a termination of the contract.

95.—(1) Section 94 shall apply to a transfer of functions from a person not acting on behalf of the Crown (in this section referred to as the transferor) to a government department or any other officer or body exercising functions on behalf of the Crown (in this section referred to as the transferee) as that section applies to a transfer of a business, but with the substitution for references to the previous owner and new owner of references to the transferor and transferee respectively.

Transfer to Crown employment.

PART VI

(2) In so far as the renewal or re-engagement of the employee by the transferee is in employment otherwise than under a contract of employment—
- (a) references in section 94 (and in sections 82(4) to (6), 84 and 90 as they apply by virtue of that section) to a contract of employment or to the terms of such a contract shall be construed as references to employment otherwise than under such a contract and to the terms of such employment; and
- (b) references in subsection (4) of section 94, as modified by subsection (1) of this section, to the substitution of the transferee for the transferor shall be construed as references to the substitution of employment by the transferee otherwise than under a contract of employment for employment by the transferor under such a contract.

Exemption orders.

96.—(1) If at any time there is in force an agreement between one or more employers or organisations of employers and one or more trade unions representing employees, whereby employees to whom the agreement applies have a right in certain circumstances to payments on the termination of their contracts of employment, and, on the application of all the parties to the agreement, the Secretary of State, having regard to the provisions of the agreement, is satisfied that section 81 should not apply to those employees, he may make an order under this section in respect of that agreement.

(2) The Secretary of State shall not make an order under this section in respect of an agreement unless the agreement indicates (in whatsoever terms) the willingness of the parties to it to submit to an industrial tribunal such questions as are mentioned in paragraph (b) of subsection (3).

(3) Where an order under this section is in force in respect of an agreement—
- (a) section 81 shall not have effect in relation to any employee who immediately before the relevant date is an employee to whom the agreement applies, but
- (b) section 91 shall have effect in relation to any question arising under the agreement as to the right of an employee to a payment on the termination of his employment, or as to the amount of such a payment, as if the payment were a redundancy payment and the question arose under this Part.

(4) Any order under this section may be revoked by a subsequent order thereunder, whether in pursuance of an application made by all or any of the parties to the agreement in question or without any such application.

97.—(1) A claim under paragraph 1 of Schedule 11 to the Employment Protection Act 1975 (claims as to recognised terms and conditions and general level of terms and conditions) may be reported to the Advisory, Conciliation and Arbitration Service in accordance with that Schedule, and may be referred by the Service to the Central Arbitration Committee, and the Committee may make an award under that Schedule, notwithstanding that the terms and conditions which it is claimed that the employer is not observing consist of or include terms and conditions as to payments to be made to employees in the circumstances specified in paragraph (a) or paragraph (b) of section 81(1) or in similar circumstances, and that provision for redundancy payments is made by this Act.

PART VI
Claims as to extension of terms and conditions.
1975 c. 71.

(2) Where a claim which is reported to the Advisory, Conciliation and Arbitration Service under the said paragraph 1 is founded upon recognised terms and conditions and relates to an agreement in respect of which an order under section 96 is for the time being in force, and the Central Arbitration Committee makes an award in pursuance of that claim, section 96(3) shall have effect in relation to all persons in respect of whom the employer is required by that award to observe the recognised terms and conditions, whether they are persons to whom section 96(3) would apply apart from this subsection or not.

98.—(1) The Secretary of State shall by regulations make provision for excluding the right to a redundancy payment, or reducing the amount of any redundancy payment, in such cases as may be prescribed by the regulations, being cases in which an employee has (whether by virtue of any statutory provision or otherwise) a right or claim (whether legally enforceable or not) to a periodical payment or lump sum by way of pension, gratuity or superannuation allowance which is to be paid by reference to his employment by a particular employer and is to be paid, or to begin to be paid, at the time when he leaves that employment or within such period thereafter as may be prescribed by the regulations.

Exclusion or reduction of redundancy payment on account of pension rights.

(2) Provision shall be made by any such regulations for securing that the right to a redundancy payment shall not be excluded, and that the amount of a redundancy payment shall not be reduced, by reason of any right or claim to a periodical payment or lump sum, in so far as that payment or lump sum represents such compensation as is mentioned in section 118(1) and is payable under a statutory provision, whether made or passed before, on or after the passing of this Act.

(3) In relation to any case where, under section 85 or 92 or 110, an industrial tribunal determines that an employer is liable

PART VI to pay part (but not the whole) of a redundancy payment, any reference in this section to a redundancy payment, or to the amount of a redundancy payment, shall be construed as a reference to that part of the redundancy payment, or to the amount of that part, as the case may be.

Public offices, etc.

99.—(1) Without prejudice to any exemption or immunity of the Crown, section 81 shall not apply to any person in respect of any employment which—

1965 c. 74.
    (*a*) is employment in a public office for the purposes of section 38 of the Superannuation Act 1965, or

    (*b*) whether by virtue of that Act or otherwise, is treated for the purposes of pensions and other superannuation benefits as service in the civil service of the State, or

    (*c*) is employment by any such body as is specified in Schedule 5.

(2) Without prejudice to any exemption or immunity of the Crown, section 81 shall not apply to any person in respect of his employment in any capacity under the Government of an overseas territory (as defined by section 114).

Domestic servants.

100.—(1) For the purposes of the application of the provisions of this Part to an employee who is employed as a domestic servant in a private household, those provisions (except section 94) shall apply as if the household were a business and the maintenance of the household were the carrying on of that business by the employer.

(2) Without prejudice to section 146(1), section 81 shall not apply to any person in respect of employment as a domestic servant in a private household, where the employer is the father, mother, grandfather, grandmother, stepfather, stepmother, son, daughter, grandson, granddaughter, stepson, stepdaughter, brother, sister, half-brother, or half-sister of the employee.

Claims for redundancy payments.

101.—(1) Notwithstanding anything in the preceding previsions of this Part, an employee shall not be entitled to a redundancy payment unless, before the end of the period of six months beginning with the relevant date—

    (*a*) the payment has been agreed and paid, or

    (*b*) the employee has made a claim for the payment by notice in writing given to the employer, or

    (*c*) a question as to the right of the employee to the payment, or as to the amount of the payment, has been referred to an industrial tribunal, or

    (*d*) a complaint relating to his dismissal has been presented by the employee under section 67.

(2) An employee shall not by virtue of subsection (1) lose his right to a redundancy payment if, during the period of six months immediately following the period mentioned in that subsection, the employee—

(a) makes such a claim as is referred to in paragraph (b) of that subsection,

(b) refers to a tribunal such a question as is referred to in paragraph (c) of that subsection, or

(c) makes such a complaint as is referred to in paragraph (d) of that subsection,

and it appears to the tribunal to be just and equitable that the employee should receive a redundancy payment having regard to the reason shown by the employee for his failure to take any such step as is referred to in paragraph (a), (b) or (c) of this subsection within the period mentioned in subsection (1), and to all the other relevant circumstances.

102.—(1) On making any redundancy payment, otherwise than in pursuance of a decision of a tribunal which specifies the amount of the payment to be made, the employer shall give to the employee a written statement indicating how the amount of the payment has been calculated.

Written particulars of redundancy payment.

(2) Any employer who without reasonable excuse fails to comply with subsection (1) shall be guilty of an offence and liable on summary conviction to a fine not exceeding £20.

(3) If an employer fails to comply with the requirements of subsection (1), then (without prejudice to any proceedings for an offence under subsection (2)) the employee may by notice in writing to the employer require him to give to the employee a written statement complying with those requirements within such period (not being less than one week beginning with the day on which the notice is given) as may be specified in the notice; and if the employer without reasonable excuse fails to comply with the notice he shall be guilty of an offence under this subsection and liable on summary conviction—

(a) if it is his first conviction of an offence under this subsection, to a fine not exceeding £20, or

(b) in any other case, to a fine not exceeding £100.

Redundancy Fund

103.—(1) The Secretary of State shall continue to have the control and management of the Redundancy Fund established under section 26 of the Redundancy Payments Act 1965 (in this Part referred to as "the fund"), and payments shall be made out of the fund in accordance with the provisions of sections 104 to 109 and 156 and Part VII.

Establishment and maintenance of fund.
1965 c. 62.

PART VI

(2) The Secretary of State shall prepare accounts of the fund in such form as the Treasury may direct, and shall send them to the Comptroller and Auditor General not later than the end of the month of November following the end of the financial year to which the accounts relate; and the Comptroller and Auditor General shall examine and certify the accounts and shall lay copies thereof, together with his report thereon, before Parliament.

(3) Any moneys forming part of the fund may from time to time be paid over to the National Debt Commissioners and by them invested, in accordance with such directions as may be given by the Treasury, in such manner as may be specified by an order of the Treasury for the time being in force under section 22(1) of the National Savings Bank Act 1971.

1971 c. 29.

Redundancy rebates.

104.—(1) Subject to the provisions of this section, the Secretary of State shall make a payment (in this Part referred to as a "redundancy rebate") out of the fund to any employer who—

(a) is liable under the foregoing provisions of this Part to pay, and has paid, a redundancy payment to an employee, or

(b) under an agreement in respect of which an order is in force under section 96, is liable to make, and has made, a payment to an employee on the termination of his contract of employment, or

(c) by virtue of any award made by the Central Arbitration Committee as mentioned in section 97(2) in relation to an agreement in respect of which such an order is in force, is liable to make, and has made, a payment to an employee on the termination of his contract of employment.

(2) No redundancy rebate shall be payable by virtue of this section in a case falling within paragraph (b) or paragraph (c) of subsection (1) if the employee's right to the payment referred to in that paragraph arises by virtue of a period of employment (computed in accordance with the provisions of the agreement in question) which is less than one hundred and four weeks.

(3) The Secretary of State may if he thinks fit pay a redundancy rebate to an employer who has paid an employee a redundancy payment in circumstances in which, owing to section 101, the employee had no right to, and the employer had no liability for, the payment, if the Secretary of State is satisfied that it would be just and equitable to do so having regard to all the relevant circumstances.

(4) The amount of any redundancy rebate shall (subject to subsection (7)) be calculated in accordance with Schedule 6.

(5) The Secretary of State shall make provision by regulations as to the making of claims for redundancy rebates; and any such regulations may in particular—

- (a) require any claim for a redundancy rebate to be made at or before a time prescribed by the regulations;
- (b) in such cases as may be so prescribed, require prior notice that such a claim may arise to be given at or before a time so prescribed, so however that, where the claim would relate to an employer's payment in respect of dismissal, the regulations shall not require the notice to be given more than four weeks before the date on which the termination of the contract of employment takes effect; and
- (c) for the purpose of determining the right of any person to, and the amount of, any redundancy rebate, require a person at any time when he makes a claim or gives prior notice as mentioned in paragraph (a) or paragraph (b) to provide such evidence and such other information, and to produce for examination on behalf of the Secretary of State documents in his custody or under his control of such descriptions, as may be determined in accordance with the regulations.

(6) In relation to any case where, under section 85 or 92 or 110, an industrial tribunal determines that an employer is liable to pay part (but not the whole) of a redundancy payment, the reference in subsection (1)(a) to a redundancy payment shall be construed as a reference to that part of the redundancy payment.

(7) If any employer who, in accordance with subsection (1), would be entitled to a redundancy rebate fails to give prior notice as required by any such regulations in accordance with paragraph (b) of subsection (5) and it appears to the Secretary of State that he has so failed without reasonable excuse, the Secretary of State may, subject to section 108, reduce the amount of the rebate by such proportion (not exceeding one-tenth) as appears to the Secretary of State to be appropriate in the circumstances.

(8) Any person who—

- (a) in providing any information required by regulations under this section, makes a statement which he knows to be false in a material particular, or recklessly makes a statement which is false in a material particular, or
- (b) produces for examination in accordance with any such regulations a document which to his knowledge has been wilfully falsified,

shall be guilty of an offence.

PART VI

(9) A person guilty of an offence under subsection (8) shall be liable on summary conviction to a fine not exceeding the prescribed sum or to imprisonment for a term not exceeding three months or both, or on conviction on indictment to a fine or to imprisonment for a term not exceeding two years or both.

(10) In subsection (9) above "the prescribed sum" means—

1977 c. 45.
(a) in England and Wales, the prescribed sum within the meaning of section 28 of the Criminal Law Act 1977 (that is to say, £1,000 or another sum fixed by order under section 61 of that Act to take account of changes in the value of money);

1975 c. 21.
(b) in Scotland, the prescribed sum within the meaning of section 289B of the Criminal Procedure (Scotland) Act 1975 (that is to say, £1,000 or another sum fixed by an order made under section 289D of that Act for that purpose).

Payments out of fund to employers in other cases.
105.—(1) The Secretary of State may make payments out of the fund to employers in respect of employees to whom this section applies.

(2) This section applies to employees to whom, by virtue of section 144(2), 145 or 149, section 81 does not apply.

(3) The Secretary of State may determine the classes of employees to whom this section applies in respect of whom payments are to be made by virtue of this section, and, with the approval of the Treasury, may determine the amounts of the payments which may be so made in respect of any class of such employees.

1975 c. 14.
(4) The payments made to an employer by virtue of this section shall not, in respect of any period, exceed the amount appearing to the Secretary of State to be equal to the amount paid into the fund from the appropriate employment protection allocation (under section 134 of the Social Security Act 1975) from all secondary Class 1 contributions paid by that employer under Part I of that Act.

Payments out of fund to employees.
106.—(1) Where an employee claims that his employer is liable to pay to him an employer's payment, and either—

(a) that the employee has taken all reasonable steps (other than legal proceedings) to recover the payment from the employer and that the employer has refused or failed to pay it, or has paid part of it and has refused or failed to pay the balance, or

(b) that the employer is insolvent and that the whole or part of the payment remains unpaid,

the employee may apply to the Secretary of State for a payment under this section.

(2) If on an application under this section the Secretary of State is satisfied—

   (a) that the employee is entitled to the employer's payment;

   (b) that either of the conditions specified in subsection (1) is fulfilled; and

   (c) that, in a case where the employer's payment is such a payment as is mentioned in paragraph (b) or paragraph (c) of section 104(1), the employee's right to the payment arises by virtue of a period of employment (computed in accordance with the provisions of the agreement in question) which is not less than one hundred and four weeks,

the Secretary of State shall pay to the employee out of the fund a sum calculated in accordance with Schedule 7, reduced by so much (if any) of the employer's payment as has been paid.

(3) Where the Secretary of State pays a sum to an employee in respect of an employer's payment—

   (a) all rights and remedies of the employee with respect to the employer's payment, or (if the Secretary of State has paid only part of it) all his rights and remedies with respect to that part of the employer's payment, shall be transferred to and vest in the Secretary of State; and

   (b) any decision of an industrial tribunal requiring the employer's payment to be paid to the employee shall have effect as if it required that payment, or, as the case may be, that part of it which the Secretary of State has paid, to be paid to the Secretary of State;

and any moneys recovered by the Secretary of State by virtue of this subsection shall be paid into the fund.

(4) Where the Secretary of State pays a sum under this section in respect of an employer's payment, then (subject to the following provisions of this subsection) section 104 shall apply as if that sum had been paid by the employer to the employee on account of that payment; but if, in a case falling within paragraph (a) of subsection (1), it appears to the Secretary of State that the refusal or failure of the employer to pay the employer's payment, or part of it, as the case may be, was without reasonable excuse, the Secretary of State may, subject to section 108, withhold any redundancy rebate to which the employer would otherwise be entitled in respect of the employer's payment, or

PART VI

may reduce the amount of any such rebate to such extent as the Secretary of State considers appropriate.

(5) For the purposes of this section an employer shall be taken to be insolvent if—

(a) he has become bankrupt or has made a composition or arrangement with his creditors or a receiving order is made against him;

1914 c. 59.

(b) he has died and an order has been made under section 130 of the Bankruptcy Act 1914 for the administration of his estate according to the law of bankruptcy, or by virtue of an order of the court his estate is being administered in accordance with the rules set out in Part I of Schedule 1 to the Administration of Estates Act 1925; or

1925 c. 23.

(c) where the employer is a company, a winding-up order has been made with respect to it or a resolution for voluntary winding-up has been passed with respect to it, or a receiver or manager of its undertaking has been duly appointed, or possession has been taken, by or on behalf of the holders of any debentures secured by a floating charge, of any property of the company comprised in or subject to the charge.

(6) In the application of this section to Scotland, for paragraphs (a), (b) and (c) of subsection (5) there shall be substituted the following paragraphs:—

(a) an award of sequestration has been made on his estate, or he has executed a trust deed for his creditors or entered into a composition contract;

1913 c. 20.

(b) he has died and a judicial factor appointed under section 163 of the Bankruptcy (Scotland) Act 1913 is required by the provisions of that section to divide his insolvent estate among his creditors; or

(c) where the employer is a company, a winding-up order has been made or a resolution for voluntary winding-up is passed with respect to it or a receiver of its undertaking is duly appointed.

(7) In this section "legal proceedings" does not include any proceedings before an industrial tribunal, but includes any proceedings to enforce a decision or award of an industrial tribunal.

Supplementary provisions relating to applications under s. 106.

107.—(1) Where an employee makes an application to the Secretary of State under section 106, the Secretary of State may, by notice in writing given to the employer, require the employer to provide the Secretary of State with such information, and to produce for examination on behalf of the Secretary of State documents in his custody or under his control of such descriptions, as the Secretary of State may reasonably require for the purpose of determining whether the application is well-founded.

PART VI

(2) If any person on whom a notice is served under this section fails without reasonable excuse to comply with a requirement imposed by the notice, he shall be guilty of an offence and liable on summary conviction to a fine not exceeding £100.

(3) Any person who—
   (a) in providing any information required by a notice under this section, makes a statement which he knows to be false in a material particular, or recklessly makes a statement which is false in a material particular, or
   (b) produces for examination in accordance with any such notice a document which to his knowledge has been wilfully falsified,

shall be guilty of an offence under this subsection.

(4) A person guilty of an offence under subsection (3) shall be liable on summary conviction to a fine not exceeding the prescribed sum or to imprisonment for a term not exceeding three months or both, or on conviction on indictment to a fine or to imprisonment for a term not exceeding two years or both.

(5) In subsection (4) above " the prescribed sum " means—
   (a) in England and Wales, the prescribed sum within the meaning of section 28 of the Criminal Law Act 1977 (that is to say, £1,000 or another sum fixed by order under section 61 of that Act to take account of changes in the value of money);
   (b) in Scotland, the prescribed sum within the meaning of section 289B of the Criminal Procedure (Scotland) Act 1975 (that is to say, £1,000 or another sum fixed by an order made under section 289D of that Act for that purpose).

1977 c. 45.

1975 c. 21.

108.—(1) Subsections (2) and (3) shall have effect where—
   (a) a claim is made for a redundancy rebate on the grounds that an employer is liable to pay, and has paid, an employer's payment, or prior notice that such a claim may arise is given in accordance with regulations made under section 104(5)(b), or

References and appeals to tribunal relating to payments out of fund.

(b) an application is made to the Secretary of State for a payment under section 106, where it is claimed that an employer is liable to pay an employer's payment.

(2) Where any such claim or application is made or such prior notice is given, there shall be referred to an industrial tribunal—

(a) any question as to the liability of the employer to pay the employer's payment;
(b) in a case falling within paragraph (a) of subsection (1), any question as to the amount of the rebate payable in accordance with Schedule 6;
(c) in a case falling within paragraph (b) of subsection (1), any question as to the amount of the sum payable in accordance with Schedule 7.

(3) For the purposes of any reference under subsection (2), an employee who has been dismissed by his employer shall, unless the contrary is proved, be presumed to have been so dismissed by reason of redundancy.

(4) Where, in any case to which section 104(3) applies, the Secretary of State refuses to pay a redundancy rebate, the employer may appeal to an industrial tribunal; and if on any such appeal the tribunal is satisfied that it is just and equitable having regard to all the relevant circumstances that a redundancy rebate should be paid, the tribunal shall determine accordingly, and the Secretary of State shall comply with any such determination of a tribunal.

(5) In any case where the Secretary of State withholds, or reduces the amount of, a redundancy rebate in pursuance of section 104(7) or section 106(4), the employer may appeal to an industrial tribunal; and if on any such appeal the tribunal is satisfied—

(a) in a case where the rebate was withheld, that it should be paid in full, or should be reduced instead of being withheld, or
(b) in a case where the rebate was reduced, that it should not be reduced, or should be reduced by a smaller or larger proportion than that which the Secretary of State has applied,

the tribunal shall determine accordingly, and the Secretary of State shall comply with any such determination.

Financial provisions relating to the fund.

109.—(1) Subject to the following provisions of this section, the Treasury may from time to time advance out of the National Loans Fund to the Secretary of State for the purposes of the fund such sums as the Secretary of State may request; and any sums advanced to the Secretary of State under this section shall be paid into the fund.

(2) The aggregate amount outstanding by way of principal in respect of sums advanced to the Secretary of State under this section shall not at any time exceed £16 million or such larger sum not exceeding £40 million as the Secretary of State may by order made with the consent of the Treasury determine.

(3) Any sums advanced to the Secretary of State under this section shall be repaid by the Secretary of State out of the fund into the National Loans Fund in such manner and at such times, and with interest thereon at such rate, as the Treasury may direct.

(4) An order shall not be made under this section unless a draft of the order has been laid before Parliament and approved by resolution of each House of Parliament.

Miscellaneous and supplemental

110.—(1) The provisions of this section shall have effect where, after an employer has given notice to an employee to terminate his contract of employment (in this section referred to as a " notice of termination ")—

Strike during currency of employer's notice to terminate contract.

    (a) the employee begins to take part in a strike of employees of the employer, and

    (b) the employer serves on him a notice in writing (in this section referred to as a " notice of extension ") requesting him to agree to extend the contract of employment beyond the time of expiry by an additional period comprising as many available days as the number of working days lost by striking (in this section referred to as " the proposed period of extension ").

(2) A notice of extension shall indicate the reasons for which the employer makes the request contained in the notice, and shall state that unless either—

    (a) the employee complies with the request, or

    (b) the employer is satisfied that, in consequence of sickness, injury or otherwise, he is unable to comply with it, or that (notwithstanding that he is able to comply with it) in the circumstances it is reasonable for him not to do so,

the employer will contest any liability to pay him a redundancy payment in respect of the dismissal effected by the notice of termination.

(3) For the purposes of this section an employee shall be taken to comply with the request contained in a notice of

PART VI extension if, but only if, on each available day within the proposed period of extension, he attends at his proper or usual place of work and is ready and willing to work, whether he has signified his agreement to the request in any other way or not.

(4) Where an employee on whom a notice of extension has been served—

   (a) complies with the request contained in the notice, or

   (b) does not comply with it, but attends at his proper or usual place of work and is ready and willing to work on one or more (but not all) of the available days within the proposed period of extension,

the notice of termination shall have effect, and shall be deemed at all material times to have had effect, as if the period specified in it had (in a case falling within paragraph (a)) been extended beyond the time of expiry by an additional period equal to the proposed period of extension or (in a case falling within paragraph (b)) had been extended beyond the time of expiry up to the end of the day (or, if more than one, the last of the days) on which he so attends and is ready and willing to work; and section 50 and Schedule 3 shall apply accordingly as if the period of notice required by section 49 were extended to a corresponding extent.

(5) Subject to subsection (6), if an employee on whom a notice of extension is served in pursuance of subsection (1) does not comply with the request contained in the notice, he shall not be entitled to a redundancy payment by reason of the dismissal effected by the notice of termination, unless the employer agrees to pay such a payment to him notwithstanding that the request has not been complied with.

(6) Where a notice of extension has been served, and on a reference to an industrial tribunal it appears to the tribunal that the employee has not complied with the request contained in the notice and the employer has not agreed to pay a redundancy payment in respect of the dismissal in question, but that the employee was unable to comply with the request, or it was reasonable for him not to comply with it, as mentioned in subsection (2)(b) the tribunal may determine that the employer shall be liable to pay to the employee—

   (a) the whole of any redundancy payment to which the employee would have been entitled apart from subsection (5), or

   (b) such part of any such redundancy payment as the tribunal thinks fit.

(7) The service of a notice of extension, and any extension, by virtue of subsection (4) of the period specified in a notice of termination,—

    (a) shall not affect any right either of the employer or of the employee to terminate the contract of employment (whether before, at or after the time of expiry) by a further notice or without notice, and

    (b) shall not affect the operation of sections 81 to 102 in relation to any such termination of the contract of employment.

(8) In this section any reference to the number of working days lost by striking is a reference to the number of working days in the period beginning with the date of service of the notice of termination and ending with the time of expiry which are days on which the employee in question takes part in a strike of employees of the employer.

(9) In this section, "strike" has the meaning given by paragraph 24 of Schedule 13, "time of expiry", in relation to a notice of termination, means the time at which the notice would expire apart from this section, "working day", in relation to an employee, means a day on which, in accordance with his contract of employment, he is normally required to work, "available day", in relation to an employee, means a working day beginning at or after the time of expiry which is a day on which he is not taking part in a strike of employees of the employer, and "available day within the proposed period of extension" means an available day which begins before the end of that period.

111.—(1) The provisions of this section shall have effect with respect to employment of any of the following descriptions, that is to say—

    (a) any such employment as is mentioned in paragraph (a), paragraph (b) or paragraph (c) of subsection (1) of section 99 (whether as originally enacted or as modified by any order under section 149(1));

    (b) any employment remunerated out of the revenue of the Duchy of Lancaster or the Duchy of Cornwall;

    (c) any employment remunerated out of the Queen's Civil List;

    (d) any employment remunerated out of Her Majesty's Privy Purse.

(2) Where the Secretary of State is satisfied that a payment has been, or will be, made in respect of the termination of any person's employment of any description specified in subsection

PART VI

1965 c. 74.

1972 c. 11.

(1), and that the payment has been, or will be, so made to or in respect of him—

(a) in accordance with the Superannuation Act 1965, as that Act continues to have effect by virtue of section 23(1) of the Superannuation Act 1972,

(b) in accordance with any provision of a scheme made under section 1 of the Superannuation Act 1972, or

(c) in accordance with any such arrangements as are mentioned in subsection (3),

the Secretary of State shall pay the appropriate sum out of the fund to the appropriate fund or authority.

(3) The arrangements referred to in paragraph (c) of subsection (2) are any arrangements made with the approval of the Minister for the Civil Service for securing that payments by way of compensation for loss of any such employment as is mentioned in subsection (1) will be made—

(a) in circumstances which in the opinion of the Minister for the Civil Service correspond (subject to the appropriate modifications) to those in which a right to a redundancy payment would have accrued if section 81 had applied, and

(b) on a scale which in the opinion of the Minister for the Civil Service, taking into account any sums which are payable as mentioned in subsection (2)(a) or (b) to or in respect of the person losing the employment in question, corresponds (subject to the appropriate modifications) to that on which a redundancy payment would have been payable if section 81 had applied.

(4) For the purposes of subsection (2) the appropriate sum is the sum appearing to the Secretary of State to be equal to the amount of the redundancy rebate which would have been payable under section 104 if such a right as is mentioned in paragraph (a) of subsection (3) had accrued, and such a redundancy payment as is mentioned in paragraph (b) of subsection (3) had been payable and had been paid.

(5) Any accounts prepared by the Secretary of State under section 103(2) shall show as a separate item the aggregate amount of sums paid under subsection (2) during the period to which the accounts relate.

(6) In this section " the appropriate fund or authority "—

(a) in relation to employment of any description falling within paragraph 7 of subsection (1) of section 39 of the Superannuation Act 1965 (whether as originally enacted or as modified by any order under that section), means the fund out of which, or the body out of whose revenues, the employment is remunerated;

(b) in relation to any employment remunerated out of the revenues of the Duchy of Lancaster, means the Chancellor of the Duchy, and, in relation to any employment remunerated out of the revenues of the Duchy of Cornwall, means such person as the Duke of Cornwall, or the possessor for the time being of the Duchy of Cornwall, appoints;

(c) in relation to any employment remunerated out of the Queen's Civil List or out of Her Majesty's Privy Purse, means the Civil List or the Privy Purse, as the case may be; and

(d) in any other case, means the Consolidated Fund.

112.—(1) This section applies to any such payment as is mentioned in subsection (3) of section 111 which is payable in accordance with any such arrangements as are mentioned in that subsection.

References to tribunal relating to equivalent payments.

(2) Where the terms and conditions (whether constituting a contract of employment or not) on which any person is employed in any such employment as is mentioned in subsection (1) of section 111 include provision—

(a) for the making of any payment to which this section applies, and

(b) for referring to a tribunal any such question as is mentioned in the following provisions of this subsection,

any question as to the right of any person to such a payment in respect of that employment, or as to the amount of such a payment shall be referred to and determined by an industrial tribunal.

113.—(1) Where the Secretary of State is satisfied that, in accordance with any such arrangements as are mentioned in subsection (3), a payment has been, or will be, made in respect of the termination of a person's employment in any capacity under the Government of an overseas territory (in this section referred to as " the relevant Government "), and that in respect of the whole or part of the period during which that person was in that employment, employer's contributions were paid in respect of him, the Secretary of State shall pay the appropriate sum out of the fund to such other fund or authority as may be designated in that behalf by the relevant Government.

Employment under Government of overseas territory.

(2) The reference in subsection (1) to employer's contributions is a reference to secondary Class 1 contributions paid in respect

PART VI

1975 c. 14.

1965 c. 51.

of the person in question by persons who were in relation to him secondary Class 1 contributors by virtue of section 4(4)(a) of the Social Security Act 1975, and in relation to any period before 6th April 1975, to employer's contributions within the meaning of the National Insurance Act 1965.

(3) The arrangements referred to in subsection (1) are any arrangements made by or on behalf of the relevant Government for securing that payments by way of compensation for loss of employment in the capacity in question will be made—

(a) in circumstances which in the opinion of the Secretary of State correspond (subject to the appropriate modifications) to those in which a right to a redundancy payment would have accrued if section 81 had applied, and

(b) on a scale which in the opinion of the Secretary of State corresponds (subject to the appropriate modifications) to that on which a redundancy payment would have been payable if that section had applied.

(4) For the purposes of subsection (1) the appropriate sum (subject to subsection (5)) is the sum appearing to the Secretary of State to be equal to the amount of the redundancy rebate which would have been payable under section 104 if such a right as is mentioned in paragraph (a) of subsection (3) had accrued, and such a redundancy payment as is mentioned in paragraph (b) of that subsection had been payable and had been paid.

(5) Where it appears to the Secretary of State that such contributions as are mentioned in subsection (1) were paid in respect of part (but not the whole) of the period of employment in question, the rebate which would have been payable as mentioned in subsection (4) shall be calculated as if the employment had been limited to that part of the period.

(6) Any accounts prepared by the Secretary of State under section 103(2) shall show as a separate item the aggregate amount of sums paid under subsection (1) during the period to which the accounts relate.

Meaning of "Government of overseas territory".

114. In this Part " overseas territory " means any territory or country outside the United Kingdom ; and any reference to the Government of an overseas territory includes a reference to a Government constituted for two or more overseas territories and to any authority established for the purpose of providing or administering services which are common to, or relate to matters of common interest to, two or more such territories.

115.—(1) This section applies to employment of any description which—

> (a) is not employment under a contract of service or of apprenticeship, and
>
> (b) is not employment of any description falling within paragraphs (a) to (d) of section 111(1),

but is employment such that secondary Class 1 contributions are payable under Part I of the Social Security Act 1975 in respect of persons engaged therein.

Part VI
Application of Part VI to employment not under contract of employment.
1975 c. 14.

(2) The Secretary of State may by regulations under this section provide that, subject to such exceptions and modifications as may be prescribed by the regulations, this Part and the provisions of this Act supplementary thereto shall have effect in relation to any such employment of a description to which this section applies as may be so prescribed as if—

> (a) it were employment under a contract of employment, and
>
> (b) any person engaged in employment of that description were an employee, and
>
> (c) such person as may be determined by or under the regulations were his employer.

(3) Without prejudice to the generality of subsection (2), regulations made under this section may provide that section 105 shall apply to persons engaged in any such employment of a description to which this section applies as may be prescribed by the regulations, as if those persons were employees to whom that section applies.

116.—(1) The Secretary of State may by regulations under this section provide that, subject to such exceptions and modifications as may be prescribed by the regulations, the provisions of this Part shall have effect in relation to any person who, by virtue of any statutory provisions,—

Provision for treating termination of certain employments by statute as equivalent to dismissal.

> (a) is transferred to, and becomes a member of, a body specified in those provisions, but
>
> (b) at a time so specified ceases to be a member of that body unless before that time certain conditions so specified have been fulfilled,

as if the cessation of his membership of that body by virtue of those provisions were dismissal by his employer by reason of redundancy.

(2) The power conferred by subsection (1) shall be exercisable whether membership of the body in question constitutes employment within the meaning of section 153 or not; and, where that membership does not constitute such employment,

PART VI

Employees paid by person other than employer.

that power may be exercised in addition to any power exercisable by virtue of section 115.

117.—(1) This section applies to any employee whose remuneration is, by virtue of any statutory provision, payable to him by a person other than his employer.

(2) For the purposes of the operation, in relation to employees to whom this section applies, of the provisions of this Part and Schedule 13 specified in column 1 of Schedule 8, any reference to the employer which is specified in column 2 of Schedule 8 shall be construed as a reference to the person responsible for paying the remuneration.

(3) In relation to employees to whom this section applies, section 119 shall have effect as if—

(a) any reference in subsection (1) or subsection (2) of that section to a notice required or authorised to be given by or to an employer included a reference to a notice which, by virtue of subsection (2), is required or authorised to be given by or to the person responsible for paying the remuneration;

(b) in relation to a notice required or authorised to be given to that person, any reference to the employer in paragraph (a) or paragraph (b) of subsection (2) of that section were a reference to that person; and

(c) the reference to the employer in subsection (5) of that section included a reference to that person.

(4) In this section and in Schedule 8, " the person responsible for paying the remuneration " means the person by whom the remuneration is payable as mentioned in subsection (1).

Statutory compensation schemes.

118.—(1) This section applies to any statutory provision which was in force immediately before 6th December 1965, whereby the holders of such situations, places or employments as are specified in that provision are, or may become, entitled to compensation for loss of employment, or for loss or diminution of emoluments or of pension rights, in consequence of the operation of any other statutory provision referred to therein.

(2) The Secretary of State may make provision by regulations for securing that where apart from this section a person is entitled to compensation under a statutory provision to which this section applies, and the circumstances are such that he is also entitled to a redundancy payment, the amount of the redundancy payment shall be set off against the compensation to which he would be entitled apart from this section; and any statutory provision to which any such regulations apply shall have effect subject to the regulations.

119.—(1) Any notice which under this Part is required or authorised to be given by an employer to an employee may be given by being delivered to the employee, or left for him at his usual or last-known place of residence, or sent by post addressed to him at that place.

PART VI
Provisions as to notices.

(2) Any notice which under this Part is required or authorised to be given by an employee to an employer may be given either by the employee himself or by a person authorised by him to act on his behalf, and, whether given by or on behalf of the employee,—

- (a) may be given by being delivered to the employer, or sent by post addressed to him at the place where the employee is or was employed by him, or
- (b) if arrangements in that behalf have been made by the employer, may be given by being delivered to a person designated by the employer in pursuance of the arrangements, or left for such a person at a place so designated, or sent by post to such a person at an address so designated.

(3) In the preceding provisions of this section, any reference to the delivery of a notice shall, in relation to a notice which is not required by this Part to be in writing, be construed as including a reference to the oral communication of the notice.

(4) Any notice which, in accordance with any provision of this section, is left for a person at a place referred to in that provision shall, unless the contrary is proved, be presumed to have been received by him on the day on which it was left there.

(5) Nothing in subsection (1) or subsection (2) shall be construed as affecting the capacity of an employer to act by a servant or agent for the purposes of any provision of this Part, including either of those subsections.

120.—(1) Where an offence under this Part committed by a body corporate is proved to have been committed with the consent or connivance of, or to be attributable to any neglect on the part of, any director, manager, secretary or other similar officer of the body corporate or any person who was purporting to act in any such capacity, he as well as the body corporate shall be guilty of that offence and shall be liable to be proceeded against and punished accordingly.

Offences.

(2) In this section "director", in relation to a body corporate established by or under any enactment for the purpose of carrying on under national ownership any industry or part of an industry or undertaking, being a body corporate whose affairs are managed by its members, means a member of that body corporate.

Part VII

Insolvency of Employer

Priority of certain debts on insolvency.
1914 c. 59.
1913 c. 20.

1948 c. 38.

1975 c. 71.

121.—(1) An amount to which this section applies shall be treated for the purposes of—

(*a*) section 33 of the Bankruptcy Act 1914;

(*b*) section 118 of the Bankruptcy (Scotland) Act 1913; and

(*c*) section 319 of the Companies Act 1948;

as if it were wages payable by the employer to the employee in respect of the period for which it is payable.

(2) This section applies to any amount owed by an employer to an employee in respect of—

(*a*) a guarantee payment;

(*b*) remuneration on suspension on medical grounds under section 19;

(*c*) any payment for time off under section 27(3) or 31(3);

(*d*) remuneration under a protective award made under section 101 of the Employment Protection Act 1975.

Employee's rights on insolvency of employer.

122.—(1) If on an application made to him in writing by an employee the Secretary of State is satisfied—

(*a*) that the employer of that employee has become insolvent; and

(*b*) that on the relevant date the employee was entitled to be paid the whole or part of any debt to which this section applies,

the Secretary of State shall, subject to the provisions of this section, pay the employee out of the Redundancy Fund the amount to which in the opinion of the Secretary of State the employee is entitled in respect of that debt.

(2) In this section the "relevant date" in relation to a debt means the date on which the employer became insolvent or the date of the termination of the employee's employment, whichever is the later.

(3) This section applies to the following debts:—

(*a*) any arrears of pay in respect of a period or periods not exceeding in the aggregate eight weeks;

(*b*) any amount which the employer is liable to pay the employee for the period of notice required by section 49(1) or (2) or for any failure of the employer to give the period of notice required by section 49(1);

(*c*) any holiday pay in respect of a period or periods of holiday, not exceeding six weeks in all, to which the employee became entitled during the twelve months immediately preceding the relevant date;

(d) any basic award of compensation for unfair dismissal (within the meaning of section 72);

(e) any reasonable sum by way of reimbursement of the whole or part of any fee or premium paid by an apprentice or articled clerk.

(4) For the purposes of subsection (3)(a), any such amount as is referred to in section 121(2) shall be treated as if it were arrears of pay.

(5) The total amount payable to an employee in respect of any debt mentioned in subsection (3), where the amount of that debt is referable to a period of time, shall not exceed £100 in respect of any one week or, in respect of a shorter period, an amount bearing the same proportion to £100 as that shorter period bears to a week.

(6) The Secretary of State may vary the limit referred to in subsection (5) after a review under section 148, by order made in accordance with that section.

(7) A sum shall be taken to be reasonable for the purposes of subsection (3)(e) in a case where a trustee in bankruptcy or liquidator has been or is required to be appointed if it is admitted to be reasonable by the trustee in bankruptcy or liquidator under section 34 of the Bankruptcy Act 1914 (preferential claims of apprentices and articled clerks), whether as originally enacted or as applied to the winding up of a company by section 317 of the Companies Act 1948.

(8) Subsection (7) shall not apply to Scotland, but in Scotland a sum shall be taken to be reasonable for the purposes of subsection (3)(e) in a case where a trustee in bankruptcy or liquidator has been or is required to be appointed if it is admitted by the trustee in bankruptcy or the liquidator for the purposes of the bankruptcy or winding up.

(9) The provisions of subsections (10) and (11) shall apply in a case where one of the following officers (hereafter in this section referred to as the "relevant officer") has been or is required to be appointed in connection with the employer's insolvency, that is to say, a trustee in bankruptcy, a liquidator, a receiver or manager, or a trustee under a composition or arrangement between the employer and his creditors or under a trust deed for his creditors executed by the employer; and in this subsection "liquidator" and "receiver" include the Official Receiver in his capacity as a provisional liquidator or interim receiver.

PART VII

(10) Subject to subsection (11), the Secretary of State shall not in such a case make any payment under this section in respect of any debt until he has received a statement from the relevant officer of the amount of that debt which appears to have been owed to the employee on the relevant date and to remain unpaid; and the relevant officer shall, on request by the Secretary of State, provide him, as soon as reasonably practicable, with such a statement.

(11) Where—
  (a) a period of six months has elapsed since the application for a payment under this section was received by the Secretary of State, but no such payment has been made;
  (b) the Secretary of State is satisfied that a payment under this section should be made; and
  (c) it appears to the Secretary of State that there is likely to be further delay before he receives a statement about the debt in question,

then, the Secretary of State may, if the applicant so requests or, if the Secretary of State thinks fit, without such a request, make a payment under this section, notwithstanding that no such statement has been received.

Payment of unpaid contributions to occupational pension scheme.

123.—(1) If, on application made to him in writing by the persons competent to act in respect of an occupational pension scheme, the Secretary of State is satisfied that an employer has become insolvent and that at the time that he did so there remained unpaid relevant contributions falling to be paid by him to the scheme, the Secretary of State shall, subject to the provisions of this section, pay into the resources of the scheme out of the Redundancy Fund the sum which in his opinion is payable in respect of the unpaid relevant contributions.

(2) In this section "relevant contributions" means contributions falling to be paid by an employer in accordance with an occupational pension scheme, either on his own account or on behalf of an employee; and for the purposes of this section a contribution of any amount shall not be treated as falling to be paid on behalf of an employee unless a sum equal to that amount has been deducted from the pay of the employee by way of a contribution from him.

(3) The sum payable under this section in respect of unpaid contributions of an employer on his own account to an occupational pension scheme shall be the least of the following amounts—
  (a) the balance of relevant contributions remaining unpaid on the date when he became insolvent and payable by

the employer on his own account to the scheme in respect of the twelve months immediately preceding that date;

(b) the amount certified by an actuary to be necessary for the purpose of meeting the liability of the scheme on dissolution to pay the benefits provided by the scheme to or in respect of the employees of the employer;

(c) an amount equal to ten per cent. of the total amount of remuneration paid or payable to those employees in respect of the twelve months immediately preceding the date on which the employer became insolvent.

(4) For the purposes of subsection (3)(c), "remuneration" includes holiday pay, maternity pay and any such payment as is referred to in section 121(2).

(5) Any sum payable under this section in respect of unpaid contributions on behalf of an employee shall not exceed the amount deducted from the pay of the employee in respect of the employee's contributions to the occupational pension scheme during the twelve months immediately preceding the date on which the employer became insolvent.

(6) The provisions of subsections (7) to (9) shall apply in a case where one of the following officers (hereafter in this section referred to as the "relevant officer") has been or is required to be appointed in connection with the employer's insolvency, that is to say, a trustee in bankruptcy, a liquidator, a receiver or manager, or a trustee under a composition or arrangement between the employer and his creditors or under a trust deed for his creditors executed by the employer; and in this subsection "liquidator" and "receiver" include the Official Receiver in his capacity as a provisional liquidator or interim receiver.

(7) Subject to subsection (9), the Secretary of State shall not in such a case make any payment under this section in respect of unpaid relevant contributions until he has received a statement from the relevant officer of the amount of relevant contributions which appear to have been unpaid on the date on which the employer became insolvent and to remain unpaid; and the relevant officer shall, on request by the Secretary of State provide him, as soon as reasonably practicable, with such a statement.

(8) Subject to subsection (9), an amount shall be taken to be payable, paid or deducted as mentioned in subsection (3)(a) or (c) or subsection (5), only if it is so certified by the relevant officer.

PART VII (9) Where—

(a) a period of six months has elapsed since the application for a payment under this section was received by the Secretary of State, but no such payment has been made;

(b) the Secretary of State is satisfied that a payment under this section should be made; and

(c) it appears to the Secretary of State that there is likely to be further delay before he receives a statement or certificate about the contributions in question,

then, the Secretary of State may, if the applicants so request or, if the Secretary of State thinks fit, without such a request, make a payment under this section, notwithstanding that no such statement or certificate has been received.

Complaint to industrial tribunal.

124.—(1) A person who has applied for a payment under section 122 may, within the period of three months beginning with the date on which the decision of the Secretary of State on that application was communicated to him or, if that is not reasonably practicable, within such further period as is reasonable, present a complaint to an industrial tribunal that—

(a) the Secretary of State has failed to make any such payment; or

(b) any such payment made by the Secretary of State is less than the amount which should have been paid.

(2) Any persons who are competent to act in respect of an occupational pension scheme and who have applied for a payment to be made under section 123 into the resources of the scheme may, within the period of three months beginning with the date on which the decision of the Secretary of State on that application was communicated to them, or, if that is not reasonably practicable, within such further period as is reasonable, present a complaint to an industrial tribunal that—

(a) the Secretary of State has failed to make any such payment; or

(b) any such payment made by him is less than the amount which should have been paid.

(3) Where an industrial tribunal finds that the Secretary of State ought to make a payment under section 122 or 123, it shall make a declaration to that effect and shall also declare the amount of any such payment which it finds the Secretary of State ought to make.

125.—(1) Where, in pursuance of section 122, the Secretary of State makes any payment to an employee in respect of any debt to which that section applies—

Part VII

Transfer to Secretary of State of rights and remedies.

    (a) any rights and remedies of the employee in respect of that debt (or, if the Secretary of State has paid only part of it, in respect of that part) shall, on the making of the payment, become rights and remedies of the Secretary of State; and

    (b) any decision of an industrial tribunal requiring an employer to pay that debt to the employee shall have the effect that the debt or, as the case may be, that part of it which the Secretary of State has paid, is to be paid to the Secretary of State.

(2) There shall be included among the rights and remedies which become rights and remedies of the Secretary of State in accordance with subsection (1)(a) any right to be paid in priority to other creditors of the employer in accordance with—

    (a) section 33 of the Bankruptcy Act 1914;

1914 c. 59.

    (b) section 118 of the Bankruptcy (Scotland) Act 1913; and

1913 c. 20.

    (c) section 319 of the Companies Act 1948,

1948 c. 38.

and the Secretary of State shall be entitled to be so paid in priority to any other unsatisfied claim of the employee; and in computing for the purposes of any of those provisions any limit on the amount of sums to be so paid any sums paid to the Secretary of State shall be treated as if they had been paid to the employee.

(3) Where in pursuance of section 123 the Secretary of State makes any payment into the resources of an occupational pension scheme in respect of any contributions to the scheme, any rights and remedies in respect of those contributions belonging to the persons competent to act in respect of the scheme shall, on the making of the payment, become rights and remedies of the Secretary of State.

(4) Any sum recovered by the Secretary of State in exercising any right or pursuing any remedy which is his by virtue of this section shall be paid into the Redundancy Fund.

126.—(1) Where an application is made to the Secretary of State under section 122 or 123 in respect of a debt owed, or contributions to an occupational pension scheme falling to be made, by an employer, the Secretary of State may require—

Power of Secretary of State to obtain information in connection with applications.

    (a) the employer to provide him with such information as the Secretary of State may reasonably require for the purpose of determining whether the application is well-founded; and

PART VII

(b) any person having the custody or control of any relevant records or other documents to produce for examination on behalf of the Secretary of State any such document in that person's custody or under his control which is of such a description as the Secretary of State may require.

(2) Any such requirement shall be made by notice in writing given to the person on whom the requirement is imposed and may be varied or revoked by a subsequent notice so given.

(3) If a person refuses or wilfully neglects to furnish any information or produce any document which he has been required to furnish or produce by a notice under this section he shall be liable on summary conviction to a fine not exceeding £100.

(4) If a person, in purporting to comply with a requirement of a notice under this section, knowingly or recklessly makes any false statement he shall be liable on summary conviction to a fine not exceeding £400.

Interpretation of ss. 122 to 126.

127.—(1) For the purposes of sections 122 to 126, an employer shall be taken to be insolvent if, but only if, in England and Wales,—

(a) he becomes bankrupt or makes a composition or arrangement with his creditors or a receiving order is made against him;

1914 c. 59.

(b) he has died and an order is made under section 130 of the Bankruptcy Act 1914 for the administration of his estate according to the law of bankruptcy, or by virtue of an order of the court his estate is being administered in accordance with rules set out in Part I of Schedule 1 to the Administration of Estates Act 1925; or

1925 c. 23.

(c) where the employer is a company, a winding up order is made or a resolution for voluntary winding up is passed with respect to it, or a receiver or manager of its undertaking is duly appointed, or possession is taken, by or on behalf of the holders of any debentures secured by a floating charge, of any property of the company comprised in or subject to the charge.

(2) For the purposes of sections 122 to 126, an employer shall be taken to be insolvent if, but only if, in Scotland,—

(a) an award of sequestration is made on his estate or he executes a trust deed for his creditors or enters into a composition contract;

1913 c. 20.

(b) he has died and a judicial factor appointed under section 163 of the Bankruptcy (Scotland) Act 1913 is required by that section to divide his insolvent estate among his creditors; or

(c) where the employer is a company, a winding-up order is made or a resolution for voluntary winding up is passed with respect to it or a receiver of its undertaking is duly appointed.

(3) In sections 122 to 126—

"holiday pay" means—

(a) pay in respect of a holiday actually taken; or

(b) any accrued holiday pay which under the employee's contract of employment would in the ordinary course have become payable to him in respect of the period of a holiday if his employment with the employer had continued until he became entitled to a holiday;

"occupational pension scheme" means any scheme or arrangement which provides or is capable of providing, in relation to employees in any description of employment, benefits (in the form of pensions or otherwise) payable to or in respect of any such employees on the termination of their employment or on their death or retirement;

and any reference in those sections to the resources of such a scheme is a reference to the funds out of which the benefits provided by the scheme are from time to time payable.

Part VIII

Resolution of Disputes Relating to Employment

Industrial tribunals

128.—(1) The Secretary of State may by regulations make provision for the establishment of tribunals, to be known as industrial tribunals, to exercise the jurisdiction conferred on them by or under this Act or any other Act, whether passed before or after this Act.

(2) Regulations made wholly or partly under section 12 of the Industrial Training Act 1964 and in force immediately before the date on which this section comes into force shall, so far as so made, continue to have effect as if they had been made under subsection (1), and tribunals established in accordance with such regulations shall continue to be known as industrial tribunals.

(3) Schedule 9, which makes provision, among other things, with respect to proceedings before industrial tribunals, shall have effect.

PART VIII

(4) Complaints, references and appeals to industrial tribunals shall be made in accordance with regulations made under paragraph 1 of Schedule 9.

Remedy for infringement of certain rights under this Act.

129. The remedy of an employee for infringement of any of the rights conferred on him by sections 8 and 53 and Parts II, III, V and VII shall, if provision is made for a complaint or for the reference of a question to an industrial tribunal, be by way of such complaint or reference and not otherwise.

Jurisdiction of referees to be exercised by tribunals.

130.—(1) There shall be referred to and determined by an industrial tribunal any question which by any statutory provision is directed (in whatsoever terms) to be determined by a referee or board of referees constituted under any of the statutory provisions specified in Schedule 10 or which is so directed to be determined in the absence of agreement to the contrary.

(2) The transfer of any jurisdiction by this section shall not affect the principles on which any question is to be determined or the persons on whom the determination is binding, or any provision which requires particular matters to be expressly dealt with or embodied in the determination, or which relates to evidence.

Power to confer jurisdiction on industrial tribunals in respect of damages, etc., for breach of contract of employment.

131.—(1) The appropriate Minister may by order provide that on any claim to which this section applies or any such claim of a description specified in the order, being in either case a claim satisfying the relevant condition or conditions mentioned in subsection (3), proceedings for the recovery of damages or any other sum, except damages or a sum due in respect of personal injuries, may be brought before an industrial tribunal.

(2) Subject to subsection (3), this section applies to any of the following claims, that is to say—

(a) a claim for damages for breach of a contract of employment or any other contract connected with employment;

(b) a claim for a sum due under such a contract;

(c) a claim for the recovery of a sum in pursuance of any enactment relating to the terms or performance of such a contract;

being in each case a claim such that a court in England and Wales or Scotland, as the case may be, would under the law for the time being in force have jurisdiction to hear and determine an action in respect of the claim.

(3) An order under this section may make provision with respect to any such claim only if it satisfies either of the following conditions, that is to say—

    (a) it arises or is outstanding on the termination of the employee's employment; or

    (b) it arises in circumstances which also give rise to proceedings already or simultaneously brought before an industrial tribunal otherwise than by virtue of this section;

or, if the order so provides, it satisfies both those conditions

(4) Where on proceedings under this section an industrial tribunal finds that the whole or part of a sum claimed in the proceedings is due, the tribunal shall order the respondent to the proceedings to pay the amount which it finds due.

(5) Without prejudice to section 154(3), an order under this section may include provisions—

    (a) as to the manner in which and time within which proceedings are to be brought by virtue of this section; and

    (b) modifying any other enactment.

(6) Any jurisdiction conferred on an industrial tribunal by virtue of this section in respect of any claim shall be exercisable concurrently with any court in England and Wales or in Scotland, as the case may be, which has jurisdiction to hear and determine an action in respect of the claim.

(7) In this section—

"appropriate Minister", as respects a claim in respect of which an action could be heard and determined in England and Wales, means the Lord Chancellor and, as respects a claim in respect of which an action could be heard and determined by a court in Scotland, means the Secretary of State;

"personal injuries" includes any disease and any impairment of a person's physical or mental condition;

and any reference to breach of a contract includes a reference to breach of—

    (a) a term implied in a contract by or under any enactment or otherwise;

    (b) a term of a contract as modified by or under any enactment or otherwise; and

    (c) a term which, although not contained in a contract, is incorporated in the contract by another term of the contract.

Recoupment of certain benefits

132.—(1) This section applies to payments which are the subject of proceedings before industrial tribunals, and which are—

(a) payments of wages or compensation for loss of wages; or

(b) payments, by employers to employees, under Part II, III or V or section 53 or in pursuance of an award under section 103 of the Employment Protection Act 1975; or

(c) payments, by employers to employees, of a nature similar to, or for a purpose corresponding to the purpose of, such payments as are mentioned in paragraph (b);

and to payments of remuneration in pursuance of a protective award under section 101 of the said Act of 1975.

(2) The Secretary of State may by regulations make provision with respect to payments to which this section applies for all or any of the following purposes—

(a) enabling the Secretary of State to recover from an employer, by way of total or partial recoupment of unemployment benefit or supplementary benefit, a sum not exceeding the amount of the prescribed element of the monetary award or, in the case of a protective award, the amount of the remuneration;

(b) requiring or authorising the tribunal to order the payment of such a sum, by way of total or partial recoupment of either benefit, to the Secretary of State instead of to the employee;

(c) requiring the tribunal to order the payment to the employee of only the excess of the prescribed element of the monetary award over the amount of any unemployment benefit or supplementary benefit shown to the tribunal to have been paid to the employee, and enabling the Secretary of State to recover from the employer, by way of total or partial recoupment of the benefit, a sum not exceeding that amount.

(3) Without prejudice to subsection (2), regulations under that subsection may—

(a) be so framed as to apply to all payments to which this section applies or one or more classes of those payments, and so as to apply both to unemployment benefit and supplementary benefit or only to one of those benefits;

(b) confer powers and impose duties on industrial tribunals, on the Supplementary Benefits Commission and on insurance officers and other persons;

(c) impose, on an employer to whom a monetary award or protective award relates, a duty to furnish particulars connected with the award and to suspend payments in pursuance of the award during any period prescribed by the regulations;

(d) provide for an employer who pays a sum to the Secretary of State in pursuance of this section to be relieved from any liability to pay the sum to another person;

(e) confer on an employee who is aggrieved by any decision of the Commission as to the total or partial recoupment of supplementary benefit in pursuance of the regulations (including any decision as to the amount of benefit) a right to appeal against the decision to an Appeal Tribunal constituted in accordance with the Supplementary Benefits Act 1976 and for that purpose apply section 15(2) and (3) of that Act (appeals) with or without modifications;

(f) provide for the proof in proceedings before industrial tribunals (whether by certificate or in any other manner) of any amount of unemployment benefit or supplementary benefit paid to an employee; and

(g) make different provision for different cases.

(4) Where in pursuance of any regulations under subsection (2) a sum has been recovered by or paid to the Secretary of State by way of total or partial recoupment of unemployment benefit or supplementary benefit—

(a) section 119(1) and (2) of the Social Security Act 1975 (repayment of benefit revised on review) shall not apply to the unemployment benefit recouped; and

(b) sections 18 and 20 of the Supplementary Benefits Act 1976 (recovery of expenditure on supplementary benefits from persons liable for maintenance and recovery in cases of misrepresentation or non-disclosure) shall not apply to the supplementary benefit recouped.

(5) Any amount found to have been duly recovered by or paid to the Secretary of State in pursuance of regulations under subsection (2) by way of total or partial recoupment of unemployment benefit shall be paid into the National Insurance Fund.

(6) In this section—

"monetary award" means the amount which is awarded, or ordered to be paid, to the employee by the tribunal

PART VIII

1976 c. 71.

1975 c. 14.

or would be so awarded or ordered apart from any provision of regulations under this section;

"the prescribed element", in relation to any monetary award, means so much of that award as is attributable to such matters as may be prescribed by regulations under subsection (2);

"supplementary benefit" has the same meaning as in the Supplementary Benefits Act 1976; and

"unemployment benefit" means unemployment benefit under the Social Security Act 1975.

Conciliation officers

General provisions as to conciliation officers.

1975 c. 71.

133.—(1) The provisions of subsections (2) to (6) shall have effect in relation to industrial tribunal proceedings, or claims which could be the subject of tribunal proceedings,—

(a) arising out of a contravention, or alleged contravention, of any of the following provisions of this Act, that is to say, sections 8, 12, 19, 23, 27, 28, 29, 31, 33 and 53; or

(b) arising out of a contravention, or alleged contravention, of section 99 or 102 of the Employment Protection Act 1975 or of a provision of any other Act specified by an order under subsection (7) as one to which this paragraph applies; or

(c) which are proceedings or claims in respect of which an industrial tribunal has jurisdiction by virtue of an order under section 131.

(2) Where a complaint has been presented to an industrial tribunal, and a copy of it has been sent to a conciliation officer, it shall be the duty of the conciliation officer—

(a) if he is requested to do so by the complainant and by the person against whom the complaint is presented, or

(b) if, in the absence of any such request, the conciliation officer considers that he could act under this subsection with a reasonable prospect of success,

to endeavour to promote a settlement of the complaint without its being determined by an industrial tribunal.

(3) Where at any time—

(a) a person claims that action has been taken in respect of which a complaint could be presented by him to an industrial tribunal, but

(b) before any complaint relating to that action has been presented by him, a request is made to a conciliation officer (whether by that person or by the person against whom the complaint could be made) to make his services available to them, the conciliation officer shall act in accordance with subsection (2) as if a complaint has been presented to an industrial tribunal.

(4) Subsections (2) and (3) shall apply, with appropriate modifications, to the presentation of a claim and the reference of a question to an industrial tribunal as they apply to the presentation of a complaint.

(5) In proceeding under subsection (2) or (3) a conciliation officer shall, where appropriate, have regard to the desirability of encouraging the use of other procedures available for the settlement of grievances.

(6) Anything communicated to a conciliation officer in connection with the performance of his functions under this section shall not be admissible in evidence in any proceedings before an industrial tribunal, except with the consent of the person who communicated it to that officer.

(7) The Secretary of State may by order—
 (a) direct that further provisions of this Act be added to the list in subsection (1)(a);
 (b) specify a provision of any other Act as one to which subsection (1)(b) applies.

134.—(1) Where a complaint has been presented to an industrial tribunal under section 67 by a person (in this section referred to as the complainant) and a copy of it has been sent to a conciliation officer, it shall be the duty of the conciliation officer— *Functions of conciliation officers on complaint under s. 67.*

 (a) if he is requested to do so by the complainant and by the employer against whom it was presented, or
 (b) if, in the absence of any such request, the conciliation officer considers that he could act under this section with a reasonable prospect of success,

to endeavour to promote a settlement of the complaint without its being determined by an industrial tribunal.

(2) For the purpose of promoting such a settlement, in a case where the complainant has ceased to be employed by the employer against whom the complaint was made,—
 (a) the conciliation officer shall in particular seek to promote the reinstatement or re-engagement of the complainant by the employer, or by a successor of the employer or by an associated employer, on terms appearing to the conciliation officer to be equitable; but

PART VIII

(b) where the complainant does not wish to be reinstated or re-engaged, or where reinstatement or re-engagement is not practicable, and the parties desire the conciliation officer to act under this section, he shall seek to promote agreement between them as to a sum by way of compensation to be paid by the employer to the complainant.

(3) Where at any time—

(a) after the complainant has ceased to be employed by an employer, in circumstances where the employee claims that he was unfairly dismissed, but

(b) before any complaint relating to that claim has been presented by the claimant under section 67,

a request is made to a conciliation officer (whether by the employer or by the employee) to make his services available to them, the conciliation officer shall act in accordance with subsections (1) and (2) as if a complaint had been presented in pursuance of that claim.

(4) In proceeding under subsections (1) to (3), a conciliation officer shall where appropriate have regard to the desirability of encouraging the use of other procedures available for the settlement of grievances.

(5) Anything communicated to a conciliation officer in connection with the performance of his functions under this section shall not be admissible in evidence in any proceedings before an industrial tribunal, except with the consent of the person who communicated it to that officer.

Employment Appeal Tribunal

Employment Appeal Tribunal.
1975 c. 71.

135.—(1) The Employment Appeal Tribunal established under section 87 of the Employment Protection Act 1975 shall continue in existence by that name for the purpose of hearing appeals under section 136.

(2) The Employment Appeal Tribunal (in this Act referred to as " the Appeal Tribunal ") shall consist of—

(a) such number of judges as may be nominated from time to time by the Lord Chancellor from among the judges (other than the Lord Chancellor) of the High Court and the Court of Appeal;

(b) at least one judge of the Court of Session nominated from time to time by the Lord President of that Court; and

(c) such number of other members as may be appointed from time to time by Her Majesty on the joint recommendation of the Lord Chancellor and the Secretary of State.

(3) The members of the Appeal Tribunal appointed under subsection (2)(c) shall be persons who appear to the Lord Chancellor and the Secretary of State to have special knowledge or experience of industrial relations, either as representatives of employers or as representatives of workers (within the meaning of the Trade Union and Labour Relations Act 1974).

(4) The Lord Chancellor shall, after consultation with the Lord President of the Court of Session, appoint one of the judges nominated under subsection (2) to be President of the Appeal Tribunal.

(5) No judge shall be nominated a member of the Appeal Tribunal except with his consent.

(6) The provisions of Schedule 11 shall have effect with respect to the Appeal Tribunal and proceedings before the Tribunal.

136.—(1) An appeal shall lie to the Appeal Tribunal on a question of law arising from any decision of, or arising in any proceedings before, an industrial tribunal under, or by virtue of, the following Acts—

(a) the Equal Pay Act 1970;

(b) the Sex Discrimination Act 1975;

(c) the Employment Protection Act 1975;

(d) the Race Relations Act 1976;

(e) this Act.

(2) The Appeal Tribunal shall hear appeals on questions of law arising in any proceedings before, or arising from any decision of, the Certification Officer under the following enactments—

(a) sections 3, 4 and 5 of the Trade Union Act 1913;

(b) section 4 of the Trade Union (Amalgamations, etc.) Act 1964.

(3) The Appeal Tribunal shall hear appeals on questions of fact or law arising in any proceedings before, or arising from any decision of, the Certification Officer under the following enactments—

(a) section 8 of the Trade Union and Labour Relations Act 1974;

(b) section 8 of the Employment Protection Act 1975.

(4) Without prejudice to section 13 of the Administration of Justice Act 1960 (appeal in case of contempt of court), an appeal shall lie on any question of law from any decision or order of the Appeal Tribunal with the leave of the Tribunal or

PART VIII

of the Court of Appeal or, as the case may be, the Court of Session,—

(a) in the case of proceedings in England and Wales, to the Court of Appeal;

(b) in the case of proceedings in Scotland, to the Court of Session.

(5) No appeal shall lie except to the Appeal Tribunal from any decision of an industrial tribunal under the Acts listed in subsection (1) or from any decision under the enactments listed in subsections (2) and (3) of the Certification Officer appointed under section 7 of the Employment Protection Act 1975.

1975 c. 71.

PART IX

MISCELLANEOUS AND SUPPLEMENTAL

Extension of employment protection legislation

Power to extend employment protection legislation.

137.—(1) Her Majesty may by Order in Council provide that—

(a) the provisions of this Act; and

(b) any legislation (that is to say any enactment of the Parliament of Northern Ireland and any provision made by or under a Measure of the Northern Ireland Assembly) for the time being in force in Northern Ireland which makes provision for purposes corresponding to any of the purposes of this Act,

shall, to such extent and for such purposes as may be specified in the Order, apply (with or without modification) to or in relation to any person in employment to which this section applies.

(2) This section applies to employment for the purposes of any activities—

(a) in the territorial waters of the United Kingdom; or

(b) connected with the exploration of the sea bed or subsoil or the exploitation of their natural resources in any area designated by order under section 1(7) of the Continental Shelf Act 1964; or

1964 c. 29.

(c) connected with the exploration or exploitation, in a foreign sector of the continental shelf, of a cross-boundary petroleum field.

(3) An Order in Council under subsection (1)—

(a) may make different provision for different cases;

(b) may provide that all or any of the enactments referred to in subsection (1), as applied by such an Order, shall apply to individuals whether or not they are British subjects and to bodies corporate whether or not they are incorporated under the law of any part of the United Kingdom (notwithstanding that the application may affect their activities outside the United Kingdom);

(c) may make provision for conferring jurisdiction on any court or class of court specified in the Order, or on industrial tribunals, in respect of offences, causes of action or other matters arising in connection with employment to which this section applies;

(d) without prejudice to the generality of subsection (1) or of paragraph (a), may provide that the enactments referred to in subsection (1), as applied by the Order, shall apply in relation to any person in employment for the purposes of such activities as are referred to in subsection (2) in any part of the areas specified in paragraphs (a) and (b) of that subsection;

(e) may exclude from the operation of section 3 of the Territorial Waters Jurisdiction Act 1878 (consents required for prosecutions) proceedings for offences under the enactments referred to in subsection (1) in connection with employment to which this section applies;

(f) may provide that such proceedings shall not be brought without such consent as may be required by the Order;

(g) may, without prejudice to the generality of the power under subsection (1) to modify the enactments referred to in that subsection in their application for the purposes of this section, modify or exclude the operation of sections 141 and 144 or paragraph 14 of Schedule 13 or of any corresponding provision in any such Northern Irish legislation as is referred to in subsection (1)(b).

(4) Any jurisdiction conferred on any court or tribunal under this section shall be without prejudice to jurisdiction exercisable apart from this section by that or any other court or tribunal.

(5) In subsection (2) above—

"cross-boundary petroleum field" means a petroleum field that extends across the boundary between a designated area and a foreign sector of the continental shelf;

"foreign sector of the continental shelf" means an area which is outside the territorial waters of any State and within which rights are exercisable by a State other than the United Kingdom with respect to the sea bed and subsoil and their natural resources;

"petroleum field" means a geological structure identified as an oil or gas field by the Order in Council concerned.

PART IX
Application of Act to Crown employment.

1953 c. 50.

Crown employment

138.—(1) Subject to the following provisions of this section, Parts I (so far as it relates to itemised pay statements), II, III (except section 44), V, VIII and this Part and section 53 shall have effect in relation to Crown employment and to persons in Crown employment as they have effect in relation to other employment and to other employees.

(2) In this section, subject to subsections (3) to (5), "Crown employment" means employment under or for the purposes of a government department or any officer or body exercising on behalf of the Crown functions conferred by any enactment.

(3) This section does not apply to service as a member of the naval, military or air forces of the Crown, or of any women's service administered by the Defence Council, but does apply to employment by any association established for the purposes of the Auxiliary Forces Act 1953.

(4) For the purposes of this section, Crown employment does not include any employment in respect of which there is in force a certificate issued by or on behalf of a Minister of the Crown certifying that employment of a description specified in the certificate, or the employment of a particular person so specified, is (or, at a time specified in the certificate, was) required to be excepted from this section for the purpose of safeguarding national security; and any document purporting to be a certificate so issued shall be received in evidence and shall, unless the contrary is proved, be deemed to be such a certificate.

(5) For the purposes of Parts I (so far as it relates to itemised pay statements), II, III (except section 44(3) and (4)), V, VII (except section 126(3) and (4)), VIII and this Part and section 53, none of the bodies referred to in Schedule 5 shall be regarded as performing functions on behalf of the Crown and accordingly employment by any such body shall not be Crown employment within the meaning of this section.

(6) For the purposes of the application of the provisions of this Act in relation to employment by any such body as is referred to in subsection (5), any reference to redundancy shall be construed as a reference to the existence of such circumstances as, in accordance with any arrangements for the time being in force as mentioned in section 111(3), are treated as equivalent to redundancy in relation to such employment.

(7) For the purposes of the application of the provisions of this Act in relation to Crown employment in accordance with subsection (1)—

(*a*) any reference to an employee shall be construed as a reference to a person in Crown employment;

(b) any reference to a contract of employment shall be construed as a reference to the terms of employment of a person in Crown employment;

(c) any reference to dismissal shall be construed as a reference to the termination of Crown employment;

(d) any reference to redundancy shall be construed as a reference to the existence of such circumstances as, in accordance with any arrangements for the time being in force as mentioned in section 111(3), are treated as equivalent to redundancy in relation to Crown employment;

(e) the reference in paragraph 1(5)(c) of Schedule 9 to a person's undertaking or any undertaking in which he works shall be construed as a reference to the national interest; and

(f) any other reference to an undertaking shall be construed, in relation to a Minister of the Crown, as a reference to his functions or (as the context may require) to the department of which he is in charge and, in relation to a government department, officer or body, shall be construed as a reference to the functions of the department, officer or body or (as the context may require) to the department, officer or body.

(8) Where the terms of employment of a person in Crown employment restrict his right to take part in—

(a) certain political activities; or

(b) activities which may conflict with his official functions,

nothing in section 29 shall require him to be allowed time off work for public duties connected with any such activities.

House of Commons staff

139.—(1) The provisions of Parts I (so far as it relates to itemised pay statements), II, III (except section 44), V and VIII, and this Part and section 53 shall apply to relevant members of House of Commons staff as they apply to persons in Crown employment within the meaning of section 138 and accordingly for the purposes of the application of those provisions in relation to any such members—

Provisions as to House of Commons staff.

(a) any reference to an employee shall be construed as a reference to any such member;

(b) any reference to a contract of employment shall be construed as including a reference to the terms of employment of any such member;

(c) any reference to dismissal shall be construed as including a reference to the termination of any such member's employment;

(d) the reference in paragraph 1(5)(c) of Schedule 9 to a person's undertaking or any undertaking in which he works shall be construed as a reference to the national interest or, if the case so requires, the interests of the House of Commons; and

(e) any other reference to an undertaking shall be construed as a reference to the House of Commons.

(2) Nothing in any rule of law or the law or practice of Parliament shall prevent a relevant member of the House of Commons staff from bringing a civil employment claim before the court or from bringing before an industrial tribunal proceedings of any description which could be brought before such a tribunal by any person who is not such a member.

(3) In this section—

"relevant member of the House of Commons staff" means—

(a) any person appointed by the House of Commons Commission (in this section referred to as the Commission) or employed in the refreshment department; and

(b) any member of Mr. Speaker's personal staff;

"civil employment claim" means a claim arising out of or relating to a contract of employment or any other contract connected with employment, or a claim in tort arising in connection with a person's employment; and

"the court" means the High Court or the county court.

(4) It is hereby declared that for the purposes of the enactments applied by subsection (1) and of Part VI (where applicable to relevant members of House of Commons staff) and for the purposes of any civil employment claim—

(a) the Commission is the employer of staff appointed by the Commission; and

(b) Mr. Speaker is the employer of his personal staff and of any person employed in the refreshment department and not falling within paragraph (a);

but the foregoing provision shall have effect subject to subsection (5).

(5) The Commission or, as the case may be, Mr. Speaker may designate for all or any of the purposes mentioned in subsection (4)—

(a) any description of staff other than Mr. Speaker's personal staff; and

(b) in relation to staff so designated, any person;

and where a person is so designated he, instead of the Commission or Mr. Speaker, shall be deemed for the purposes to which the designation relates to be the employer of the persons in relation to whom he is so designated.

(6) Where any proceedings are brought by virtue of this section against the Commission or Mr. Speaker or any person designated under subsection (5), the person against whom the proceedings are brought may apply to the court or the industrial tribunal, as the case may be, to have some other person against whom the proceedings could at the time of the application be properly brought substituted for him as a party to those proceedings.

(7) For the purposes mentioned in subsection (4) a person's employment in or for the purposes of the House of Commons shall not, provided he continues to be employed in such employment, be treated as terminated by reason only of a change (whether effected before or after the passing of the House of Commons (Administration) Act 1978, and whether effected by virtue of that Act or otherwise) in his employer and (provided he so continues) his first appointment to such employment shall be deemed after the change to have been made by his employer for the time being, and accordingly—

(a) he shall be treated for the purposes so mentioned as being continuously employed by that employer from the commencement of such employment until its termination; and

(b) anything done by or in relation to his employer for the time being in respect of such employment before the change shall be so treated as having been done by or in relation to the person who is his employer for the time being after the change.

(8) In subsection (7) "employer for the time being", in relation to a person who has ceased to be employed in or for the purposes of the House of Commons, means the person who was his employer immediately before he ceased to be so employed, except that where some other person would have been his employer for the time being if he had not ceased to be so employed, it means that other person.

(9) If the House of Commons resolves at any time that any provision of subsections (3) to (6) should be amended in its application to any member of the staff of that House, Her Majesty may by Order in Council amend that provision accordingly.

PART IX

Contracting out of provisions of Act

Restrictions on contracting out.

140.—(1) Except as provided by the following provisions of this section, any provision in an agreement (whether a contract of employment or not) shall be void in so far as it purports—

    (a) to exclude or limit the operation of any provision of this Act; or

    (b) to preclude any person from presenting a complaint to, or bringing any proceedings under this Act before, an industrial tribunal.

(2) Subsection (1) shall not apply—

    (a) to any provision in a collective agreement excluding rights under section 12 if an order under section 18 is for the time being in force in respect of it;

    (b) to any union membership agreement so far as it affects the rights of an employee—

        (i) under section 23 in accordance with subsection (4) of that section;

        (ii) under section 58 in accordance with subsection (3) of that section;

    (c) to any provision in a dismissal procedures agreement excluding rights under section 54 if that provision is not to have effect unless an order under section 65 is for the time being in force in respect of it;

    (d) to any agreement to refrain from presenting a complaint under section 67, where in compliance with a request under section 134(3) a conciliation officer has taken action in accordance with that subsection;

    (e) to any agreement to refrain from proceeding with a complaint presented under section 67 where a conciliation officer has taken action in accordance with section 134(1) and (2);

    (f) to any provision in an agreement if an order under section 96 is for the time being in force in respect of it;

    (g) to any agreement to refrain from instituting or continuing any proceedings before an industrial tribunal where a conciliation officer has taken action in accordance with section 133(2) or (3);

    (h) to any provision of an agreement relating to dismissal from employment such as is mentioned in section 142(1) or (2).

Excluded classes of employment

Employment outside Great Britain.

141.—(1) Sections 1 to 4 and 49 to 51 do not apply in relation to employment during any period when the employee is engaged in work wholly or mainly outside Great Britain unless the employee ordinarily works in Great Britain and the work outside Great Britain is for the same employer.

(2) Sections 8 and 53 and Parts II, III, V and VII do not apply to employment where under his contract of employment the employee ordinarily works outside Great Britain.

(3) An employee shall not be entitled to a redundancy payment if on the relevant date he is outside Great Britain, unless under his contract of employment he ordinarily worked in Great Britain.

(4) An employee who under his contract of employment ordinarily works outside Great Britain shall not be entitled to a redundancy payment unless on the relevant date he is in Great Britain in accordance with instructions given to him by his employer.

(5) For the purpose of subsection (2), a person employed to work on board a ship registered in the United Kingdom (not being a ship registered at a port outside Great Britain) shall, unless—

(a) the employment is wholly outside Great Britain, or
(b) he is not ordinarily resident in Great Britain,

be regarded as a person who under his contract ordinarily works in Great Britain.

142.—(1) Section 54 does not apply to dismissal from employment under a contract for a fixed term of two years or more, where the dismissal consists only of the expiry of that term without its being renewed, if before the term so expires the employee has agreed in writing to exclude any claim in respect of rights under that section in relation to that contract.

Contracts for a fixed term.

(2) An employee employed under a contract of employment for a fixed term of two years or more entered into after 5th December 1965 shall not be entitled to a redundancy payment in respect of the expiry of that term without its being renewed (whether by the employer or by an associated employer of his), if before the term so expires he has agreed in writing to exclude any right to a redundancy payment in that event.

(3) Such an agreement as is mentioned in subsection (1) or (2) may be contained either in the contract itself or in a separate agreement.

(4) Where an agreement under subsection (2) is made during the currency of a fixed term, and that term is renewed, the agreement under that subsection shall not be construed as applying to the term as renewed, but without prejudice to the making of a further agreement under that subsection in relation to the term so renewed.

PART IX
Minimum periods of employment.

143.—(1) An employee shall not be entitled to a guarantee payment in respect of any day unless he has been continuously employed for a period of four weeks ending with the last complete week before that day.

(2) An employee shall not be entitled to remuneration under section 19 unless he has been continuously employed for a period of four weeks ending with the last complete week before the day on which the suspension begins.

(3) Subject to subsection (4)—

(*a*) sections 12 and 19 do not apply to employment under a contract for a fixed term of twelve weeks or less; and

(*b*) sections 12, 19 and 49 do not apply to employment under a contract made in contemplation of the performance of a specific task which is not expected to last for more than twelve weeks.

(4) Subsection (3) does not apply where the employee has been continuously employed for a period of more than twelve weeks.

Mariners.

144.—(1) Sections 1 to 6 and 49 to 51 do not apply to—

(*a*) a person employed as a master of or a seaman on a sea-going British ship having a gross registered tonnage of eighty tons or more, including a person ordinarily employed as a seaman who is employed in or about such a ship in port by the owner or charterer of the ship to do work of a kind ordinarily done by a seaman on such a ship while it is in port, or

1894 c. 60.

(*b*) a person employed as a skipper of or a seaman on a fishing boat for the time being required to be registered under section 373 of the Merchant Shipping Act 1894.

(2) Sections 8 and 53 and Parts II, III and V to VII do not apply to employment as master or as a member of the crew of a fishing vessel where the employee is remunerated only by a share in the profits or gross earnings of the vessel.

(3) Section 141(3) and (4) do not apply to an employee, and section 142(2) does not apply to a contract of employment, if the employee is employed as a master or seaman in a British ship and is ordinarily resident in Great Britain.

(4) Sections 8, 29, 31, 122 and 123 do not apply to employment as a merchant seaman.

(5) Employment as a merchant seaman does not include employment in the fishing industry or employment on board a ship otherwise than by the owner, manager or charterer of that

ship except employment as a radio officer, but, save as aforesaid, it includes employment as master or a member of the crew of any ship and as a trainee undergoing training for the sea service, and employment in or about a ship in port by the owner, manager or charterer of the ship to do work of the kind ordinarily done by a merchant seaman on a ship while it is in port.

145.—(1) Sections 1 to 6 and 49 to 51 do not apply to any registered dock worker except when engaged in work which is not dock work.

(2) Sections 12, 19, 31, 53, 54, 122 and 123 do not apply to employment as a registered dock worker other than employment by virtue of which the employee is wholly or mainly engaged in work which is not dock work.

(3) Subject to subsection (4), section 81 does not apply to any person in respect of his employment as a registered dock worker, unless it is employment by virtue of which he is wholly or mainly engaged in work which is not dock work.

(4) Subsection (3) does not apply where—

(a) the person became a registered dock worker in consequence of having been employed on work which became classified;

(b) at the date of the termination of his employment he has been continuously employed since a time before that work was classified; and

(c) as a result of the termination he ceases to be a registered dock worker,

and, for the purposes of this subsection, Schedule 13 shall have effect subject to the provisions of the new Scheme.

(5) In this section—

" classified " means classified as dock work for the purposes of the new Scheme by an order under section 11 of the Dock Work Regulation Act 1976;

" dock work ", in relation to a dock worker registered under the 1967 Scheme, means the same as in that Scheme and in relation to one registered under the new Scheme means any work which, by reference to what it is or where it is done, is classified;

" registered " means registered under the 1967 Scheme or under the new Scheme, and in relation to a worker who is registered under the new Scheme, means registered in a main register thereunder, and not in an extension register;

PART IX

1946 c. 22.
S.I. 1967/1252.

"the 1967 Scheme" means the Scheme made under the Dock Workers (Regulation of Employment) Act 1946 and set out, as varied, in Schedule 2 to the Dock Workers (Regulation of Employment) (Amendment) Order 1967;

1976 c. 79.

"the new Scheme" means the Scheme made and in force under section 4 of the Dock Work Regulation Act 1976.

Miscellaneous classes of employment.

146.—(1) The following provisions of this Act do not apply to employment where the employer is the husband or wife of the employee, that is to say, sections 1, 4, 8, 53, 122 and 123 and Parts II, III, V and VI.

(2) Parts II, III, V and VII and sections 8, 9, 53 and 86 do not apply to employment under a contract of employment in police service or to persons engaged in such employment.

(3) In subsection (2), " police service " means service—

(a) as a member of any constabulary maintained by virtue of any enactment, or

(b) in any other capacity by virtue of which a person has the powers or privileges of a constable.

(4) Subject to subsections (5), (6) and (7), the following provisions of this Act (which confer rights which do not depend upon an employee having a qualifying period of continuous employment) do not apply to employment under a contract which normally involves employment for less than sixteen hours weekly, that is to say, sections 8, 27, 28 and 29.

(5) If the employee's relations with his employer cease to be governed by a contract which normally involves work for sixteen hours or more weekly and become governed by a contract which normally involves employment for eight hours or more, but less than sixteen hours, weekly, the employee shall nevertheless for a period of twenty-six weeks, computed in accordance with subsection (6), be treated for the purposes of subsection (4) as if his contract normally involved employment for sixteen hours or more weekly.

(6) In computing the said period of twenty-six weeks no account shall be taken of any week—

(a) during which the employee is in fact employed for sixteen hours or more;

(b) during which the employee takes part in a strike (as defined by paragraph 24 of Schedule 13) or is absent from work because of a lock-out (as so defined) by his employer; or

(c) during which there is no contract of employment but which, by virtue of paragraph 9(1) of Schedule 13, counts in computing a period of continuous employment.

(7) An employee whose relations with his employer are governed by a contract of employment which normally involves employment for eight hours or more, but less than sixteen hours, weekly shall nevertheless, if he has been continuously employed for a period of five years or more be treated for the purposes of subsection (4) as if his contract normally involved employment for sixteen hours or more weekly.

147. Sections 1 to 4 shall apply to an employee who at any time comes or ceases to come within the exceptions from those sections provided for by or under sections 3(1), 143 to 146 and 149 as if a period of employment terminated or began at that time.

Application of ss. 1 to 4 to excluded employment.

Supplementary provisions

148.—(1) The Secretary of State shall in each calendar year review—

Review of limits.

(a) the limits referred to in section 15;

(b) the limit referred to in section 122(5); and

(c) the limits imposed by paragraph 8(1) of Schedule 14 on the amount of a week's pay for the purposes of those provisions;

and shall determine whether any of those limits should be varied.

(2) In making a review under this section the Secretary of State shall consider—

(a) the general level of earnings obtaining in Great Britain at the time of the review;

(b) the national economic situation as a whole; and

(c) such other matters as he thinks relevant.

(3) If on a review under this section the Secretary of State determines that, having regard to the considerations mentioned in subsection (2), any of those limits should be varied, he shall prepare and lay before each House of Parliament the draft of an order giving effect to his decision.

(4) Where a draft of an order under this section is approved by resolution of each House of Parliament the Secretary of State shall make an order in the form of the draft.

(5) If, following the completion of an annual review under this section, the Secretary of State determines that any of the limits referred to in subsection (1) shall not be varied, he shall

PART IX lay before each House of Parliament a report containing a statement of his reasons for that determination.

(6) The Secretary of State may at any time, in addition to the annual review provided for in subsection (1), conduct a further review of the limits mentioned in subsection (1) so as to determine whether any of those limits should be varied, and subsections (2) to (4) shall apply to such a review as if it were a review under subsection (1).

General power to amend Act.

149.—(1) Subject to the following provisions of this section, the Secretary of State may by order—
   (a) provide that any enactment contained in this Act which is specified in the order shall not apply to persons or to employments of such classes as may be prescribed in the order;
   (b) provide that any such enactment shall apply to persons or employments of such classes as may be prescribed in the order subject, except in relation to section 54 (but without prejudice to paragraph (a)), to such exceptions and modifications as may be so prescribed;
   (c) vary, or exclude the operation of, any of the following provisions of this Act, that is to say, sections 64(1), 99, 141(2) and (5), 143(3) and (4), 144(1), (2), (4) and (5), 145(1), (2) and (3) and 146(1) and (4) to (7);
   (d) add to, vary or delete any of the provisions of Schedule 5.

(2) Subsection (1) does not apply to the following provisions of this Act, namely, sections 7, 52, 55, 57, 58, 59, 62, 63, 65, 66, 67, 75, 80, 103 to 120, 128, 134, 141(1) and 142(1) and Schedules 3, 9 and 13, and, in addition, paragraph (b) of subsection (1) does not apply to sections 1 to 6 and 49 to 51 and paragraph (c) of subsection (1) does not apply to section 143 as that section applies in relation to section 49.

(3) The provisions of this section are without prejudice to any other power of the Secretary of State to amend, vary or repeal any provision of this Act or to extend or restrict its operation in relation to any person or employment.

(4) No order under subsection (1) shall be made unless a draft of the order has been laid before Parliament and approved by a resolution of each House of Parliament.

Death of employee or employer.

150. Schedule 12 shall have effect for the purpose of supplementing and modifying the provisions of Part I (so far as it relates to itemised pay statements), section 53 and Parts II, III, and V to VII as respects the death of an employee or employer.

151.—(1) Subject to sections 104(2) and 106(2), Schedule 13 shall have effect for the purposes of this Act for ascertaining the length of an employee's period of employment and whether that employment has been continuous, and references in this Act to a period of employment shall be construed accordingly.

PART IX
Continuous employment.

(2) For the purposes of any proceedings under this Act, other than proceedings for a breach of section 1, 2, 4 or 49, a person's employment during any period shall, unless the contrary is shown, be presumed to have been continuous.

152. Schedule 14 shall have effect for the purposes of this Act for calculating the normal working hours and the amount of a week's pay of any employee.

Calculation of normal working hours and a week's pay.

153.—(1) In this Act, except so far as the context otherwise requires—

Interpretation.

" act " and " action " each includes omission and references to doing an act or taking action shall be construed accordingly;

" business " includes a trade or profession and includes any activity carried on by a body of persons, whether corporate or unincorporate;

" certified midwife " means a midwife certified under the Midwives Act 1951 or the Midwives (Scotland) Act 1951;

1951 c. 53.
1951 c. 54.

" collective agreement " has the meaning given by section 30(1) of the Trade Union and Labour Relations Act 1974;

1974 c. 52.

" confinement " means the birth of a living child or the birth of a child whether living or dead after twenty-eight weeks of pregnancy;

" contract of employment " means a contract of service or apprenticeship, whether express or implied, and (if it is express) whether it is oral or in writing;

" dismissal procedures agreement " means an agreement in writing with respect to procedures relating to dismissal made by or on behalf of one or more independent trade unions and one or more employers or employers' associations;

" effective date of termination " has the meaning given by section 55(4) and (5);

" employee " means an individual who has entered into or works under (or, where the employment has ceased, worked under) a contract of employment;

" employer ", in relation to an employee, means the person by whom the employee is (or, in a case where the employment has ceased, was) employed;

PART IX
1974 c. 52.

"employers' association" has the same meaning as it has for the purposes of the Trade Union and Labour Relations Act 1974;

"employer's payment" means a payment falling within paragraph (a), (b) or (c) of section 104(1);

"employment", except for the purposes of sections 111 to 115, means employment under a contract of employment;

"expected week of confinement" means the week, beginning with midnight between Saturday and Sunday, in which it is expected that confinement will take place;

"government department", except in section 138 and paragraph 19 of Schedule 13, includes a Minister of the Crown;

"guarantee payment" has the meaning given by section 12(1);

"inadmissible reason" has the meaning given by section 58(5);

"independent trade union" means a trade union which—
  (a) is not under the domination or control of an employer or a group of employers or of one or more employers' associations; and
  (b) is not liable to interference by an employer or any such group or association (arising out of the provision of financial or material support or by any other means whatsoever) tending towards such control;

and, in relation to a trade union, "independent" and "independence" shall be construed accordingly;

"job", in relation to an employee, means the nature of the work which he is employed to do in accordance with his contract and the capacity and place in which he is so employed;

"maternity pay" has the meaning given by section 33(1);

"Maternity Pay Fund" means the fund referred to in section 37;

"maternity pay rebate" has the meaning given by section 39;

"notice of intention to claim" has the meaning given by section 88;

"notified day of return" has the meaning given by section 47(1) and (8);

"official", in relation to a trade union, has the meaning given by section 30(1) of the Trade Union and Labour Relations Act 1974;

"original contract of employment", in relation to an employee who is absent from work wholly or partly because of pregnancy or confinement, means the contract under which she worked immediately before the beginning of her absence or, if she entered into that contract during her pregnancy by virtue of section 60(2) or otherwise by reason of her pregnancy, the contract under which she was employed immediately before she entered into the later contract or, if there was more than one later contract, the first of the later contracts;

"position", in relation to an employee, means the following matters taken as a whole, that is to say, his status as an employee, the nature of his work and his terms and conditions of employment;

"Redundancy Fund" means the fund referred to in section 103;

"redundancy payment" has the meaning given by section 81(1);

"redundancy rebate" has the meaning given by section 104;

"relevant date", for the purposes of the provisions of this Act which relate to redundancy payments, has the meaning given by section 90;

"renewal" includes extension, and any reference to renewing a contract or a fixed term shall be construed accordingly;

"statutory provision" means a provision, whether of a general or a special nature, contained in, or in any document made or issued under, any Act, whether of a general or special nature;

"successor" has the meaning given by section 30(3) and (4) of the Trade Union and Labour Relations Act 1974; 1974 c. 52.

"trade dispute" has the meaning given by section 29 of the said Act of 1974;

"trade union" has the meaning given by section 28 of the said Act of 1974;

"union membership agreement" has the meaning given by section 30(1) of the said Act of 1974 and "employees", in relation thereto, has the meaning given by section 30(5A) of that Act;

"week" means, in relation to an employee whose remuneration is calculated weekly by a week ending with a day other than Saturday, a week ending with that other day, and in relation to any other employee, a week ending with Saturday.

PART IX

(2) References in this Act to dismissal by reason of redundancy, and to cognate expressions, shall be construed in accordance with section 81.

(3) In sections 33, 47, 56, 61 and 86 and Schedule 2, except where the context otherwise requires, "to return to work" means to return to work in accordance with section 45(1), and cognate expressions shall be construed accordingly.

(4) For the purposes of this Act, any two employers are to be treated as associated if one is a company of which the other (directly or indirectly) has control, or if both are companies of which a third person (directly or indirectly) has control; and the expression "associated employer" shall be construed accordingly.

(5) For the purposes of this Act it is immaterial whether the law which (apart from this Act) governs any person's employment is the law of the United Kingdom, or of a part of the United Kingdom, or not.

(6) In this Act, except where otherwise indicated—

(a) a reference to a numbered Part, section or Schedule is a reference to the Part or section of, or the Schedule to, this Act so numbered, and

(b) a reference in a section to a numbered subsection is a reference to the subsection of that section so numbered, and

(c) a reference in a section, subsection or Schedule to a numbered paragraph is a reference to the paragraph of that section, subsection or Schedule so numbered, and

(d) a reference to any provision of an Act (including this Act) includes a Schedule incorporated in the Act by that provision.

(7) Except so far as the context otherwise requires, any reference in this Act to an enactment shall be construed as a reference to that enactment as amended or extended by or under any other enactment, including this Act.

Orders, rules and regulations.

154.—(1) Any power conferred by any provision of this Act to make an order (other than an Order in Council or an order under section 65 or 66) or to make rules or regulations shall be exercisable by statutory instrument.

(2) Any statutory instrument made under any power conferred by this Act to make an Order in Council or other order or to make rules or regulations, except—

(a) an instrument required to be laid before Parliament in draft; and

(b) an order under section 18,

shall be subject to annulment in pursuance of a resolution of either House of Parliament.

(3) Any power conferred by this Act which is exercisable by statutory instrument shall include power to make such incidental, supplementary or transitional provisions as appear to the authority exercising the power to be necessary or expedient.

(4) An order made by statutory instrument under any provision of this Act may be revoked or varied by a subsequent order made under that provision.

This subsection does not apply to an order under section 96 but is without prejudice to subsection (4) of that section.

155.—(1) Where an offence under section 44 or 126 committed by a body corporate is proved to have been committed with the consent or connivance of, or to be attributable to any neglect on the part of, any director, manager, secretary or other similar officer of the body corporate, or any person who was purporting to act in any such capacity, he as well as the body corporate shall be guilty of that offence and shall be liable to be proceeded against and punished accordingly. *Offences by bodies corporate.*

(2) Where the affairs of a body corporate are managed by its members, subsection (1) shall apply in relation to the acts and defaults of a member in connection with his functions of management as if he were a director of the body corporate.

156.—(1) There shall be paid out of the Maternity Pay Fund into the Consolidated Fund sums equal to the amount of any expenses incurred by the Secretary of State in exercising his functions under this Act relating to maternity pay. *Payments into the Consolidated Fund.*

(2) There shall be paid out of the Redundancy Fund into the Consolidated Fund sums equal to the amount of any expenses incurred—

(a) by the Secretary of State in consequence of Part VI, except expenses incurred in the payment of sums in accordance with any such arrangements as are mentioned in section 111(3);

(b) by the Secretary of State (or by persons acting on his behalf) in exercising his functions under sections 122 to 126.

(3) There shall be paid out of the Redundancy Fund into the Consolidated Fund such sums as the Secretary of State may estimate in accordance with directions given by the Treasury to be the amount of any expenses incurred by any government department other than the Secretary of State in consequence of the provisions of sections 103 to 109.

PART IX
Northern Ireland.

157.—(1) If provision is made by Northern Irish legislation (that is to say by or under a Measure of the Northern Ireland Assembly) for purposes corresponding to any of the purposes of this Act, except sections 1 to 7 and 49 to 51, the Secretary of State may, with the consent of the Treasury, make reciprocal arrangements with the appropriate Northern Irish authority for co-ordinating the relevant provisions of this Act with the corresponding provisions of the Northern Irish legislation, so as to secure that they operate, to such extent as may be provided by the arrangements, as a single system.

(2) For the purpose of giving effect to any such arrangements the Secretary of State shall have power, in conjunction with the appropriate Northern Irish authority—

(a) where the arrangements relate to the provisions of this Act relating to maternity pay, to make any necessary financial adjustments between the Maternity Pay Fund and any fund established under Northern Irish legislation; and

(b) where the arrangements relate to Part VI or to sections 122 to 126, to make any necessary financial adjustments between the Redundancy Fund and the Northern Ireland Redundancy Fund.

(3) The Secretary of State may make regulations for giving effect in Great Britain to any such arrangements, and any such regulations may make different provision for different cases, and may provide that the relevant provisions of this Act shall have effect in relation to persons affected by the arrangements subject to such modifications and adaptations as may be specified in the regulations, including provision—

(a) for securing that acts, omissions and events having any effect for the purposes of the Northern Irish legislation shall have a corresponding effect for the purposes of this Act (but not so as to confer a right to double payment in respect of the same act, omission or event); and

(b) for determining, in cases where rights accrue both under this Act and under the Northern Irish legislation, which of those rights shall be available to the person concerned.

(4) In this section "the appropriate Northern Irish authority" means such authority as may be specified in that behalf in the Northern Irish legislation.

The Isle of Man.

158.—(1) If an Act of Tynwald is passed for purposes similar to the purposes of Part VI, the Secretary of State may, with the consent of the Treasury, make reciprocal arrangements with the appropriate Isle of Man authority for co-ordinating the provisions of Part VI with the corresponding provisions of the Act of Tynwald so as to secure that they operate, to such extent as may be provided by the arrangements, as a single system.

(2) For the purpose of giving effect to any such arrangements, the Secretary of State shall have power, in conjunction with the appropriate Isle of Man authority, to make any necessary financial adjustments between the Redundancy Fund and any fund established under the Act of Tynwald.

(3) The Secretary of State may make regulations for giving effect in Great Britain to any such arrangements, and any such regulations may provide that Part VI shall have effect in relation to persons affected by the arrangements subject to such modifications and adaptations as may be specified in the regulations, including provision—

(a) for securing that acts, omissions and events having any effect for the purposes of the Act of Tynwald shall have a corresponding effect for the purposes of Part VI (but not so as to confer a right to double payment in respect of the same act, omission or event); and

(b) for determining, in cases where rights accrue both under this Act and under the Act of Tynwald, which of those rights shall be available to the person concerned.

(4) In this section "the appropriate Isle of Man authority" means such authority as may be specified in that behalf in an Act of Tynwald.

159.—(1) The transitional provisions and savings in Schedule 15 shall have effect but nothing in that Schedule shall be construed as prejudicing section 38 of the Interpretation Act 1889 (effect of repeals).

(2) The enactments specified in Schedule 16 shall have effect subject to the amendments specified in that Schedule.

(3) The enactments specified in the first column of Schedule 17 are hereby repealed to the extent specified in column 3 of that Schedule.

160.—(1) This Act may be cited as the Employment Protection (Consolidation) Act 1978.

(2) This Act, except section 139(2) to (9) and the repeals in section 122 of the Employment Protection Act 1975 provided for in Schedule 17 to this Act, shall come into force on 1st November 1978, and section 139(2) to (9) and those repeals shall come into force on 1st January 1979.

(3) This Act, except sections 137 and 157 and paragraphs 12 and 28 of Schedule 16, shall not extend to Northern Ireland.

SCHEDULES

Section 19.

SCHEDULE 1

Provisions Leading to Suspension on Medical Grounds

1. The Paints and Colours Manufacture Regulations 1907.	S.R. & O. 1907 No. 17...	Reg. 5.
2. The Yarn (Dyed by Lead Compounds) Heading Regulations 1907.	S.R. & O. 1907 No. 616	Reg. 4.
3. The Vitreous Enamelling Regulations 1908.	S.R. & O. 1908 No. 1258	Reg. 10.
4. The Tinning of Metal Hollow-ware, Iron Drums and Harness Furniture Regulations 1909.	S.R. & O. 1909 No. 720	Reg. 6.
5. The Lead Smelting and Manufacture Regulations 1911.	S.R. & O. 1911 No. 752	Reg. 13.
6. The Lead Compounds Manufacture Regulations 1921.	S.R. & O. 1921 No. 1443	Reg. 11.
7. The Indiarubber Regulations 1922.	S.R. & O. 1922 No. 329	Reg. 12.
8. The Chemical Works Regulations 1922.	S.R. & O. 1922 No. 731	Reg. 30.
9. The Electric Accumulator Regulations 1925.	S.R. & O. 1925 No. 28...	Reg. 13.
10. The Lead Paint Regulations 1927...	S.R. & O. 1927 No. 847	Reg. 6.
11. The Pottery (Health and Welfare) Special Regulations 1950.	S.I. 1950 No. 65 ...	Reg. 7.
12. The Factories Act 1961	1961 c. 34	Section 75(2) (including that section as extended by section 128).
13. The Ionising Radiations (Unsealed Radioactive Substances) Regulations 1968.	S.I. 1968 No. 780 ...	Regs. 12 and 33.
14. The Ionising Radiations (Sealed Sources) Regulations 1969.	S.I. 1969 No. 808 ...	Regs. 11 and 30.
15. The Radioactive Substances (Road Transport Workers) (Great Britain) Regulations 1970.	S.I. 1970 No. 1827 ...	Reg. 14.

SCHEDULE 2

Section 33.

Supplementary Provisions Relating to Maternity

Part I

Unfair Dismissal

Introductory

1. References in this Part to provisions of this Act relating to unfair dismissal are references to those provisions as they apply by virtue of section 56.

Adaptation of unfair dismissal provisions

2.—(1) Section 57 shall have effect as if for subsection (3) there were substituted the following subsection:—

" (3) Where the employer has fulfilled the requirements of subsection (1), then, subject to sections 58(1), 59, 60 and 62, the determination of the question whether the dismissal was fair or unfair, having regard to the reason shown by the employer, shall depend on whether the employer can satisfy the tribunal that in the circumstances (having regard to equity and the substantial merits of the case) he would have been acting reasonably in treating it as a sufficient reason for dismissing the employee if she had not been absent from work.".

(2) If in the circumstances described in section 45(3) no offer is made of such alternative employment as is referred to in that subsection, then the dismissal which by virtue of section 56 is treated as taking place shall, notwithstanding anything in section 57 or 58, be treated as an unfair dismissal for the purposes of Part V of this Act.

(3) The following references shall be construed as references to the notified day of return, that is to say—

(a) references in Part V of this Act to the effective date of termination;

(b) references in sections 69 and 70 to the date of termination of employment.

(4) The following provisions of this Act shall not apply, that is to say, sections 55, 58(3), 64(1), 65, 66, 73(5) and (6), 141(2), 142(1), 144(2), 145(2) and 146(1), paragraph 11(1) of Schedule 13, paragraphs 7(1)(f) to (i) and (2) and 8(3) of Schedule 14 and paragraph 10 of Schedule 15.

(5) For the purposes of Part II of Schedule 14 as it applies for the calculation of a week's pay for the purposes of section 71 or 73, the calculation date is the last day on which the employee worked under the original contract of employment.

Part II

Redundancy Payments

Introductory

3. References in this Part to provisions of this Act relating to redundancy are references to those provisions as they apply by virtue of section 86.

Adaptation of redundancy payments provisions

4.—(1) References in Part VI of this Act shall be adapted as follows, that is to say—

(a) references to the relevant date, wherever they occur, shall be construed, except where the context otherwise requires, as references to the notified day of return;

(b) references in sections 82(4) and 84(1) to a renewal or re-engagement taking effect immediately on the ending of employment under the previous contract or after an interval of not more than four weeks thereafter, shall be construed as references to a renewal or re-engagement taking effect on the notified day of return or not more than four weeks after that day; and

(c) references in section 84(3) to the provisions of the previous contract shall be construed as references to the provisions of the original contract of employment.

(2) Nothing in section 86 shall prevent an employee from being treated, by reason of the operation of section 84(1), as not having been dismissed for the purposes of Part VI of this Act.

(3) The following provisions of this Act shall not apply, that is to say, sections 81(1)(b), 82(1) and (2), 83(1) and (2), 85, 87 to 89, 90(3), 92, 93, 96, 110, 144(2), 146(1) and 150, paragraph 4 of Schedule 4, Schedule 12 and paragraphs 7(1)(j) and (k) and 8(4) of Schedule 14.

(4) For the purposes of Part II of Schedule 14 as it applies for the calculation of a week's pay for the purposes of Schedule 4, the calculation date is the last day on which the employee worked under the original contract of employment.

Prior redundancy

5. If, in proceedings arising out of a failure to permit an employee to return to work, the employer shows—

(a) that the reason for the failure is that the employee is redundant; and

(b) that the employee was dismissed or, had she continued to be employed by him, would have been dismissed, by reason of redundancy during her absence on a day earlier than the notified day of return and falling after the beginning of the eleventh week before the expected week of confinement,

then, for the purposes of Part VI of this Act the employee—
   (i) shall not be treated as having been dismissed with effect from the notified day of return; but
   (ii) shall, if she would not otherwise be so treated, be treated as having been continuously employed until that earlier day and as having been dismissed by reason of redundancy with effect from that day.

Part III

General

Dismissal during period of absence

6.—(1) This paragraph applies to the dismissal of an employee who is under this Act entitled to return to work and whose contract of employment continues to subsist during the period of her absence but who is dismissed by her employer during that period after the beginning of the eleventh week before the expected week of confinement.

(2) For the purposes of sub-paragraph (1), an employee shall not be taken to be dismissed during the period of her absence if the dismissal occurs in the course of the employee's attempting to return to work in accordance with her contract in circumstances in which section 48 applies.

(3) In the application of Part V of this Act to a dismissal to which this paragraph applies, the following provisions shall not apply, that is to say, sections 58(3), 64, 65, 66, 141(2), 144(2), 145 and 146(1).

(4) Any such dismissal shall not affect the employee's right to return to work, but—
   (a) compensation in any unfair dismissal proceedings arising out of that dismissal shall be assessed without regard to the employee's right to return; and
   (b) that right shall be exercisable only on her repaying any redundancy payment or compensation for unfair dismissal paid in respect of that dismissal, if the employer requests such repayment.

Power to amend or modify

7.—(1) The Secretary of State may by order amend the provisions of this Schedule and section 48 or modify the application of those provisions to any description of case.

(2) No order under this paragraph shall be made unless a draft of the order has been laid before Parliament and approved by a resolution of each House of Parliament.

Section 50.

SCHEDULE 3

RIGHTS OF EMPLOYEE IN PERIOD OF NOTICE

Preliminary

1. In this Schedule the "period of notice" means the period of notice required by section 49(1) or, as the case may be, section 49(2).

Employments for which there are normal working hours

2.—(1) If an employee has normal working hours under the contract of employment in force during the period of notice, and if during any part of those normal working hours—

   (a) the employee is ready and willing to work but no work is provided for him by his employer; or

   (b) the employee is incapable of work because of sickness or injury; or

   (c) the employee is absent from work in accordance with the terms of his employment relating to holidays,

then the employer shall be liable to pay the employee for the part of normal working hours covered by paragraphs (a), (b) and (c) a sum not less than the amount of remuneration for that part of normal working hours calculated at the average hourly rate of remuneration produced by dividing a week's pay by the number of normal working hours.

(2) Any payments made to the employee by his employer in respect of the relevant part of the period of notice whether by way of sick pay, holiday pay or otherwise, shall go towards meeting the employer's liability under this paragraph.

(3) Where notice was given by the employee, the employer's liability under this paragraph shall not arise unless and until the employee leaves the service of the employer in pursuance of the notice.

Employments for which there are no normal working hours

3.—(1) If an employee does not have normal working hours under the contract of employment in force in the period of notice the employer shall be liable to pay the employee for each week of the period of notice a sum not less than a week's pay.

(2) Subject to sub-paragraph (3), the employer's obligation under this paragraph shall be conditional on the employee being ready and willing to do work of a reasonable nature and amount to earn a week's pay.

(3) Sub-paragraph (2) shall not apply—

   (a) in respect of any period during which the employee is incapable of work because of sickness or injury, or

   (b) in respect of any period during which the employee is absent from work in accordance with the terms of his employment relating to holidays, and any payment made to an employee by his employer in respect of such a period, whether by way of sick pay, holiday pay or otherwise, shall be taken into account for the purposes of this paragraph as if it were remuneration paid by the employer in respect of that period.

(4) Where the notice was given by the employee, the employer's liability under this paragraph shall not arise unless and until the employee leaves the service of the employer in pursuance of the notice.

Sickness or industrial injury benefit

4.—(1) The following provisions of this paragraph shall have effect where the arrangements in force relating to the employment are such that—

(a) payments by way of sick pay are made by the employer to employees to whom the arrangements apply, in cases where any such employees are incapable of work because of sickness or injury, and

(b) in calculating any payment so made to any such employee an amount representing, or treated as representing, sickness benefit or industrial injury benefit is taken into account, whether by way of deduction or by way of calculating the payment as a supplement to that amount.

(2) If during any part of the period of notice the employee is incapable of work because of sickness or injury, and—

(a) one or more payments, by way of sick pay are made to him by the employer in respect of that part of the period of notice, and

(b) in calculating any such payment such an amount as is referred to in sub-paragraph (1)(b) is taken into account as therein mentioned,

then for the purposes of this Schedule the amount so taken into account shall be treated as having been paid by the employer to the employee by way of sick pay in respect of that part of that period, and shall go towards meeting the liability of the employer under paragraph 2 or paragraph 3 accordingly.

Absence on leave granted at request of employee

5. The employer shall not be liable under the foregoing provisions of this Schedule to make any payment in respect of a period during which the employee is absent from work with the leave of the employer granted at the request of the employee (including any period of time off taken in accordance with section 27, 28, 29 or 31).

Notice given before a strike

6. No payment shall be due under this Schedule in consequence of a notice to terminate a contract given by an employee if, after the notice is given and on or before the termination of the contract, the employee takes part in a strike of employees of the employer.

SCH. 3 In this paragraph " strike " has the meaning given by paragraph 24 of Schedule 13.

Termination of employment during period of notice

7.—(1) If, during the period of notice, the employer breaks the contract of employment, payments received under this Schedule in respect of the part of the period after the breach shall go towards mitigating the damages recoverable by the employee for loss of earnings in that part of the period of notice.

(2) If, during the period of notice, the employee breaks the contract and the employer rightfully treats the breach as terminating the contract, no payment shall be due to the employee under this Schedule in respect of the part of the period of notice falling after the termination of the contract.

Section 81.

SCHEDULE 4

CALCULATION OF REDUNDANCY PAYMENTS

1. The amount of a redundancy payment to which an employee is entitled in any case shall, subject to the following provisions of this Schedule, be calculated by reference to the period, ending with the relevant date, during which he has been continuously employed.

2. Subject to paragraphs 3 and 4, the amount of the redundancy payment shall be calculated by reference to the period specified in paragraph 1 by starting at the end of that period and reckoning backwards the number of years of employment falling within that period, and allowing—

   (a) one and a half weeks' pay for each such year of employment which consists wholly of weeks (within the meaning of Schedule 13) in which the employee was not below the age of forty-one;

   (b) one week's pay for each such year of employment (not falling within the preceding sub-paragraph) which consists wholly of weeks (within the meaning of Schedule 13) in which the employee was not below the age of twenty-two; and

   (c) half a week's pay for each such year of employment not falling within either of the preceding sub-paragraphs.

3. Where, in reckoning the number of years of employment in accordance with paragraph 2, twenty years of employment have been reckoned, no account shall be taken of any year of employment earlier than those twenty years.

4.—(1) Where in the case of an employee the relevant date is after the specified anniversary, the amount of the redundancy payment, calculated in accordance with the preceding provisions of this Schedule, shall be reduced by the appropriate fraction.

(2) In this paragraph " the specified anniversary ", in relation to a man, means the sixty-fourth anniversary of the day of his birth, and, in relation to a woman, means the fifty-ninth anniversary

of the day of her birth, and "the appropriate fraction" means the fraction of which—

(a) the numerator is the number of whole months, reckoned from the specified anniversary, in the the period beginning with that anniversary and ending with the relevant date, and

(b) the denominator is twelve.

5. For the purposes of any provision contained in Part VI whereby an industrial tribunal may determine that an employer shall be liable to pay to an employee either—

(a) the whole of the redundancy payment to which the employee would have been entitled apart from another provision therein mentioned, or

(b) such part of that redundancy payment as the tribunal thinks fit,

the preceding provisions of this Schedule shall apply as if in those provisions any reference to the amount of a redundancy payment were a reference to the amount of the redundancy payment to which the employee would have been so entitled.

6. The preceding provisions of this Schedule shall have effect without prejudice to the operation of any regulations made under section 98 whereby the amount of a redundancy payment, or part of a redundancy payment, may be reduced.

7. Where the relevant date does not occur on a Saturday, any reference in the preceding provisions of this Schedule to the relevant date shall be construed as a reference to the Saturday immediately following that date.

SCHEDULE 5
NATIONAL HEALTH SERVICE EMPLOYERS

1. A Regional Health Authority, Area Health Authority, special health authority, Health Board or the Common Services Agency for the Scottish Health Service.

2. The Dental Estimates Board.

3. Any joint committee constituted under section 13(8) of the National Health Service (Scotland) Act 1972.

4. The Public Health Laboratory Service Board.

SCHEDULE 6
CALCULATION OF REDUNDANCY REBATES
PART I
REBATES IN RESPECT OF REDUNDANCY PAYMENTS

1. Subject to sections 104(7) and 108 and to the following provisions of this Part, the amount of any redundancy rebate payable in respect of a redundancy payment shall be calculated by taking the number of years of employment by reference to which the redundancy payment falls to be calculated in accordance with Schedule 4 and allowing—

(a) 123/200 of one week's pay for each year of employment falling within sub-paragraph (a) of paragraph 2 of that Schedule;

Sch. 6

(b) 41/100 of one week's pay for each year of employment falling within sub-paragraph (b) of that paragraph; and

(c) 41/200 of one week's pay for each year of employment falling within sub-paragraph (c) of that paragraph.

2. Where the amount of the redundancy payment, calculated in accordance with paragraphs 1, 2 and 3 of Schedule 4, is reduced by virtue of paragraph 4 of that Schedule, the amount of the rebate shall be 41/100 of the amount of the redundancy payment as so reduced.

3.—(1) The provisions of this paragraph shall have effect in relation to any case where—

(a) under section 85, 92 or 110 an industrial tribunal is empowered to determine that an employer shall be liable to pay to an employee either the whole or part of the redundancy payment to which the employee would have been entitled apart from another provision therein mentioned, and

(b) the tribunal determines that the employer shall be liable to pay part (but not the whole) of that redundancy payment.

(2) There shall be ascertained what proportion that part of the redundancy payment bears to the whole of it (in this paragraph referred to as "the relevant proportion").

(3) There shall also be ascertained what, in accordance with the preceding provisions of this Part, would have been the amount of the redundancy rebate payable in respect of that redundancy payment if the employer had been liable to pay the whole of it.

(4) Subject to paragraph 4, the amount of the rebate payable in that case shall then be an amount equal to the relevant proportion of the amount referred to in sub-paragraph (3).

4. Where the amount of a redundancy payment or part of a redundancy payment is reduced in accordance with regulations made under section 98,—

(a) the proportion by which it is so reduced shall be ascertained, and

(b) the amount of any redundancy rebate calculated by reference to that payment shall be reduced by that proportion.

Part II

Rebates in Respect of other Payments

Introductory

5. The provisions of this Part shall have effect for the purpose of calculating the amount of any redundancy rebate payable in respect of an employer's payment which is not a redundancy payment or part of a redundancy payment (in this Part referred to as "the agreed payment").

6. In this Part " the agreement ", in relation to the agreed payment, means the agreement referred to in paragraph (*b*) or paragraph (*c*) of section 104(1) by reference to which that payment is payable ; and " the relevant provisions of the agreement " means those provisions of the agreement which relate to either of the following matters, that is to say—

(*a*) the circumstances in which the continuity of an employee's period of employment is to be treated as broken, and

(*b*) the weeks which are to count in computing a period of employment.

7. In this Part any reference to the amount of the relevant redundancy payment, in relation to the agreed payment, shall be construed as a reference to the amount of the redundancy payment which the employer would have been liable to pay to the employee if—

(*a*) the order referred to in paragraph (*b*) of subsection (1) of section 104, or (as the case may be) the order and the award referred to in paragraph (*c*) of that subsection, had not been made ;

(*b*) the circumstances in which the agreed payment is payable had been such that the employer was liable to pay a redundancy payment to the employee in those circumstances ;

(*c*) in relation to that redundancy payment, the relevant date had been the date on which the termination of the employee's contract of employment is treated for the purposes of the agreement as having taken effect ; and

(*d*) in so far as the relevant provisions of the agreement are inconsistent with the provisions of Schedule 13 as to the matters referred to in sub-paragraphs (*a*) and (*b*) of paragraph 6, those provisions of the agreement were substituted for those provisions of that Schedule ;

and " the assumed conditions " means the conditions specified in sub-paragraphs (*a*) to (*d*) of this paragraph.

Method of calculation

8. Subject to sections 104(7) and 108, and to the following provisions of this Part, the amount of any redundancy rebate payable in respect of the agreed payment shall be an amount calculated as follows, that is to say, by taking the number of years of employment by reference to which the amount of the relevant redundancy payment would fall to be calculated in accordance with Schedule 4 (as that Schedule would have applied if the assumed conditions were fulfilled), and allowing—

(*a*) 123/200 of one week's pay for each such year of employment falling within sub-paragraph (*a*) of paragraph 2 of that Schedule ;

(*b*) 41/100 of one week's pay for each such year of employment falling within sub-paragraph (*b*) of that paragraph ; and

(*c*) 41/200 of one week's pay for each such year of employment falling within sub-paragraph (*c*) of that paragraph.

Sch. 6

9. For the purposes of paragraph 8, Schedule 13 shall have effect as if paragraphs 11(2), 12 and 14 were omitted.

10. Where the amount of the agreed payment is less than the amount of the relevant redundancy payment—
- (a) the proportion which it bears to the amount of the relevant redundancy payment shall be ascertained, and
- (b) the amount of the rebate shall (except as provided by the next following paragraph) be that proportion of the amount calculated in accordance with the preceding provisions of this Part of this Schedule.

11. Where the amount of the relevant redundancy payment calculated in accordance with paragraphs 1, 2 and 3 of Schedule 4 would (if the assumed conditions were fulfilled) have been reduced by virtue of paragraph 4 of that Schedule, the amount of the rebate shall be 41/100 of the amount of the relevant redundancy payment as so reduced.

Savings

12.—(1) This Schedule shall have effect in relation to redundancy rebates of a kind specified in sub-paragraph (2), as if—
- (a) in paragraphs 1 and 8, for the reference to 123/200, 41/100 and 41/200 there were substituted a reference to 3/4, 1/2 and 1/4 respectively, and
- (b) in paragraphs 2 and 11 for each reference to 41/100 there were substituted a reference to 1/2.

(2) The redundancy rebates referred to in sub-paragraph (1) are—
- (a) any rebate payable in respect of the whole or part of a redundancy payment in relation to which the relevant date is or would but for the operation of section 90(3) be earlier than 14th August 1977;
- (b) any rebate payable in respect of a payment to an employee on the termination of his contract of employment which is paid—
  - (i) in pursuance of an agreement in respect of which an order under section 96 is in operation; or
  - (ii) in pursuance of an award made under Schedule 11 to the Employment Protection Act 1975 in connection with such an agreement,

where, under the agreement in question, the employee's contract is treated for the purposes of the agreement as having been terminated on a date earlier than 14th August 1977.

1975 c. 71.

Power to modify paragraphs 1, 2, 8 and 11

13.—(1) The Secretary of State may from time to time by order modify this Schedule—
- (a) by substituting for the three fractions of a week's pay for the time being specified in sub-paragraphs (a), (b) and (c)

of paragraphs 1 and 8 one of the other sets of three fractions specified in the following Table; and

(b) by substituting for the fraction for the time being specified in paragraphs 2 and 11 for the purpose of calculating the amount of the rebates in respect of reduced payments the like fraction as, by virtue of paragraph (a) is substituted for the fraction in paragraphs 1(b) and 8(b).

TABLE

	Fraction in paragraphs 1(a) and 8(a)	Fraction in paragraphs 1(b), 2, 8(b) and 11	Fraction in paragraphs 1(c) and 8(c)
1	21/40	7/20	7/40
2	123/200	41/100	41/200
3	27/40	9/20	9/40
4	3/4	1/2	1/4
5	33/40	11/20	11/40
6	9/10	3/5	3/10
7	39/40	13/20	13/40
8	21/20	7/10	7/20
9	9/8	3/4	3/8
10	6/5	4/5	2/5

In this Table—

(a) the three fractions specified in paragraph 2 are those which, at the passing of this Act, are specified in sub-paragraphs (a), (b) and (c) of paragraphs 1 and 8;

(b) the second of the fractions specified in paragraph 2 is the fraction which, at the passing of this Act, is specified in paragraphs 2 and 11.

(2) No order shall be made under sub-paragraph (1) unless a draft thereof has been laid before and approved by a resolution of each House of Parliament.

SCHEDULE 7

CALCULATION OF PAYMENTS TO EMPLOYEES OUT OF REDUNDANCY FUND

1.—(1) Where the employer's payment is a redundancy payment, the sum referred to in section 106(2) is a sum equal to the amount of that payment.

(2) Where, in a case falling within section 104(6), the employer's payment is part of a redundancy payment, the sum referred to in section 106(2) is a sum equal to the amount of that part of the payment.

2.—(1) The provisions of this paragraph shall have effect for the purpose of determining the sum referred to in section 106(2) in relation to an employer's payment which is not a redundancy payment or part of a redundancy payment.

SCH. 7

(2) Paragraphs 6 and 7 of Schedule 6 shall have effect for the purposes of this paragraph as they have effect for the purposes of Part II of that Schedule; and in the application of those paragraphs in accordance with this sub-paragraph the employer's payment in relation to which the sum referred to in section 106(2) falls to be determined shall be taken to be the agreed payment.

(3) In relation to any such employer's payment, the sum in question shall be a sum equal to—

(a) the amount of the employer's payment, or

(b) the amount of the relevant redundancy payment,

whichever is the less.

Section 117.

SCHEDULE 8

EMPLOYEES PAID BY VIRTUE OF STATUTORY PROVISION BY PERSON OTHER THAN EMPLOYER

Provision of Act	Reference to be construed as reference to the person responsible for paying the remuneration
Section 81(1)	The second reference to the employer.
Section 85(3)	The reference to the employer in paragraph (b).
Section 85(4)	The last reference to the employer.
Section 88(4)	The reference to the employer.
Section 89(1)	The first reference to the employer.
Section 89(4) and (5)	The references to the employer.
Section 92(3)	The second reference to the employer.
Section 98(3)	The reference to the employer.
Section 101(1)	The reference to the employer.
Section 102	The references to the employer.
Section 104	The references to the employer.
Section 106	The references to the employer.
Section 107(1)	The reference to the employer.
Section 108(1), (2), (4) and (5)	The references to the employer.
Section 110(2)	The third reference to the employer.
Section 110(5) and (6)	The reference to the employer.
Schedule 13, paragraph 12(3)	The references to the employer.

Section 128.

SCHEDULE 9

INDUSTRIAL TRIBUNALS

Regulations as to tribunal procedure

1.—(1) The Secretary of State may by regulations (in this Schedule referred to as "the regulations") make such provision as appears to him to be necessary or expedient with respect to proceedings before industrial tribunals.

(2) The regulations may in particular include provision—
  (a) for determining by which tribunal any appeal, question or complaint is to be determined;
  (b) for enabling an industrial tribunal to hear and determine proceedings brought by virtue of section 131 concurrently with proceedings brought before the tribunal otherwise than by virtue of that section;
  (c) for treating the Secretary of State (either generally or in such circumstances as may be prescribed by the regulations) as a party to any proceedings before an industrial tribunal, where he would not otherwise be a party to them, and entitling him to appear and to be heard accordingly;
  (d) for requiring persons to attend to give evidence and produce documents, and for authorising the administration of oaths to witnesses;
  (e) for granting to any person such discovery or inspection of documents or right to further particulars as might be granted by a county court in England and Wales or, in Scotland, for granting to any person such recovery or inspection of documents as might be granted by the sheriff;
  (f) for prescribing the procedure to be followed on any appeal, reference or complaint or other proceedings before an industrial tribunal, including provisions as to the persons entitled to appear and to be heard on behalf of parties to such proceedings, and provisions for enabling an industrial tribunal to review its decisions, and revoke or vary its orders and awards, in such circumstances as may be determined in accordance with the regulations;
  (g) for the appointment of one or more assessors for the purposes of any proceedings before an industrial tribunal, where the proceedings are brought under an enactment which provides for one or more assessors to be appointed;
  (h) for the award of costs or expenses, including any allowances payable under paragraph 10 other than allowances payable to members of industrial tribunals or assessors;
  (i) for taxing or otherwise settling any such costs or expenses (and, in particular, in England and Wales, for enabling such costs to be taxed in the county court); and
  (j) for the registration and proof of decisions, orders and awards of industrial tribunals.

(3) In relation to proceedings on complaints under section 67 or any other enactment in relation to which there is provision for conciliation, the regulations shall include provision—
  (a) for requiring a copy of any such complaint, and a copy of any notice relating to it which is lodged by or on behalf of the employer against whom the complaint is made, to be sent to a conciliation officer;
  (b) for securing that the complainant and the employer against whom the complaint is made are notified that the services of a conciliation officer are available to them; and

(c) for postponing the hearing of any such complaint for such period as may be determined in accordance with the regulations for the purpose of giving an opportunity for the complaint to be settled by way of conciliation and withdrawn.

(4) In relation to proceedings under section 67—

(a) where the employee has expressed a wish to be reinstated or re-engaged which has been communicated to the employer at least seven days before the hearing of the complaint; or

(b) where the proceedings arise out of the employer's failure to permit the employee to return to work after an absence due to pregnancy or confinement,

regulations shall include provision for requiring the employer to pay the costs or expenses of any postponement or adjournment of the hearing caused by his failure, without a special reason, to adduce reasonable evidence as to the availability of the job from which the complainant was dismissed, or, as the case may be, which she held before her absence, or of comparable or suitable employment.

(5) Without prejudice to paragraph 2, the regulations may enable an industrial tribunal to sit in private for the purpose of hearing evidence which in the opinion of the tribunal relates to matters of such a nature that it would be against the interests of national security to allow the evidence to be given in public or of hearing evidence from any person which in the opinion of the tribunal is likely to consist of—

(a) information which he could not disclose without contravening a prohibition imposed by or under any enactment; or

(b) any information which has been communicated to him in confidence, or which he has otherwise obtained in consequence of the confidence reposed in him by another person; or

(c) information the disclosure of which would, for reasons other than its effect on negotiations with respect to any of the matters mentioned in section 29(1) of the Trade Union and Labour Relations Act 1974 (matters to which trade disputes relate) cause substantial injury to any undertaking of his or in which he works.

(6) The regulations may include provision authorising or requiring an industrial tribunal, in circumstances specified in the regulations, to send notice or a copy of any document so specified relating to any proceedings before the tribunal, or of any decision, order or award of the tribunal, to any government department or other person or body so specified.

(7) Any person who without reasonable excuse fails to comply with any requirement imposed by the regulations by virtue of subparagraph (2)(d) or any requirement with respect to the discovery, recovery or inspection of documents so imposed by virtue of subparagraph (2)(e) shall be liable on summary conviction to a fine not exceeding £100.

National security

2.—(1) If on a complaint under section 24 or 67 it is shown that the action complained of was taken for the purpose of safeguarding national security, the industrial tribunal shall dismiss the complaint.

(2) A certificate purporting to be signed by or on behalf of a Minister of the Crown, and certifying that the action specified in the certificate was taken for the purpose of safeguarding national security, shall for the purposes of sub-paragraph (1) be conclusive evidence of that fact.

Payment of certain sums into Redundancy Fund

3. Any sum recovered by the Secretary of State in pursuance of any such award as is mentioned in paragraph 1(2)(*h*) where the award was made in proceedings in pursuance of Part VI of this Act shall be paid into the Redundancy Fund.

Exclusion of Arbitration Act 1950

4. The Arbitration Act 1950 shall not apply to any proceedings before an industrial tribunal.

Presumption as to dismissal for redundancy

5. Where in accordance with the regulations an industrial tribunal determines in the same proceedings—

(*a*) a question referred to it under sections 81 to 102, and

(*b*) a complaint presented under section 67,

section 91(2) shall not have effect for the purposes of the proceedings in so far as they relate to the complaint under section 67.

Right of appearance

6. Any person may appear before an industrial tribunal in person or be represented by counsel or by a solicitor or by a representative of a trade union or an employers' association or by any other person whom he desires to represent him.

Recovery of sums awarded

7.—(1) Any sum payable in pursuance of a decision of an industrial tribunal in England and Wales which has been registered in accordance with the regulations shall, if a county court so orders, be recoverable by execution issued from the county court or otherwise as if it were payable under an order of that court.

(2) Any order for the payment of any sum made by an industrial tribunal in Scotland may be enforced in like manner as a recorded decree arbitral.

(3) In this paragraph any reference to a decision or order of an industrial tribunal—

(*a*) does not include a decision or order which, on being reviewed, has been revoked by the tribunal, and

SCH. 9   (*b*) in relation to a decision or order which, on being reviewed, has been varied by the tribunal, shall be construed as a reference to the decision or order as so varied.

Constitution of tribunals for certain cases

8. An industrial tribunal hearing an application under section 77 or 79 may consist of a President of Industrial Tribunals, the chairman of the tribunal or a member of a panel of chairmen of such tribunals for the time being nominated by a President to hear such applications.

Remuneration for presidents and full-time chairmen of industrial tribunals

9. The Secretary of State may pay such remuneration as he may with the consent of the Minister for the Civil Service determine to the President of the Industrial Tribunals (England and Wales), the President of the Industrial Tribunals (Scotland) and any person who is a member on a full-time basis of a panel of chairmen of tribunals which is appointed in accordance with regulations under subsection (1) of section 128.

Remuneration etc. for members of industrial tribunals and for assessors and other persons

10. The Secretary of State may pay to members of industrial tribunals and to any assessors appointed for the purposes of proceedings before industrial tribunals such fees and allowances as he may with the consent of the Minister for the Civil Service determine and may pay to any other persons such allowances as he may with the consent of that Minister determine for the purposes of, or in connection with, their attendance at industrial tribunals.

Pensions for full-time presidents or chairmen of industrial tribunals

11.—(1) The Secretary of State may from time to time make to the Minister for the Civil Service, as respects any holder on a full-time basis of any of the following offices established by regulations under section 128 who is remunerated, apart from any allowances, on an annual basis, namely—

(*a*) President of the Industrial Tribunals (England and Wales);

(*b*) President of the Industrial Tribunals (Scotland);

(*c*) member of a panel of chairmen so established,

a recommendation that the Minister shall pay to that holder (hereafter in this paragraph referred to as " the pensioner ") out of moneys provided by Parliament an annual sum by way of superannuation allowance calculated in accordance with sub-paragraph (3).

(2) No such allowance shall be payable unless—

(*a*) the pensioner is at the time of his retirement over the age of seventy-two or, where he retires after fifteen years service, over the age of sixty-five; or

(*b*) the Secretary of State is satisfied by means of a medical certificate that at the time of the pensioner's retirement the pensioner is, by reason of infirmity of mind or body, incapable of discharging the duties of his office and that the incapacity is likely to be permanent.

(3) The said annual sum shall be a sum not exceeding such proportion of the pensioner's last annual remuneration (apart from any allowances) as in the following Table corresponds with the number of the pensioner's completed years of relevant service.

TABLE

Years of service	Fraction of remuneration
Less than 5	six-fortieths
5	ten-fortieths
6	eleven-fortieths
7	twelve-fortieths
8	thirteen-fortieths
9	fourteen-fortieths
10	fifteen-fortieths
11	sixteen-fortieths
12	seventeen-fortieths
13	eighteen-fortieths
14	nineteen-fortieths
15 or more	twenty-fortieths

(4) In this paragraph the expression "relevant service" means service on a full-time basis as holder of any of the offices referred to in sub-paragraph (1) (including such service remunerated otherwise than on an annual basis) or service in any such other capacity under the Crown as may be prescribed by regulations made by the Minister for the Civil Service; and regulations under this sub-paragraph—

(a) may be made generally or subject to specified exceptions or in relation to specified cases or classes of case and may make different provision for different cases or classes of cases; and

(b) may provide that in calculating relevant service either the whole of a person's prescribed service of any description shall be taken into account or such part thereof only as may be determined by or under the regulations.

(5) The decision of the Minister shall be final on any question arising as to—

(a) the amount of any superannuation allowance under sub-paragraph (1); or

(b) the reckoning of any service for the purpose of calculating such an allowance.

(6) Sections 2 to 8 of the Administration of Justice (Pensions) Act 1950 (which provide for the payment of lump sums on retirement or death and of widows' and children's pensions in the case of persons eligible for pensions for service in any of the capacities listed in Schedule 1 to that Act) shall have effect as if— 1950 c. 11 (14 & 15 Geo. 6).

(a) the capacity of holder on a full-time basis of any of the offices referred to in sub-paragraph (1) were listed in the said Schedule 1; and

Sch. 9

　　　(*b*) in relation to that capacity the expression " relevant service " in the said sections 2 to 8 had the meaning assigned by sub-paragraph (4) ; and

　　　(*c*) in relation to such a holder of such an office, any reference in the said section 2 to his last annual salary were a reference to his last annual remuneration apart from any allowances.

(7) Where the rate of the superannuation allowance payable to any person under sub-paragraph (1) is or would be increased by virtue of regulations made under sub-paragraph (4) in respect of relevant service in some capacity other than as holder of one of the offices referred to in sub-paragraph (1), and a pension payable to him wholly in respect of service in that other capacity would have been paid and borne otherwise than out of moneys provided by Parliament, any pension benefits paid to or in respect of him as having been the holder of such an office shall, to such extent as the Minister for the Civil Service may determine, having regard to the relative length of service and rate of remuneration in each capacity, be paid and borne in like manner as that in which a pension payable to him wholly in respect of service in that other capacity would have been paid and borne.

(8) In this paragraph the expression " pension " includes any superannuation or other retiring allowance or gratuity, and the expression " pensionable " shall be construed accordingly, and the expression " pension benefits " includes benefits payable to or in respect of the pensioner by virtue of sub-paragraph (6).

Section 130.

SCHEDULE 10

Statutory Provisions Relating to Referees and Boards of Referees

1946 c. 59.　　1. Regulations under section 37 of the Coal Industry Nationalisation Act 1946.

1946 c. 67.　　2. Regulations under section 67 of the National Insurance Act 1946.

1946 c. 81.　　3. Regulations under section 68 of the National Health Service Act 1946, and orders under section 11(9) or section 31(5) of that Act.

1947 c. 27.　　4. Regulations under section 67 of the National Health Service (Scotland) Act 1947.

1947 c. 41.　　5. Regulations under Schedule 5 to the Fire Services Act 1947.

1947 c. 49.　　6. Regulations under section 101 of the Transport Act 1947.

1947 c. 54.　　7. Subsections (3) and (5) of section 54 of the Electricity Act 1947, and regulations under section 55 of that Act or under that section
1957 c. 48.　　as applied by section 27 of the Electricity Act 1957.

1948 c. 26.　　8. Regulations under section 140 of the Local Government Act 1948, and such regulations as applied by any local Act, whether passed before or after this Act.

9. Regulations under subsection (1) or subsection (2) of section 60 of the National Assistance Act 1948.   SCH. 10
1948 c. 29.

10. Rules under section 3 of the Superannuation (Miscellaneous Provisions) Act 1948.   1948 c. 33.

11. Subsections (3) and (5) of section 58 of the Gas Act 1948, and regulations under section 60 of that Act.   1948 c. 67.

12. Subsection (4) of section 6 of the Commonwealth Telegraphs Act 1949 and regulations under that section.   1949 c. 39.

13. Regulations under section 25 of the Prevention of Damage by Pests Act 1949.   1949 c. 55.

14. Regulations under section 42 of the Justices of the Peace Act 1949.   1949 c. 101.

15. Regulations under section 27 or section 28 of the Transport Act 1953.   1953 c. 13.

16. Regulations under section 24 of the Iron and Steel Act 1953.   1953 c. 15.

17. Regulations under section 12 of the Electricity Reorganisation (Scotland) Act 1954.   1954 c. 60.

18. Orders under section 23 of the Local Government Act 1958 and regulations under section 60 of that Act.   1958 c. 55.

19. Regulations under section 1 of the Water Officers Compensation Act 1960.   1960 c. 15.

20. Regulations under section 18(6) of the Land Drainage Act 1961.   1961 c. 48.

21. Subsection (6) of section 74 of the Transport Act 1962 and orders under that section, regulations under section 81 of that Act, and paragraph 17(3) of Schedule 7 to that Act.   1962 c. 46.

22. Orders under section 84 of the London Government Act 1963 and regulations under section 85 of that Act.   1963 c. 33.

23. Regulations under section 106 of the Water Resources Act 1963.   1963 c. 38.

SCHEDULE 11

Section 135.

EMPLOYMENT APPEAL TRIBUNAL

PART I

PROVISIONS AS TO MEMBERSHIP, SITTINGS, PROCEEDINGS AND POWERS

Tenure of office of appointed members of Appeal Tribunal

1. Subject to paragraphs 2 and 3, a member of the Appeal Tribunal appointed by Her Majesty under section 135(2)(*c*) (in this Schedule referred to as an " appointed member ") shall hold and vacate office as such a member in accordance with the terms of his appointment.

SCH. 11

2. An appointed member may at any time resign his membership by notice in writing addressed to the Lord Chancellor and the Secretary of State.

3.—(1) If the Lord Chancellor, after consultation with the Secretary of State, is satisfied that an appointed member—

(a) has been absent from sittings of the Appeal Tribunal for a period longer than six consecutive months without the permission of the President of the Tribunal; or

(b) has become bankrupt or made an arrangement with his creditors; or

(c) is incapacitated by physical or mental illness; or

(d) is otherwise unable or unfit to discharge the functions of a member;

the Lord Chancellor may declare his office as a member to be vacant and shall notify the declaration in such manner as the Lord Chancellor thinks fit; and thereupon the office shall become vacant.

(2) In the application of this paragraph to Scotland for the references in sub-paragraph (1)(b) to a member's having become bankrupt and to a member's having made an arrangement with his creditors there shall be substituted respectively references to a member's estate having been sequestrated and to a member's having made a trust deed for behoof of his creditors or a composition contract.

Temporary membership of Appeal Tribunal

4. At any time when the office of President of the Appeal Tribunal is vacant, or the person holding that office is temporarily absent or otherwise unable to act as President of the Tribunal, the Lord Chancellor may nominate another judge nominated under section 135(2)(a) to act temporarily in his place.

5. At any time when a judge of the Appeal Tribunal nominated by the Lord Chancellor is temporarily absent or otherwise unable to act as a judge of that Tribunal, the Lord Chancellor may nominate another person who is qualified to be nominated under section 135(2)(a) to act temporarily in his place.

6. At any time when a judge of the Appeal Tribunal nominated by the Lord President of the Court of Session is temporarily absent or otherwise unable to act as a judge of the Appeal Tribunal, the Lord President may nominate another judge of the Court of Session to act temporarily in his place.

7. At any time when an appointed member is temporarily absent or otherwise unable to act as a member of the Appeal Tribunal, the Lord Chancellor and the Secretary of State may jointly appoint a person appearing to them to have the qualifications for appointment as such a member to act temporarily in his place.

8.—(1) At any time when it appears to the Lord Chancellor that it is expedient to do so in order to facilitate in England and Wales the disposal of business in the Appeal Tribunal, he may appoint a qualified person to be a temporary additional judge of the Tribunal during such period or on such occasions as the Lord Chancellor thinks fit.

(2) In this paragraph " qualified person " means a person qualified for appointment as a puisne judge of the High Court under section 9 of the Supreme Court of Judicature (Consolidation) Act 1925 or any person who has held office as a judge of the Court of Appeal or of the High Court.

9. A person appointed to act temporarily in place of the President or any other member of the Appeal Tribunal shall, when so acting, have all the functions of the person in whose place he acts.

10. A person appointed to be a temporary additional judge of the Appeal Tribunal shall have all the functions of a judge nominated under section 135(2)(a).

11. No judge shall be nominated under paragraph 5 or 6 except with his consent.

Organisation and sittings of Appeal Tribunal

12. The Appeal Tribunal shall be a superior court of record and shall have an official seal which shall be judicially noticed.

13. The Appeal Tribunal shall have a central office in London.

14. The Appeal Tribunal may sit at any time and in any place in Great Britain.

15. The Appeal Tribunal may sit, in accordance with directions given by the President of the Tribunal, either as a single tribunal or in two or more divisions concurrently.

16. With the consent of the parties to any proceedings before the Appeal Tribunal, the proceedings may be heard by a judge and one appointed member, but, in default of such consent, any proceedings before the Tribunal shall be heard by a judge and either two or four appointed members, so that in either case there are equal numbers of persons whose experience is as representatives of employers and whose experience is as representatives of workers.

Rules

17.—(1) The Lord Chancellor, after consultation with the Lord President of the Court of Session, shall make rules with respect to proceedings before the Appeal Tribunal.

(2) Subject to those rules, the Tribunal shall have power to regulate its own procedure.

18. Without prejudice to the generality of paragraph 17 the rules may include provision—
- (a) with respect to the manner in which an appeal may be brought and the time within which it may be brought;

Sch. 11

(b) for requiring persons to attend to give evidence and produce documents, and for authorising the administration of oaths to witnesses;

(c) enabling the Appeal Tribunal to sit in private for the purpose of hearing evidence to hear which an industrial tribunal may sit in private by virtue of paragraph 1 of Schedule 9.

19.—(1) Without prejudice to the generality of paragraph 17 the rules may empower the Appeal Tribunal to order a party to any proceedings before the Tribunal to pay to any other party to the proceedings the whole or part of the costs or expenses incurred by that other party in connection with the proceedings, where in the opinion of the Tribunal—

(a) the proceedings were unnecessary, improper or vexatious, or

(b) there has been unreasonable delay or other unreasonable conduct in bringing or conducting the proceedings.

(2) Except as provided by sub-paragraph (1), the rules shall not enable the Appeal Tribunal to order the payment of costs or expenses by any party to proceedings before the Tribunal.

20. Any person may appear before the Appeal Tribunal in person or be represented by counsel or by a solicitor or by a representative of a trade union or an employers' association or by any other person whom he desires to represent him.

Powers of Tribunal

21.—(1) For the purpose of disposing of an appeal the Appeal Tribunal may exercise any powers of the body or officer from whom the appeal was brought or may remit the case to that body or officer.

(2) Any decision or award of the Appeal Tribunal on an appeal shall have the same effect and may be enforced in the same manner as a decision or award of a body or officer from whom the appeal was brought.

22.—(1) The Appeal Tribunal shall, in relation to the attendance and examination of witnesses, the production and inspection of documents and all other matters incidental to its jurisdiction, have the like powers, rights, privileges and authority—

(a) in England and Wales, as the High Court,

(b) in Scotland, as the Court of Session.

(2) No person shall be punished for contempt of the Tribunal except by, or with the consent of, a judge.

1948 c. 58.
1967 c. 80.

23.—(1) In relation to any fine imposed by the Appeal Tribunal for contempt of the Tribunal, section 14 of the Criminal Justice Act 1948 and section 47 of the Criminal Justice Act 1967 (which relate to fines imposed and recognizances forfeited at certain courts) shall have effect as if in those provisions any reference to the Crown Court included a reference to the Tribunal.

(2) A magistrates' court shall not remit the whole or any part of a fine imposed by the Appeal Tribunal except with the consent of a judge who is a member of the Tribunal.

(3) This paragraph does not extend to Scotland.

Staff

24. The Secretary of State may appoint such officers and servants of the Appeal Tribunal as he may determine, subject to the approval of the Minister for the Civil Service as to numbers and as to terms and conditions of service.

Part II

Supplementary

Remuneration and allowances

25. The Secretary of State shall pay the appointed members of the Appeal Tribunal, the persons appointed to act temporarily as appointed members, and the officers and servants of the Tribunal such remuneration and such travelling and other allowances as he may with the approval of the Minister for the Civil Service determine

26. A person appointed to be a temporary additional judge of the Appeal Tribunal shall be paid such remuneration and allowances as the Lord Chancellor may, with the approval of the Minister for the Civil Service, determine.

Pensions, etc.

27. If the Secretary of State determines, with the approval of the Minister for the Civil Service, that this paragraph shall apply in the case of an appointed member, the Secretary of State shall pay such pension, allowance or gratuity to or in respect of that member on his retirement or death or make that member such payments towards the provision of such a pension, allowance or gratuity as the Secretary of State may with the like approval determine.

28. Where a person ceases to be an appointed member otherwise than on his retirement or death and it appears to the Secretary of State that there are special circumstances which make it right for him to receive compensation, the Secretary of State may make him a payment of such amount as the Secretary of State may, with the approval of the Minister for the Civil Service, determine.

SCHEDULE 12

Death of Employee or Employer

Part I

General

Introductory

1. In this Schedule " the relevant provisions " means Part I (so far as it relates to itemised pay statements), section 53 and Parts II, III, V, VI and VII of this Act and this Schedule.

SCH. 12

Institution or continuance of tribunal proceedings

2. Where an employee or employer has died, tribunal proceedings arising under any of the relevant provisions may be instituted or continued by a personal representative of the deceased employee or, as the case may be, defended by a personal representative of the deceased employer.

3.—(1) If there is no personal representative of a deceased employee, tribunal proceedings arising under any of the relevant provisions (or proceedings to enforce a tribunal award made in any such proceedings) may be instituted or continued on behalf of the estate of the deceased employee by such other person as the industrial tribunal may appoint being either—

(*a*) a person authorised by the employee to act in connection with the proceedings before the employee's death ; or

(*b*) the widower, widow, child, father, mother, brother or sister of the deceased employee,

and references in this Schedule to a personal representative shall be construed as including such a person.

(2) In such a case any award made by the industrial tribunal shall be in such terms and shall be enforceable in such manner as may be provided by regulations made by the Secretary of State.

4.—(1) Subject to any specific provision of this Schedule to the contrary, in relation to an employee or employer who has died—

(*a*) any reference in the relevant provisions to the doing of anything by or in relation to an employee or employer shall be construed as including a reference to the doing of that thing by or in relation to any personal representative of the deceased employee or employer ; and

(*b*) any reference in the said provisions to a thing required or authorised to be done by or in relation to an employee or employer shall be construed as including a reference to any thing which, in accordance with any such provision as modified by this Schedule (including sub-paragraph (*a*)), is required or authorised to be done by or in relation to any personal representative of the deceased employee or employer.

(2) Nothing in this paragraph shall prevent references in the relevant provisions to a successor of an employer from including a personal representative of a deceased employer.

Rights and liabilities accruing after death

5. Any right arising under any of the relevant provisions as modified by this Schedule shall, if it had not accrued before the death of the employee in question, nevertheless devolve as if it had so accrued.

6. Where by virtue of any of the relevant provisions as modified by this Schedule a personal representative of a deceased employer

is liable to pay any amount and that liability had not accrued before the death of the employer, it shall be treated for all purposes as if it were a liability of the deceased employer which had accrued immediately before the death.

PART II

UNFAIR DISMISSAL

Introductory

7. In this Part of this Schedule "the unfair dismissal provisions" means Part V of this Act and this Schedule.

Death during notice period

8. Where an employer has given notice to an employee to terminate his contract of employment and before that termination the employee or the employer dies, the unfair dismissal provisions shall apply as if the contract had been duly terminated by the employer by notice expiring on the date of the death.

9. Where the employee's contract of employment has been terminated by the employer and by virtue of section 55(5) a date later than the effective date of termination as defined by subsection (4) of that section is to be treated as the effective date of termination for the purposes of certain of the unfair dismissal provisions, and before that later date the employee or the employer dies, section 55(5) shall have effect as if the notice referred to in that subsection as required to be given by the employer would have expired on the date of the death.

Remedies for unfair dismissal

10. Where an employee has died, then, unless an order for reinstatement or re-engagement has already been made, section 69 shall not apply; and accordingly if the industrial tribunal finds that the grounds of the complaint are well-founded the case shall be treated as falling within section 68(2) as a case in which no order is made under section 69.

11. If an order for reinstatement or re-engagement has been made and the employee dies before the order is complied with—

(a) if the employer has before the death refused to reinstate or re-engage the employee in accordance with the order, section 71(2) and (3) shall apply and an award shall be made under section 71(2)(b) unless the employer satisfies the tribunal that it was not practicable at the time of the refusal to comply with the order;

(b) if there has been no such refusal, section 71(1) shall apply if the employer fails to comply with any ancillary terms of the order which remain capable of fulfilment after the employee's death as it would apply to such a failure to comply fully with the terms of an order where the employee had been reinstated or re-engaged.

Part III

Redundancy Payments: Death of Employer

Introductory

12. The provisions of this Part shall have effect in relation to an employee where his employer (in this Part referred to as "the deceased employer") dies.

13. Section 94 shall not apply to any change whereby the ownership of the business, for the purposes of which the employee was employed by the deceased employer, passes to a personal representative of the deceased employer.

Dismissal

14. Where by virtue of subsection (1) of section 93 the death of the deceased employer is to be treated for the purposes of Part VI of this Act as a termination by him of the contract of employment, section 84 shall have effect subject to the following modifications:—

   (a) for subsection (1) there shall be substituted the following subsection—

   "(1) If an employee's contract of employment is renewed, or he is re-engaged under a new contract of employment, by a personal representative of the deceased employer and the renewal or re-engagement takes effect not later than eight weeks after the death of the deceased employer, then, subject to subsections (3) and (6), the employee shall not be regarded as having been dismissed by reason of the ending of his employment under the previous contract.";

   (b) in subsection (2), paragraph (a) shall be omitted and in paragraph (b) for the words "four weeks" there shall be substituted the words "eight weeks";

   (c) in subsections (5) and (6), references to the employer shall be construed as references to the personal representative of the deceased employer.

15. Where by reason of the death of the deceased employer the employee is treated for the purposes of Part VI of this Act as having been dismissed by him, section 82 shall have effect subject to the following modifications—

   (a) for subsection (3) there shall be substituted the following subsection—

   "(3) If a personal representative of the deceased employer makes an employee an offer (whether in writing or not) to renew his contract of employment, or to re-engage him under a new contract of employment, so that the renewal or re-engagement would take effect not later than eight weeks after the death of the deceased employer the provisions of subsections (5) and (6) shall have effect.";

(b) in subsection (4), paragraph (a) shall be omitted and in paragraph (b) for the words "four weeks" there shall be substituted the words "eight weeks";

(c) in subsection (5), the reference to the employer shall be construed as a reference to the personal representative of the deceased employer.

16. For the purposes of section 82 as modified by paragraph 15—

(a) an offer shall not be treated as one whereby the provisions of the contract as renewed, or of the new contract, as the case may be, would differ from the corresponding provisions of the contract as in force immediately before the death of the deceased employer by reason only that the personal representative would be substituted as the employer for the deceased employer, and

(b) no account shall be taken of that substitution in determining whether the refusal of the offer was unreasonable, or, as the case may be, whether the employee acted reasonably in terminating the renewed, or new, employment during the trial period referred to in section 84.

Lay-off and short-time

17. Where the employee has before the death of the deceased employer been laid off or kept on short-time for one or more weeks, but has not given to the deceased employer notice of intention to claim, then if after the death of the deceased employer—

(a) his contract of employment is renewed, or he is re-engaged under a new contract by a personal representative of the deceased employer, and

(b) after the renewal or re-engagement, he is laid off or kept on short-time for one or more weeks by the personal representative of the deceased employer,

the provisions of sections 88 and 89 shall apply as if the week in which the deceased employer died and the first week of the employee's employment by the personal representative were consecutive weeks, and any reference in those sections to four weeks or thirteen weeks shall be construed accordingly.

18. The provisions of paragraph 19 or (as the case may be) paragraph 20 shall have effect where the employee has given to the deceased employer notice of intention to claim, and—

(a) the deceased employer has died before the end of the next four weeks after the service of that notice, and

(b) the employee has not terminated the contract of employment by notice expiring before the death of the deceased employer.

19. If in the circumstances specified in paragraph 18 the employee's contract of employment is not renewed by a personal representative of the deceased employer before the end of the next four weeks after the service of the notice of intention to claim,

SCH. 12 and he is not re-engaged under a new contract by such a personal representative before the end of those four weeks, section 88(1) and (2) and (in relation to subsection (1) of that section) section 89(2) and (3) shall apply as if—

(a) the deceased employer had not died, and

(b) the employee had terminated the contract of employment by a week's notice (or, if under the contract he is required to give more than a week's notice to terminate the contract, he had terminated it by the minimum notice which he is so required to give) expiring at the end of those four weeks,

but sections 88(3) and (4) and 89(1) and (4) shall not apply.

20.—(1) The provisions of this paragraph shall have effect where, in the circumstances specified in paragraph 18, the employee's contract of employment is renewed by a personal representative of the deceased employer before the end of the next four weeks after the service of the notice of intention to claim, or he is re-engaged under a new contract by such a personal representative before the end of those four weeks, and—

(a) he was laid off or kept on short-time by the deceased employer for one or more of those weeks, and

(b) he is laid off or kept on short-time by the personal representative for the week, or for the next two or more weeks, following the renewal or re-engagement.

(2) Where the conditions specified in sub-paragraph (1) are fulfilled, sections 88 and 89 shall apply as if—

(a) all the weeks for which the employee was laid off or kept on short-time as mentioned in sub-paragraph (1) were consecutive weeks during which he was employed (but laid off or kept on short-time) by the same employer, and

(b) each of the periods specified in paragraphs (a) and (b) of subsection (5) of section 89 were extended by any week or weeks any part of which was after the death of the deceased employer and before the date on which the renewal or re-engagement took effect.

Continuity of period of employment

21. For the purposes of the application, in accordance with section 100(1), of any provisions of Part VI of this Act in relation to an employee who was employed as a domestic servant in a private household, any reference to a personal representative in—

(a) this Part of this Schedule, or

(b) paragraph 17 of Schedule 13,

shall be construed as including a reference to any person to whom, otherwise than in pursuance of a sale or other disposition for valuable consideration, the management of the household has passed in consequence of the death of the deceased employer.

Part IV

Redundancy Payments: Death of Employee

22.—(1) Where an employer has given notice to an employee to terminate his contract of employment, and before that notice expires the employee dies, the provisions of Part VI of this Act shall apply as if the contract had been duly terminated by the employer by notice expiring on the date of the employee's death.

(2) Where the employee's contract of employment has been terminated by the employer and by virtue of section 90(3) a date later than the relevant date as defined by subsection (1) of that section is to be treated as the relevant date for the purposes of certain provisions of Part VI of this Act, and before that later date the employee dies, section 90(3) shall have effect as if the notice referred to in that subsection as required to be given by an employer would have expired on the employee's death.

23.—(1) Where an employer has given notice to an employee to terminate his contract of employment, and has offered to renew his contract of employment, or to re-engage him under a new contract, then if—

(a) the employee dies without having either accepted or refused the offer, and

(b) the offer has not been withdrawn before his death,

section 82 shall apply as if for the words "the employee unreasonably refuses" there were substituted the words "it would have been unreasonable on the part of the employee to refuse".

(2) Where an employee's contract of employment has been renewed, or he has been re-engaged under a new contract of employment, and during the trial period the employee dies without having terminated or having given notice to terminate the contract, subsection (6) of that section shall apply as if for the words from "and during the trial period" to "terminated" there were substituted the words "and it would have been unreasonable for the employee, during the trial period referred to in section 84, to terminate or give notice to terminate the contract".

24. Where an employee's contract of employment has been renewed, or he has been re-engaged under a new contract of employment, and during the trial period he gives notice to terminate the contract but dies before the expiry of that notice, sections 82(6) and 84(6)(a) shall have effect as if the notice had expired and the contract had thereby been terminated on the date of the employee's death.

25.—(1) Where, in the circumstances specified in paragraphs (a) and (b) of subsection (1) of section 85, the employee dies before the notice given by him under paragraph (b) of that subsection is due to expire and before the employer has given him notice under subsection (3) of that section, subsection (4) of that section shall apply as if the employer had given him such notice and he had not complied with it.

Sch. 12

(2) Where, in the said circumstances, the employee dies before his notice given under section 85(1)(b) is due to expire but after the employer has given him notice under subsection (3) of section 85, subsections (3) and (4) of that section shall apply as if the circumstances were that the employee had not died, but did not comply with the last-mentioned notice.

26.—(1) Where an employee has given notice of intention to claim and dies before he has given notice to terminate his contract of employment and before the period allowed for the purposes of subsection (2)(a) of section 88 has expired, the said subsection (2)(a) shall not apply.

(2) Where an employee, who has given notice of intention to claim, dies within seven days after the service of that notice, and before the employer has given a counter-notice, the provisions of sections 88 and 89 shall apply as if the employer had given a counter-notice within those seven days.

(3) In this paragraph "counter-notice" has the same meaning as in section 89(1).

27.—(1) In relation to the making of a claim by a personal representative of a deceased employee who dies before the end of the period of six months beginning with the relevant date, subsection (1) of section 101 shall apply with the substitution for the words "six months", of the words "one year".

(2) In relation to the making of a claim by a personal representative of a deceased employee who dies after the end of the period of six months beginning with the relevant date and before the end of the following period of six months, subsection (2) of section 101 shall apply with the substitution for the words "six months", of the words "one year".

28. In relation to any case where, under any provision contained in Part VI of this Act as modified by this Schedule, an industrial tribunal has power to determine that an employer shall be liable to pay to a personal representative of a deceased employee either—

(a) the whole of a redundancy payment to which he would have been entitled apart from another provision therein mentioned, or

(b) such part of such a redundancy payment as the tribunal thinks fit,

any reference in paragraph 5 to a right shall be construed as including a reference to any right to receive the whole or part of a redundancy payment if the tribunal determines that the employer shall be liable to pay it.

SCHEDULE 13

Computation of Period of Employment

Preliminary

1.—(1) Where an employee's period of employment is, for the purposes of any enactment (including any enactment contained in this Act), to be computed in accordance with this Schedule, it shall be computed in weeks, and in any such enactment which refers to a period of employment expressed in years, a year means fifty-two weeks (whether continuous or discontinuous) which count in computing a period of employment.

(2) For the purpose of computing an employee's period of employment (but not for any other purpose), the provisions of this Schedule apply, subject to paragraph 14, to a period of employment notwithstanding that during that period the employee was engaged in work wholly or mainly outside Great Britain or was excluded by or under this Act from any right conferred by this Act.

2. Except so far as otherwise provided by the following provisions of this Schedule, any week which does not count under paragraphs 3 to 13 breaks the continuity of the period of employment.

Normal working weeks

3. Any week in which the employee is employed for sixteen hours or more shall count in computing a period of employment.

Employment governed by contract

4. Any week during the whole or part of which the employee's relations with the employer are governed by a contract of employment which normally involves employment for sixteen hours or more weekly shall count in computing a period of employment.

5.—(1) If the employee's relations with his employer cease to be governed by a contract which normally involves work for sixteen hours or more weekly and become governed by a contract which normally involves employment for eight hours or more, but less than sixteen hours, weekly and, but for that change, the later weeks would count in computing a period of employment, or would not break the continuity of a period of employment, then those later weeks shall count in computing a period of employment or, as the case may be, shall not break the continuity of a period of employment, notwithstanding that change.

(2) Not more than twenty-six weeks shall count under this paragraph between any two periods falling under paragraph 4, and in computing the said figure of twenty-six weeks no account shall be taken of any week which counts in computing a period of

Sch. 13 employment, or does not break the continuity of a period of employment, otherwise than by virtue of this paragraph.

6.—(1) An employee whose relations with his employer are governed, or have been from time to time governed, by a contract of employment which normally involves employment for eight hours or more, but less than sixteen hours, weekly shall nevertheless, if he satisfies the condition referred to in sub-paragraph (2), be treated for the purposes of this Schedule (apart from this paragraph) as if his contract normally involved employment for sixteen hours or more weekly, and had at all times at which there was a contract during the period of employment of five years or more referred to in sub-paragraph (2) normally involved employment for sixteen hours or more weekly.

(2) Sub-paragraph (1) shall apply if the employee, on the date by reference to which the length of any period of employment falls to be ascertained in accordance with the provisions of this Schedule, has been continuously employed within the meaning of sub-paragraph (3) for a period of five years or more.

(3) In computing for the purposes of sub-paragraph (2) an employee's period of employment, the provisions of this Schedule (apart from this paragraph) shall apply but as if, in paragraphs 3 and 4, for the words " sixteen hours " wherever they occur, there were substituted the words " eight hours ".

7.—(1) If an employee has, at any time during the relevant period of employment, been continuously employed for a period which qualifies him for any right which requires a qualifying period of continuous employment computed in accordance with this Schedule, then he shall be regarded for the purposes of qualifying for that right as continuing to satisfy that requirement until the condition referred to in sub-paragraph (3) occurs.

(2) In this paragraph the relevant period of employment means the period of employment ending on the date by reference to which the length of any period of employment falls to be ascertained which would be continuous (in accordance with the provisions of this Schedule) if at all relevant times the employee's relations with the employer had been governed by a contract of employment which normally involved employment for sixteen hours or more weekly.

(3) The condition which defeats the operation of sub-paragraph (1) is that in a week subsequent to the time at which the employee qualified as referred to in that sub-paragraph—

(a) his relations with his employer are governed by a contract of employment which normally involves employment for less than eight hours weekly ; and

(b) he is employed in that week for less than sixteen hours.

(4) If, in a case in which an employee is entitled to any right by virtue of sub-paragraph (1), it is necessary for the purpose of

ascertaining the amount of his entitlement to determine for what period he has been continuously employed, he shall be regarded for that purpose as having been continuously employed throughout the relevant period.

Orders under section 7

8. The foregoing provisions of this Schedule shall have effect subject to any order made under section 7 and an order under that section shall affect the operation of this Schedule as respects periods before the order takes effect as well as respects later periods.

Periods in which there is no contract of employment

9.—(1) If in any week the employee is, for the whole or part of the week—

(*a*) incapable of work in consequence of sickness or injury, or

(*b*) absent from work on account of a temporary cessation of work, or

(*c*) absent from work in circumstances such that, by arrangement or custom, he is regarded as continuing in the employment of his employer for all or any purposes, or

(*d*) absent from work wholly or partly because of pregnancy or confinement,

that week shall, notwithstanding that it does not fall under paragraph 3, 4 or 5, count as a period of employment.

(2) Not more than twenty-six weeks shall count under paragraph (*a*) or, subject to paragraph 10, under paragraph (*d*) of sub-paragraph (1) between any periods falling under paragraph 3, 4 or 5.

Maternity

10. If an employee returns to work in accordance with section 47 after a period of absence from work wholly or partly occasioned by pregnancy or confinement, every week during that period shall count in computing a period of employment, notwithstanding that it does not fall under paragraph 3, 4 or 5.

Intervals in employment where section 55(5) or 84(1) or 90(3) applies

11.—(1) In ascertaining, for the purposes of section 64(1)(*a*) and of section 73(3), the period for which an employee has been continuously employed, where by virtue of section 55(5) a date is treated as the effective date of termination which is later than the effective date of termination as defined by section 55(4), the period of the interval between those two dates shall count as a period of employment notwithstanding that it does not otherwise count under this Schedule.

(2) Where by virtue of section 84(1) an employee is treated as not having been dismissed by reason of a renewal or re-engagement taking effect after an interval, then, in determining for the purposes of section 81(1) or Schedule 4 whether he has been continuously employed for the requisite period, the period of that interval shall

Sch. 13 count as a period of employment except in so far as it is to be disregarded under paragraphs 12 to 14 (notwithstanding that it does not otherwise count under this Schedule).

(3) Where by virtue of section 90(3) a date is to be treated as the relevant date for the purposes of section 81(4) which is later than the relevant date as defined by section 90(1), then in determining for the purposes of section 81(1) or Schedule 4 whether the employee has been continuously employed for the requisite period, the period of the interval between those two dates shall count as a period of employment except in so far as it is to be disregarded under paragraphs 12 to 14 (notwithstanding that it does not otherwise count under this Schedule).

Payment of previous redundancy payment or equivalent payment

12.—(1) Where the conditions mentioned in sub-paragraph (2)(*a*) or (2)(*b*) are fulfilled in relation to a person, then in determining, for the purposes of section 81(1) or Schedule 4, whether at any subsequent time he has been continuously employed for the requisite period, or for what period he has been continuously employed, the continuity of the period of employment shall be treated as having been broken—

    (*a*) in so far as the employment was under a contract of employment, at the date which was the relevant date in relation to the payment mentioned in sub-paragraph (2)(*a*) or, as the case may be, sub-paragraph (2)(*b*); or

    (*b*) in so far as the employment was otherwise than under a contract of employment, at the date which would have been the relevant date in relation to that payment had the employment been under a contract of employment,

and accordingly no account shall be taken of any time before that date.

(2) Sub-paragraph (1) has effect—

    (*a*) where—

        (i) a redundancy payment is paid to an employee, whether in respect of dismissal or in respect of lay-off or short-time; and

        (ii) the contract of employment under which he was employed (in this section referred to as "the previous contract") is renewed, whether by the same or another employer, or he is re-engaged under a new contract of employment, whether by the same or another employer; and

        (iii) the circumstances of the renewal or re-engagement are such that, in determining for the purposes of section 81(1) or Schedule 4 whether at any subsequent time he has been continuously employed for the requisite period, or for what period he has been continuously employed, the continuity of his period of employment would, apart from this paragraph, be treated as not having been broken by the termination of the previous contract and the renewal or re-engagement; or

(b) where—

    (i) a payment has been made, whether in respect of the termination of any person's employment or in respect of lay-off or short-time, either in accordance with any provisions of a scheme under section 1 of the Superannuation Act 1972 or in accordance with any such arrangements as are mentioned in section 111(3); and

    (ii) he commences new, or renewed, employment; and

    (iii) the circumstances of the commencement of the new, or renewed, employment are such that, in determining for the purposes of section 81(1) or Schedule 4 whether at any subsequent time he has been continuously employed for the requisite period, or for what period he has been continuously employed, the continuity of his period of employment would, apart from this paragraph, be treated as not having been broken by the termination of the previous employment and the commencement of the new, or renewed, employment.

1972 c. 11.

(3) For the purposes of this paragraph, a redundancy payment shall be treated as having been paid if—

(a) the whole of the payment has been paid to the employee by the employer, or, in a case where a tribunal has determined that the employer is liable to pay part (but not the whole) of the redundancy payment, that part of the redundancy payment has been paid in full to the employee by the employer, or

(b) the Secretary of State has paid a sum to the employee in respect of the redundancy payment under section 106.

Certain weeks of employment to be disregarded for purposes of Schedule 4

13. In ascertaining for the purposes of Schedule 4 the period for which an employee has been continuously employed, any week which began before he attained the age of eighteen shall not count under this Schedule.

Redundancy payments: employment wholly or partly abroad

14.—(1) In computing in relation to an employee the period specified in section 81(4) or the period specified in paragraph 1 of Schedule 4, a week of employment shall not count if—

(a) the employee was employed outside Great Britain during the whole or part of that week, and

(b) he was not during that week, or during the corresponding contribution week,—

    (i) where the week is a week of employment after 1st June 1976, an employed earner for the purposes of the Social Security Act 1975 in respect of whom a secondary Class 1 contribution was payable under that Act; or

    (ii) where the week is a week of employment after 6th

1975 c. 14.

April 1975 and before 1st June 1976, an employed earner for the purposes of the Social Security Act 1975 ; or

(iii) where the week is a week of employment before 6th April 1975, an employee in respect of whom an employer's contribution was payable in respect of the corresponding contribution week ;

whether or not the contribution mentioned in paragraph (i) or (iii) of this sub-paragraph was in fact paid.

(2) For the purposes of the application of sub-paragraph (1) to a week of employment where the corresponding contribution week began before 5th July 1948, an employer's contribution shall be treated as payable as mentioned in sub-paragraph (1) if such a contribution would have been so payable if the statutory provisions relating to national insurance which were in force on 5th July 1948 had been in force in that contribution week.

(3) Where by virtue of sub-paragraph (1) a week of employment does not count in computing such a period as is mentioned in that sub-paragraph, the continuity of that period shall not be broken by reason only that that week of employment does not count in computing that period.

(4) Any question arising under this paragraph whether—

(a) an employer's contribution was or would have been payable, as mentioned in sub-paragraph (1) or (2), or

(b) a person was an employed earner for the purposes of the Social Security Act 1975 and if so whether a secondary Class 1 contribution was payable in respect of him under that Act,

shall be determined by the Secretary of State ; and any legislation (including regulations) as to the determination of questions which under that Act the Secretary of State is empowered to determine (including provisions as to the reference of questions for decision, or as to appeals, to the High Court or the Court of Session) shall apply to the determination of any question by the Secretary of State under this paragraph.

(5) In this paragraph "employer's contribution" has the same meaning as in the National Insurance Act 1965, and "corresponding contribution week", in relation to a week of employment, means a contribution week (within the meaning of the said Act of 1965) of which so much as falls within the period beginning with midnight between Sunday and Monday and ending with Saturday also falls within that week of employment.

(6) The provisions of this paragraph shall not apply in relation to a person who is employed as a master or seaman in a British ship and is ordinarily resident in Great Britain.

Industrial disputes

15.—(1) A week shall not count under paragraph 3, 4, 5, 9 or 10 if in that week, or any part of that week, the employee takes part in a strike.

(2) The continuity of an employee's period of employment is not broken by a week which does not count under this Schedule, and which begins after 5th July 1964 if in that week, or any part of that week, the employee takes part in a strike.

(3) Sub-paragraph (2) applies whether or not the week would, apart from sub-paragraph (1), have counted under this Schedule.

(4) The continuity of the period of employment is not broken by a week which begins after 5th July 1964 and which does not count under this Schedule, if in that week, or any part of that week, the employee is absent from work because of a lock-out by the employer.

Reinstatement after service with the armed forces, etc.

16.—(1) If a person who is entitled to apply to his former employer under Part II of the National Service Act 1948 (reinstatement in civil employment) enters the employment of that employer not later than the end of the six month period mentioned in section 35(2)(*b*) of that Act, his previous period of employment with that employer (or if there was more than one such period, the last of those periods) and the period of employment beginning in the said period of six months shall be treated as continuous.

(2) The reference in this paragraph to Part II of the National Service Act 1948 includes a reference to that Part of that Act as amended, applied or extended by any other Act passed before or after this Act.

Change of employer

17.—(1) Subject to this paragraph and paragraph 18, the foregoing provisions of this Schedule relate only to employment by the one employer.

(2) If a trade or business or an undertaking (whether or not it be an undertaking established by or under an Act of Parliament) is transferred from one person to another, the period of employment of an employee in the trade or business or undertaking at the time of the transfer shall count as a period of employment with the transferee, and the transfer shall not break the continuity of the period of employment.

(3) If by or under an Act of Parliament, whether public or local and whether passed before or after this Act, a contract of employment between any body corporate and an employee is modified and some other body corporate is substituted as the employer, the employee's period of employment at the time when the modification takes effect shall count as a period of employment with the second-mentioned body corporate, and the change of employer shall not break the continuity of the period of employment.

(4) If on the death of an employer the employee is taken into the employment of the personal representatives or trustees of the deceased, the employee's period of employment at the time of the death shall count as a period of employment with the employer's

SCH. 13 personal representatives or trustees, and the death shall not break the continuity of the period of employment.

(5) If there is a change in the partners, personal representatives or trustees who employ any person, the employee's period of employment at the time of the change shall count as a period of employment with the partners, personal representatives or trustees after the change, and the change shall not break the continuity of the period of employment.

18. If an employee of an employer is taken into the employment of another employer who, at the time when the employee enters his employment is an associated employer of the first-mentioned employer, the employee's period of employment at that time shall count as a period of employment with the second-mentioned employer and the change of employer shall not break the continuity of the period of employment.

Crown employment

19.—(1) Subject to the following provisions of this paragraph, the provisions of this Schedule shall have effect (for the purpose of computing an employee's period of employment, but not for any other purpose) in relation to Crown employment and to persons in Crown employment as they have effect in relation to other employment and to other employees, and accordingly, except where the context otherwise requires, references to an employer shall be construed as including a reference to the Crown.

(2) In this paragraph, subject to sub-paragraph (3), " Crown employment" means employment under or for the purposes of a government department or any officer or body exercising on behalf of the Crown functions conferred by any enactment.

(3) This paragraph does not apply to service as a member of the naval, military or air forces of the Crown, or of any women's service administered by the Defence Council, but does apply to employment by any association established for the purposes of the Auxiliary Forces Act 1953.

1953 c. 50.

(4) In so far as a person in Crown employment is employed otherwise than under a contract of employment, references in this Schedule to an employee's relations with his employer being governed by a contract of employment which normally involves employment for a certain number of hours weekly shall be modified accordingly.

(5) The reference in paragraph 17(2) to an undertaking shall be construed as including a reference to any function of (as the case may require) a Minister of the Crown, a government department, or any other officer or body performing functions on behalf of the Crown.

Reinstatement or re-engagement of dismissed employee

20.—(1) Regulations made by the Secretary of State may make provision—

    (a) for preserving the continuity of a person's period of employment for the purposes of this Schedule or for the purposes of this Schedule as applied by or under any other enactment specified in the regulations, or

(b) for modifying or excluding the operation of paragraph 12 subject to the recovery of any such payment as is mentioned in sub-paragraph (2) of that paragraph,

in cases where, in consequence of action to which sub-paragraph (2) applies, a dismissed employee is reinstated or re-engaged by his employer or by a successor or associated employer of that employer.

(2) This sub-paragraph applies to any action taken in relation to the dismissal of an employee which consists—

(a) of the presentation by him of a complaint under section 67, or

(b) of his making a claim in accordance with a dismissal procedures agreement designated by an order under section 65, or

(c) of any action taken by a conciliation officer under section 134(3).

Employment before the commencement of Act

21. Save as otherwise expressly provided, the provisions of this Schedule apply to periods before it comes into force as they apply to later periods.

22. If, in any week beginning before 6th July 1964, the employee was, for the whole or any part of the week, absent from work—

(a) because he was taking part in a strike, or

(b) because of a lock-out by the employer,

the week shall count as a period of employment.

23. Without prejudice to the foregoing provisions of this Schedule, any week which counted as a period of employment in the computation of a period of employment in accordance with the Contracts of Employment Act 1972 whether for the purposes of that Act, the Redundancy Payments Act 1965, the Trade Union and Labour Relations Act 1974 or the Employment Protection Act 1975, shall count as a period of employment for the purposes of this Act, and any week which did not break the continuity of a person's employment for the purposes of those Acts shall not break the continuity of a period of employment for the purposes of this Act.

1972 c. 53.
1965 c. 62.
1974 c. 52.
1975 c. 71.

Interpretation

24.—(1) In this Schedule, unless the context otherwise requires,—

"lock-out" means the closing of a place of employment, or the suspension of work, or the refusal by an employer to continue to employ any number of persons employed by him in consequence of a dispute, done with a view to compelling those persons, or to aid another employer in compelling persons employed by him, to accept terms or conditions of or affecting employment;

"strike" means the cessation of work by a body of persons employed acting in combination, or a concerted refusal

Sch. 13

or a refusal under a common understanding of any number of persons employed to continue to work for an employer in consequence of a dispute, done as a means of compelling their employer or any person or body of persons employed, or to aid other employees in compelling their employer or any person or body of persons employed, to accept or not to accept terms or conditions of or affecting employment;

" week " means a week ending with Saturday.

(2) For the purposes of this Schedule the hours of employment of an employee who is required by the terms of his employment to live on the premises where he works shall be the hours during which he is on duty or during which his services may be required.

Section 152.

SCHEDULE 14

CALCULATION OF NORMAL WORKING HOURS AND A WEEK'S PAY

PART I

NORMAL WORKING HOURS

1. For the purposes of this Schedule the cases where there are normal working hours include cases where the employee is entitled to overtime pay when employed for more than a fixed number of hours in a week or other period, and, subject to paragraph 2, in those cases that fixed number of hours shall be the normal working hours.

2. If in such a case—
    (a) the contract of employment fixes the number, or the minimum number, of hours of employment in the said week or other period (whether or not it also provides for the reduction of that number or minimum in certain circumstances), and
    (b) that number or minimum number of hours exceeds the number of hours without overtime,

that number or minimum number of hours (and not the number of hours without overtime) shall be the normal working hours.

PART II

A WEEK'S PAY

Employments for which there are normal working hours

3.—(1) This paragraph and paragraph 4 shall apply if there are normal working hours for an employee when employed under the contract of employment in force on the calculation date.

(2) Subject to paragraph 4, if an employee's remuneration for employment in normal working hours, whether by the hour or week or other period, does not vary with the amount of work done in the period, the amount of a week's pay shall be the amount which is payable by the employer under the contract of employment in

force on the calculation date if the employee works throughout his normal working hours in a week.

(3) Subject to paragraph 4, if sub-paragraph (2) does not apply, the amount of a week's pay shall be the amount of remuneration for the number of normal working hours in a week calculated at the average hourly rate of remuneration payable by the employer to the employee in respect of the period of twelve weeks—
    (a) where the calculation date is the last day of a week, ending with that week;
    (b) in any other case, ending with the last complete week before the calculation date.

(4) References in this paragraph to remuneration varying with the amount of work done include references to remuneration which may include any commission or similar payment which varies in amount.

4.—(1) This paragraph shall apply if there are normal working hours for an employee when employed under the contract of employment in force on the calculation date, and he is required under that contract to work during those hours on days of the week or at times of the day which differ from week to week or over a longer period so that the remuneration payable for, or apportionable to, any week varies according to the incidence of the said days or times.

(2) The amount of a week's pay shall be the amount of remuneration for the average weekly number of normal working hours (calculated in accordance with sub-paragraph (3)) at the average hourly rate of remuneration (calculated in accordance with sub-paragraph (4)).

(3) The average number of weekly hours shall be calculated by dividing by twelve the total number of the employee's normal working hours during the period of twelve weeks—
    (a) where the calculation date is the last day of a week, ending with that week;
    (b) in any other case, ending with the last complete week before the calculation date.

(4) The average hourly rate of remuneration shall be the average hourly rate of remuneration payable by the employer to the employee in respect of the period of twelve weeks—
    (a) where the calculation date is the last day of a week, ending with that week;
    (b) in any other case, ending with the last complete week before the calculation date.

5.—(1) For the purpose of paragraphs 3 and 4, in arriving at the average hourly rate of remuneration only the hours when the employee was working, and only the remuneration payable for, or apportionable to, those hours of work, shall be brought in; and if for any of the twelve weeks mentioned in either of those paragraphs no such remuneration was payable by the employer to the employee, account shall be taken of remuneration in earlier weeks so as to bring the number of weeks of which account is taken up to twelve.

SCH. 14   (2) Where, in arriving at the said hourly rate of remuneration, account has to be taken of remuneration payable for, or apportionable to, work done in hours other than normal working hours, and the amount of that remuneration was greater than it would have been if the work had been done in normal working hours, account shall be taken of that remuneration as if—

    (a) the work had been done in normal working hours; and

    (b) the amount of that remuneration had been reduced accordingly.

(3) For the purpose of the application of sub-paragraph (2) to a case falling within paragraph 2, sub-paragraph (2) shall be construed as if for the words " had been done in normal working hours ", in each place where those words occur, there were substituted the words " had been done in normal working hours falling within the number of hours without overtime ".

Employments for which there are no normal working hours

6.—(1) This paragraph shall apply if there are no normal working hours for an employee when employed under the contract of employment in force on the calculation date.

(2) The amount of a week's pay shall be the amount of the employee's average weekly remuneration in the period of twelve weeks—

    (a) where the calculation date is the last day of a week, ending with that week;

    (b) in any other case, ending with the last complete week before the calculation date.

(3) In arriving at the said average weekly rate of remuneration no account shall be taken of a week in which no remuneration was payable by the employer to the employee and remuneration in earlier weeks shall be brought in so as to bring the number of weeks of which account is taken up to twelve.

The calculation date

7.—(1) For the purposes of this Part, the calculation date is,—

    (a) where the calculation is for the purposes of section 14, the day in respect of which the guarantee payment is payable, or, where an employee's contract has been varied, or a new contract entered into, in connection with a period of short-time working, the last day on which the original contract was in force;

    (b) where the calculation is for the purposes of section 21, the day before that on which the suspension referred to in section 19(1) begins;

    (c) where the calculation is for the purposes of section 31, the day on which the employer's notice was given;

    (d) where the calculation is for the purposes of section 35, the last day on which the employee worked under the contract of employment in force immediately before the beginning of her absence;

    (e) where the calculation is for the purposes of Schedule 3, the day immediately preceding the first day of the period of notice required by section 49(1) or, as the case may be, section 49(2);

(f) where the calculation is for the purposes of section 53 or 71(2)(b) and the dismissal was with notice, the date on which the employer's notice was given;

(g) where the calculation is for the purposes of section 53 or 71(2)(b) but sub-paragraph (f) does not apply, the effective date of termination;

(h) where the calculation is for the purposes of section 73 and by virtue of section 55(5) a date is to be treated as the effective date of termination for the purposes of section 73(3) which is later than the effective date of termination as defined by section 55(4), the effective date of termination as defined by section 55(4);

(i) where the calculation is for the purposes of section 73 but section 55(5) does not apply in relation to the date of termination, the date on which notice would have been given had the conditions referred to in sub-paragraph (2) been fulfilled (whether those conditions were in fact fulfilled or not);

(j) where the calculation is for the purposes of section 87(2), the day immediately preceding the first of the four or, as the case may be, the six weeks referred to in section 88(1);

(k) where the calculation is for the purposes of Schedule 4 and by virtue of section 90(3) a date is to be treated as the relevant date for the purposes of certain provisions of this Act which is later than the relevant date as defined by section 90(1), the relevant date as defined by section 90(1);

(l) where the calculation is for the purposes of Schedule 4 but sub-paragraph (k) does not apply, the date on which notice would have been given had the conditions referred to in sub-paragraph (2) been fulfilled (whether those conditions were in fact fulfilled or not).

(2) The conditions referred to in sub-paragraphs (1)(i) and (l) are that the contract was terminable by notice and was terminated by the employer giving such notice as is required to terminate that contract by section 49 and that the notice expired on the effective date of termination or on the relevant date, as the case may be.

Maximum amount of week's pay for certain purposes

8.—(1) Notwithstanding the preceding provisions of this Schedule, the amount of a week's pay for the purpose of calculating—

(a) an additional award of compensation (within the meaning of section 71(2)(b), shall not exceed £100;

(b) a basic award of compensation (within the meaning of section 72) shall not exceed £100;

(c) a redundancy payment shall not exceed £100;

(2) The Secretary of State may after a review under section 148 vary the limit referred to in sub-paragraph (1)(a) or (b) or (c) by an order made in accordance with that section.

(3) Without prejudice to the generality of the power to make transitional provision in an order under section 148, such an order

SCH. 14 may provide that it shall apply in the case of a dismissal in relation to which the effective date of termination for the purposes of this sub-paragraph, as defined by section 55(5), falls after the order comes into operation, notwithstanding that the effective date of termination, as defined by section 55(4), for the purposes of other provisions of this Act falls before the order comes into operation.

(4) Without prejudice to the generality of the power to make transitional provision in an order under section 148, such an order may provide that it shall apply in the case of a dismissal in relation to which the relevant date for the purposes of this sub-paragraph falls after the order comes into operation, notwithstanding that the relevant date for the purposes of other provisions of this Act falls before the order comes into operation.

Supplemental

9. In any case in which an employee has not been employed for a sufficient period to enable a calculation to be made under any of the foregoing provisions of this Part, the amount of a week's pay shall be an amount which fairly represents a week's pay; and in determining that amount the tribunal shall apply as nearly as may be such of the foregoing provisions of this Part as it considers appropriate, and may have regard to such of the following considerations as it thinks fit, that is to say—

(a) any remuneration received by the employee in respect of the employment in question;

(b) the amount offered to the employee as remuneration in respect of the employment in question;

(c) the remuneration received by other persons engaged in relevant comparable employment with the same employer;

(d) the remuneration received by other persons engaged in relevant comparable employment with other employers;

10. In arriving at an average hourly rate or average weekly rate of remuneration under this Part account shall be taken of work for a former employer within the period for which the average is to be taken if, by virtue of Schedule 13, a period of employment with the former employer counts as part of the employee's continuous period of employment with the later employer.

11. Where under this Part account is to be taken of remuneration or other payments for a period which does not coincide with the periods for which the remuneration or other payments are calculated, then the remuneration or other payments shall be apportioned in such manner as may be just.

12. The Secretary of State may by regulations provide that in prescribed cases the amount of a week's pay shall be calculated in such manner as the regulations may prescribe.

Section 159.

SCHEDULE 15

TRANSITIONAL PROVISIONS AND SAVINGS

General

1. So far as anything done or treated as done under or for the purposes of any enactment repealed by this Act could have been done

under a corresponding provision of this Act it shall not be invalidated by the repeal but shall have effect as if done under or for the purposes of that provision().

SCH. 15

2. Where any period of time specified in an enactment repealed by this Act is current immediately before the corresponding provision of this Act comes into force, this Act shall have effect as if the corresponding provision had been in force when that period began to run.

3. Nothing in this Act shall affect the enactments repealed by this Act in their operation in relation to offences committed before the commencement of this Act.

4. Any reference in an enactment or document, whether express or implied, to—

(a) an enactment which is re-enacted in a corresponding provision of this Act;

(b) an enactment replaced or amended by a provision of the Employment Protection Act 1975 which is re-enacted in a corresponding provision of this Act;

1975 c. 71

(c) an enactment in the Industrial Relations Act 1971 which was re-enacted with or without amendment in a corresponding provision in Schedule 1 to the Trade Union and Labour Relations Act 1974 and that corresponding provision is re-enacted by a corresponding provision of this Act;

1971 c. 72.

1974 c. 52.

shall, except so far as the context otherwise requires, be construed as, or as including, a reference to the corresponding provision of this Act.

5. Paragraphs 1 to 4 have effect subject to the following provisions of this Schedule.

Guarantee payments

6. Section 15(1) shall have effect in relation to any day before 1st February 1978 as if for " £6·60 " there were substituted " £6 ".

Maternity pay

7. No employee is entitled to receive maternity pay in respect of a payment period or payment periods beginning before 6th April 1977.

Termination of employment

8. Sections 49 and 50 apply in relation to any contract made before the commencement of this Act.

Unfair dismissal

9.—(1) The repeal by this Act of the provisions relating to unfair dismissals of the Employment Protection Act 1975, of Schedule 1 to the Trade Union and Labour Relations Act 1974 and of the Trade Union and Labour Relations (Amendment) Act 1976 shall not have effect in relation to dismissals where the effective date of

1976 c. 7.

SCH. 15

1975 c. 71.

termination is earlier than 1st October 1976 and, accordingly, those provisions shall continue to apply to such dismissals as they applied thereto before this Act came into force.

(2) Without prejudice to the generality of sub-paragraph (1), the provisions of paragraphs 17(2) and (3) and 19 of Schedule 1 to the said Act of 1974 shall, notwithstanding the repeal of those provisions by the Employment Protection Act 1975, continue to apply to dismissals where the effective date of termination falls before 1st June 1976.

(3) Where the notice required to be given by an employer to terminate a contract of employment by section 49(1) would, if duly given when notice of termination was given by the employer, or (where no notice was given) when the contract of employment was terminated by the employer, expire on a date later than the effective date of termination as defined by section 55(4), that later date shall be treated as the effective date of termination for the purposes of sub-paragraphs (1) and (2).

10.—(1) Section 54 does not apply to a dismissal from employment under a contract for a fixed term of two years or more, where the contract was made before 28th February 1972 and is not a contract of apprenticeship, and the dismissal consists only of the expiry of that term without its being renewed.

(2) Sub-paragraph (1) in its application to an employee treated as unfairly dismissed by virtue of subsection (1) or (2) of section 60 shall have effect as if for the reference to 28th February 1972 there were substituted a reference to 1st June 1976.

Redundancy

1965 c. 62.

11.—(1) The repeal by this Act of any provision of the Redundancy Payments Act 1965 and of any enactment amending that Act shall not have effect in relation to dismissals and to lay-off and short-time where the relevant date falls before 1st June 1976, and, accordingly, a person's entitlement to or the computation of a redundancy payment or the reference of questions to industrial tribunals concerning such entitlement or computation in cases where the relevant date falls before 1st June 1976 shall continue to be determined as if this Act were not in force.

(2) Where the notice required to be given by an employer to terminate a contract of employment by section 49 would, if duly given when notice of termination was given by the employer, or (where no notice was given) when the contract of employment was terminated by the employer, expire on a date later than the relevant date as defined by section 90(1), that later date shall be treated as the relevant date for the purposes of sub-paragraph (1).

12. Section 81 shall not apply to an employee who immediately before the relevant date (within the meaning of section 90) is employed under a contract of employment for a fixed term of two years or more, if that contract was made before 6th December 1965 and is not a contract of apprenticeship.

13. Sections 104 and 107 shall have effect in relation to an offence committed before 17th July 1978 as if—

    (a) for each reference to the prescribed sum in subsection (9) of section 104 and subsection (4) of section 107 there were substituted a reference to £100, and

    (b) subsection (10) of section 104 and subsection (5) of section 107 were omitted.

14. Schedule 5 shall have effect as if there were added at the end the following paragraph—

" 5. The Boards of Governors of the hospitals specified in Schedule 1 to the National Health Service (Preservation of Boards of Governors) Order 1974.".

S.I 1974/281.

This paragraph shall cease to have effect on 22nd February 1979 or, if the said Order of 1974 is revoked on an earlier date, on that date.

Insolvency

15.—(1) Subject to sub-paragraph (2), the provisions of sections 122 and 123 shall apply in relation to an employer who becomes insolvent (within the meaning of section 127) after 19th April 1976, and shall in such a case apply to any debts mentioned in section 122 and to any unpaid relevant contribution (within the meaning of section 123), whether falling due before or after that date.

(2) Section 122 shall have effect in relation to any case where the employer became insolvent before 1st February 1978 as if for each reference to £100 there were substituted a reference to £80.

Calculation of a week's pay

16. Paragraph 8 of Schedule 14 shall have effect—

    (a) for the purpose of calculating an additional award of compensation in any case where the date by which the order for re-instatement or re-engagement was required to be complied with fell before 1st February 1978;

    (b) for the purpose of calculating a basic award of compensation in any case where the effective date of determination (as defined by subsection (5) of section 55 or, if the case is not within that subsection, by subsection (4) of that section) fell before 1st February 1978;

    (c) in relation to a claim for a redundancy payment, where the relevant date fell before 1st February 1978,

as if for each reference to £100 there were substituted a reference to £80.

Sch. 15

Computation of period of continuous employment

17. For the purposes of the computation of a period of continuous employment falling to be made before 1st February 1977—

(*a*) paragraphs 3 and 4 of Schedule 13 shall have effect as if for the word "sixteen" there were substituted the word "twenty-one", and

(*b*) paragraphs 5, 6 and 7 of that Schedule shall not apply.

Legal proceedings

18. Notwithstanding the repeal of any enactment by this Act, the Employment Appeal Tribunal and the industrial tribunals may continue to exercise the jurisdiction conferred on them by or under any enactment which is repealed by this Act with respect to matters arising out of or in connection with the repealed enactments.

House of Commons staff

1975 c. 71.

19. Section 122 of the Employment Protection Act 1975 shall, until 1st January 1979, have effect as if it applied the enactments which are mentioned in subsection (1) of section 139 of this Act to relevant members of the House of Commons staff (within the meaning of the said section 122).

Section 159.

SCHEDULE 16

Consequential Amendments

House of Commons Offices Act 1846 (9 & 10 Vict. c.77)

1. In section 5 of the House of Commons Offices Act 1846, after the words "Employment Protection Act 1975" there are inserted the words "the Employment Protection (Consolidation) Act 1978".

Trade Union Act 1913 (2 & 3 Geo. 5. c.30)

2. In section 5A of the Trade Union Act 1913, for the words "section 88(2) of the Employment Protection Act 1975" there are substituted the words "section 136(2) of the Employment Protection (Consolidation) Act 1978".

Iron and Steel Act 1949 (12, 13 & 14 Geo. 6. c.72)

3.—(1) In section 40 of the Iron and Steel Act 1949, in subsection (3), for the words from "a tribunal" to the end there are substituted the words "an industrial tribunal.".

(2) In section 41 of the said Act of 1949, in subsection (3), for the words from "a tribunal" to the end there are substituted the words "an industrial tribunal".

Industrial Training Act 1964 (c. 16)

4.—(1) In section 4(7) of the Industrial Training Act 1964, for the words from "a tribunal" to "Act" there are substituted the words "an industrial tribunal".

(2) For subsection (1) of section 12 of the said Act of 1964 there is substituted the following subsection—

"(1) A person assessed to levy imposed under this Act may appeal to an industrial tribunal.".

Trade Union (Amalgamations, etc.) Act 1964 (c.24)

5. In section 4(8) of the Trade Union (Amalgamations, etc.) Act 1964, for the words "section 88(2) of the Employment Protection Act 1975" there are substituted the words "section 136(2) of the Employment Protection (Consolidation) Act 1978".

Transport Act 1968 (c. 73)

6. In section 135(4)(b) of the Transport Act 1968, for the words from "a tribunal" to the end there are substituted the words "an industrial tribunal.".

Transport (London) Act 1969 (c.35)

7.—(1) In section 37(4)(b) of the Transport (London) Act 1969, for the words from "a tribunal" to the end there are substituted the words "an industrial tribunal.".

(2) In paragraph 6 of Schedule 2 to the said Act of 1969, for the words "paragraph 10(3) of Schedule 1 to the Contracts of Employment Act 1963 and section 8(2) of the Redundancy Payments Act 1965, for the purposes of those Acts" there are substituted the words "section 151(1) of and paragraph 17(3) of Schedule 13 to the Employment Protection (Consolidation) Act 1978, for the purposes of that Act".

Post Office Act 1969 (c.48)

8. In paragraph 33 of Schedule 9 to the Post Office Act 1969—

(a) in sub-paragraph (1) for the words "sections 1 and 2 of the Contracts of Employment Act 1963, Schedule 1" there are substituted the words "sections 49 and 50 and Part VI of the Employment Protection (Consolidation) Act 1978, Schedule 13", for the words "the said Act of 1963" there are substituted the words "the said Act of 1978"; and for the words "twenty-one hours" there are substituted the words "sixteen hours";

(b) in sub-paragraph (2), for the words "Schedule 1 to the said Act of 1963" there are substituted the words "Schedule 13 to the said Act of 1978";

(c) in sub-paragraph (3), for the words "7 of Schedule 2 to the said Act of 1963" there are substituted the words "10 of Schedule 14 to the said Act of 1978" and for the words from "paragraph 10" to the end there are substituted the words "Schedule 13 to that Act shall be construed as a reference to that Schedule as it has effect by virtue of sub-paragraph (1) above.";

(d) in sub-paragraph (4), for the words "the said Act of 1963" and "Schedule 1" there are substituted respectively the words "the said Act of 1978" and "Schedule 13";

Sch. 16

(e) at the end there is added the following sub-paragraph—
"(6) This paragraph applies notwithstanding the provisions of section 99 of the Employment Protection (Consolidation) Act 1978.".

Income and Corporation Taxes Act 1970 (c.10)

9.—(1) In section 412(6) of the Income and Corporation Taxes Act 1970, for the words " section 32 of the Redundancy Payments Act 1965 " there are substituted the words " section 106 of the Employment Protection (Consolidation) Act 1978 ".

(2) In section 412(7) of the said Act of 1970—
  (a) for the words " Part II of the Redundancy Payments Act 1965 " there are substituted the words " the Employment Protection (Consolidation) Act 1978 " ;
  (b) for the words " section 30(2) of the Redundancy Payments Act 1965 " there are substituted the words " section 104(2) of the Employment Protection (Consolidation) Act 1978 " ;
  (c) for the words " Schedule 5 to the Redundancy Payments Act 1965 " there are substituted the words " Schedule 6 to the Employment Protection (Consolidation) Act 1978 " ;
  (d) for the words " the Redundancy Payments Act 1965 " in paragraph (c) of the said section 412(7), there are substituted the words " the Employment Protection (Consolidation) Act 1978 ".

Atomic Energy Authority Act 1971 (c.11)

10.—(1) In subsection (1) of section 10 of the Atomic Energy Authority Act 1971, for the words " section 22 of the Redundancy Payments Act 1965 " there are substituted the words " section 93 of the Employment Protection (Consolidation) Act 1978 ".

(2) In subsection (2) of the said section 10—
  (a) for the words " section 4 of the Contracts of Employment Act 1963 " there are substituted the words " sections 1 to 4 of the Employment Protection (Consolidation) Act 1978 " ;
  (b) for the words " subsection (8) of that section ", in both places where they occur, there are substituted the words " section 5 of the said Act of 1978 " ;
  (c) for the words " the said section 4 " there are substituted the words " the said sections 1 to 4 ".

(3) In subsection (3) of the said section 10—
  (a) for the words " Section 4A(1) of the Contracts of Employment Act 1963 " there are substituted the words " Section 11 of the Employment Protection (Consolidation) Act 1978 " ;
  (b) for the words " section 4 " there are substituted the words " sections 1 to 4 ".

(4) In subsection (4) of the said section 10—
  (a) for the words from the beginning to " Redundancy Payments Act 1965 " there are substituted the words " For the

purposes of Schedule 13 to the said Act of 1978 (computation of period of employment)";

(b) for the words "paragraph 10" there are substituted the words "paragraph 17".

Tribunals and Inquiries Act 1971 (c.62)

11. In section 13 of the Tribunals and Inquiries Act 1971, the following subsection is inserted after subsection (1)—

"(1A) Subsection (1) of this section shall not apply in relation to proceedings before industrial tribunals which arise under or by virtue of any of the enactments mentioned in section 136(1) of the Employment Protection (Consolidation) Act 1978.".

Civil Aviation Act 1971 (c.75)

12.—(1) In paragraph 1 of Schedule 9 to the Civil Aviation Act 1971—

(a) in sub-paragraph (1) for the words "sections 1 and 2 of the Contracts of Employment Act 1963, Schedule 1" there are substituted the words "sections 49 and 50 and Part VI of the Employment Protection (Consolidation) Act 1978, Schedule 13", for the words "the said Act of 1963" there are substituted the words "the said Act of 1978"; and for the words "twenty-one hours" there are substituted the words "sixteen hours";

(b) in sub-paragraph (2), for the words "Schedule 1 to the said Act of 1963" there are substituted the words "Schedule 13 to the said Act of 1978";

(c) in sub-paragraph (3), for the words "7 of Schedule 2 to the said Act of 1963" there are substituted the words "10 of Schedule 14 to the said Act of 1978" and for the words from "paragraph 10" to the end there are substituted the words "Schedule 13 to that Act shall be construed as a reference to that Schedule as it has effect by virtue of sub-paragraph (1) above.";

(d) in sub-paragraph (4), for the words "the said Act of 1963" and "Schedule 1" there are substituted respectively the words "the said Act of 1978" and "Schedule 13";

(e) at the end there is added the following sub-paragraph—

"(6) This paragraph applies notwithstanding the provisions of section 99 of the Employment Protection (Consolidation) Act 1978.".

(2) In paragraph 4 of the said Schedule 9—

(a) for the words "paragraph 10(2) of Schedule 1 to the Contracts of Employment Act 1963 and section 13(1) of the Redundancy Payments Act 1965" there are substituted the words "section 94(1) of and paragraph 17(2) of Schedule 13 to the Employment Protection (Consolidation) Act 1978";

(b) for the words "the said section 13(1)" there are substituted the words "the said section 94(1)";

SCH. 16

(c) for the words from "the said Act of 1963" to "Act of 1965" there are substituted the words "the said paragraph 17(2) and the references to the said section 94(1)", and after the words "a reference" there are inserted the words "to paragraph 10(2) of Schedule 1".

Transport Holding Company Act 1972 (c.14)

13.—(1) In section 2(3)(c) of the Transport Holding Company Act 1972, for the words from "a tribunal" to the end there are substituted the words "an industrial tribunal.".

(2) In section 2(7) of the said Act of 1972, for the words "a tribunal established under section 12 of the Industrial Training Act 1964" there are substituted the words "an industrial tribunal".

Finance Act 1972 (c.41)

14. In paragraph 1(b) of Part V of Schedule 12 to the Finance Act 1972, for the words "Redundancy Payments Act 1965" there are substituted the words "Employment Protection (Consolidation) Act 1978".

British Library Act 1972 (c.54)

15. In paragraph 13(3)(a) of the Schedule to the British Library Act 1972, for the words "the Acts of 1963 and 1965" there are substituted the words "the Employment Protection (Consolidation) Act 1978".

Gas Act 1972 (c.60)

16. In section 36(5) of the Gas Act 1972, for the words from "a tribunal" to the end there are substituted the words "an industrial tribunal.".

Health and Safety at Work etc. Act 1974 (c. 37)

17. The following subsection is inserted in section 80 of the Health and Safety at Work etc. Act 1974 after subsection (2)—

"(2A) Subsection (1) above shall apply to provisions in the Employment Protection (Consolidation) Act 1978 which re-enact provisions previously contained in the Redundancy Payments Act 1965, the Contracts of Employment Act 1972 or the Trade Union and Labour Relations Act 1974 as it applies to provisions contained in Acts passed before or in the same Session as this Act.".

Trade Union and Labour Relations Act 1974 (c.52)

18. In section 8(7) of the Trade Union and Labour Relations Act 1974, for the words "section 88(3) of the Employment Protection Act 1975" there are substituted the words "section 136(3) of the Employment Protection (Consolidation) Act 1978".

Social Security Act 1975 (c. 14)

19.—(1) In section 114 of the Social Security Act 1975, the following subsection is inserted after subsection (2)—

"(2A) It is hereby declared for the avoidance of doubt that the power to make regulations under subsection (1) above includes power to make regulations for the determination of any question arising as to the total or partial recoupment of unemployment benefit in pursuance of regulations under section 132 of the Employment Protection (Consolidation) Act 1978 (including any decision as to the amount of benefit).".

(2) In section 139 of the said Act of 1975, after subsection (2) there is inserted the following subsection—

"(2A) Subsection (1) above does not apply to regulations made under this Act and contained in a statutory instrument which states that the regulations provide only that a day in respect of which there is payable a particular description of any payment to which section 132 of the Employment Protection (Consolidation) Act 1978 (recoupment of unemployment and supplementary benefits) applies shall not be treated as a day of unemployment for the purposes of entitlement to unemployment benefit.".

Sex Discrimination Act 1975 (c.65)

20.—(1) In section 65(2) of the Sex Discrimination Act 1975, for the words "paragraph 20 of Schedule 1 to the Trade Union and Labour Relations Act 1974" there are substituted the words "section 75 of the Employment Protection (Consolidation) Act 1978".

(2) In section 75(5)(c) of the said Act of 1975 for the words "paragraph 21 of Schedule 1 to the Trade Union and Labour Relations Act 1974." there are substituted the words "paragraph 1 of Schedule 9 to the Employment Protection (Consolidation) Act 1978.".

Scottish Development Agency Act 1975 (c. 69)

21. In paragraph 6 of Schedule 3 to the Scottish Development Agency Act 1975, for sub-paragraphs (a), (b) and (c) there are substituted the words "the Employment Protection (Consolidation) Act 1978".

Welsh Development Agency Act 1975 (c. 70)

22. In paragraph 7 of Schedule 2 to the Welsh Development Agency Act 1975, for sub-paragraphs (a), (b) and (c) there are substituted the words "the Employment Protection (Consolidation) Act 1978".

Employment Protection Act 1975 (c.71)

23.—(1) The Employment Protection Act 1975 shall be amended in accordance with the following provisions of this paragraph.

(2) In section 6(2)—

(a) the words from "in relation to" to "that is to say" shall be omitted;

(b) for the words "section 57 below; and" there are substituted the words "section 27 of the Employment Protection (Consolidation) Act 1978, including guidance on the circumstances in which a trade union official is to be permitted to take time off under that section in respect of duties connected with industrial action; and";

SCH. 16

(c) for the words " section 58 below " there are substituted the words " section 28 of the said Act of 1978, including guidance on the question whether, and the circumstances in which, a trade union member is to be permitted to take time off under that section for trade union activities connected with industrial action.".

(3) In section 8(9), for the words " section 88(3) below " there are substituted the words " section 136(3) of the Employment Protection (Consolidation) Act 1978 ".

(4) In section 102(4), for the words " Schedule 2 to the Contracts of Employment Act 1972 " there are substituted the words " Schedule 3 to the Employment Protection (Consolidation) Act 1978 ", and for the words " section 1(1) " there are substituted the words " section 49(1) ".

(5) In section 104(1)(a), for the words " section 30(1) of the Redundancy Payments Act 1965 " there are substituted the words " section 104(1) of the Employment Protection (Consolidation) Act 1978 ".

(6) In section 106(3), for the words from the beginning to " Redundancy Payments Act 1965 " there are substituted the words " Schedule 14 to the Employment Protection (Consolidation) Act 1978 shall apply for the calculation of a week's pay for the purposes of section 102 above, and, for the purposes of Part II of that Schedule, the calculation date is—

(a) in the case of an employee who was dismissed before the date on which the protective award was made, the date which by virtue of paragraph 7(1)(k) or (l) of the said Schedule 14 ".

(7) In section 108(1), for the words " paragraph 21 of Schedule 1 to the 1974 Act " there are substituted the words " paragraph 1 of Schedule 9 to the Employment Protection (Consolidation) Act 1978 ".

(8) In section 119(1), for the words " Parts II and IV of this Act apply " there are substituted the words " Part IV of this Act applies ".

(9) In section 119, the following subsection is added at the end—

" (17) Schedule 13 to the Employment Protection (Consolidation) Act 1978 and, so far as they modify that Schedule, any order under section 7 of that Act and any regulations under paragraph 20 of that Schedule, shall have effect for the purposes of this section in determining for what period an employee has been continuously employed; and, for the purposes of any proceedings brought under or by virtue of this Act, a person's employment during any period shall, unless the contrary is shown, be presumed to have been continuous.".

(10) In section 121(5), for the words " Schedule 3 to the Redundancy Payments Act 1965 " there are substituted the words " Schedule 5 to the Employment Protection (Consolidation) Act 1978 ".

(11) In section 121(6) and (7), for the words "section 41(3) of the Redundancy Payments Act 1965" there are substituted the words "section 111(3) of the Employment Protection (Consolidation) Act 1978".

SCH. 16

(12) In section 125(1) for the words from the beginning to "Part III of that Schedule" there are substituted the words "The provisions of the 1974 Act specified in Part III of Schedule 16 to this Act".

(13) In section 126(1), for the words "paragraph 5 of Schedule 1 to the 1974 Act" there are substituted the words "section 55 of the Employment Protection (Consolidation) Act 1978".

New Towns (Amendment) Act 1976 (c. 68)

24. In section 13 of the New Towns (Amendment) Act 1976—
   (a) in subsection (5), for the words "Schedule 1 to the Contracts of Employment Act 1972" there are substituted the words "Schedule 13 to the Employment Protection (Consolidation) Act 1978";
   (b) in subsection (6), for the words "section 13 of the Redundancy Payments Act 1965" there are substituted the words "section 94 of the Employment Protection (Consolidation) Act 1978".

Race Relations Act 1976 (c.74)

25.—(1) The Race Relations Act 1976 shall be amended in accordance with the following provisions of this paragraph.

(2) In section 56(2) for the words "paragraph 20 of Schedule 1 to the Trade Union and Labour Relations Act 1974" there are substituted the words "section 75 of the Employment Protection (Consolidation) Act 1978".

(3) In section 66(7) for the words "paragraph 21 of Schedule 1 to the Trade Union and Labour Relations Act 1974" there are substituted the words "paragraph 1 of Schedule 9 to the Employment Protection (Consolidation) Act 1978".

(4) In paragraph 11 of Schedule 2—
   (a) in sub-paragraph (3) for the words "the Redundancy Payments Act 1965" there are substituted the words "Part VI of the Employment Protection (Consolidation) Act 1978";
   (b) for sub-paragraph (4)(a) and (b) there is substituted the following paragraph—
      "(a) the Employment Protection (Consolidation) Act 1978 except Part VI of that Act;".

Development of Rural Wales Act 1976 (c. 75)

26. In both paragraph 6 of Schedule 2 and paragraph 6 of Schedule 6 to the Development of Rural Wales Act 1976, for sub-paragraphs (a), (b) and (c) there are substituted the words "the Employment Protection (Consolidation) Act 1978".

SCH. 16

Dock Work Regulation Act 1976 (c. 79)

27.—(1) In section 14(7) of the Dock Work Regulation Act 1976 for the words " subsections (1), (5) and (6) above " there are substituted the words " subsection (6) above ".

(2) In paragraph 17(1) of Schedule 1 to the said Act of 1976, for the words " Schedule 1 to the Contracts of Employment Act 1972 " there are substituted the words " Schedule 13 to the Employment Protection (Consolidation) Act 1978 ".

Aircraft and Shipbuilding Industries Act 1977 (c. 3)

28. In both section 49(10) and section 50(3)(*b*) of the Aircraft and Shipbuilding Industries Act 1977, for the words " a tribunal established under section 12 of the Industrial Training Act 1964 or, as the case may require " there are substituted the words " an industrial tribunal or, as the case may require, a tribunal established under ".

Social Security (Miscellaneous Provisions) Act 1977 (c. 5)

29. In section 18 of the Social Security (Miscellaneous Provisions) Act 1977—

(*a*) in subsection (1)(*c*), for " Act 1975 " there shall be substituted " (Consolidation) Act 1978 " ;

(*b*) in subsection (2)(*a*), for the words " section 43 of the Employment Protection Act 1975 " there are substituted the words " section 40 of the Employment Protection (Consolidation) Act 1978 " ;

(*c*) in subsection (2)(*b*), for " 64(3)(*a*) " and " 45(1) " there are substituted " 122(3)(*a*) " and " 42(1) " respectively ;

(*d*) in subsection (2)(*e*), for the words " that Act " there are substituted the words " the Employment Protection Act 1975 ".

New Towns (Scotland) Act 1977 (c. 16)

30. In section 3(6) of the New Towns (Scotland) Act 1977 for paragraphs (*a*), (*b*) and (*c*) there are substituted the words " Parts I, IV, V and VI of the Employment Protection (Consolidation) Act 1978 ".

Housing (Homeless Persons) Act 1977 (c. 48)

31. In section 14(4) of the Housing (Homeless Persons) Act 1977—

(*a*) in paragraph (*a*), for the words " section 13 of the Redundancy Payments Act 1965 " there are substituted the words " section 94 of the Employment Protection (Consolidation) Act 1978 " ;

(*b*) in paragraph (*b*), for the words " Schedule 1 to the Contracts of Employment Act 1972 " there are substituted the words " Schedule 13 to the said Act of 1978 ", and the words " sections 1 and 2 of " shall cease to have effect.

National Health Service Act 1977 (c. 49)

32. In paragraph 13(1)(b) of Schedule 14 to the National Health Service Act 1977, the reference to paragraph 106 of Schedule 4 to the National Health Service Reorganisation Act 1973 shall cease to have effect, and, accordingly, for that reference to paragraph 106 there is substituted a reference to paragraph 107 of the said Schedule 4.

Scotland Act 1978 (c. 00)

33. In section 33 of the Scotland Act 1978—

(a) in subsection (1), for paragraphs (a) and (b) there is substituted the following paragraph—

"(a) Parts I (so far as it relates to itemised pay statements), II, III (except section 44), V, VIII and IX and section 53 of the Employment Protection (Consolidation) Act 1978 ; and ",

and for the words " section 121 of the Employment Protection Act 1975 " there are substituted the words " section 138 of the Employment Protection (Consolidation) Act 1978 " ;

(b) in subsection (2), for the words " paragraph 21(5)(c) of Schedule 1 to the Act of 1974 " there are substituted the words " paragraph 1(5)(c) of Schedule 9 to the Employment Protection (Consolidation) Act 1978 ".

House of Commons (Administration) Act 1978 (c.36)

34. In paragraph 1 of Schedule 2 to the House of Commons (Administration) Act 1978, after the words " the Employment Protection Act 1975 " there are inserted the words " and section 139 of the Employment Protection (Consolidation) Act 1978 ".

Section 159.

SCHEDULE 17

Repeals

Chapter	Short title	Extent of repeal
1964 c. 16.	Industrial Training Act 1964.	Section 12(2B), (3) and (4).
1965 c. 62.	Redundancy Payments Act 1965.	Sections 1 to 26. Sections 30 to 44. Sections 46 to 55 except section 55(6)(*b*). Sections 56 to 58. In section 59, subsection (2) and in subsection (3) the words " except the last preceding section ". Schedules 1 to 9.
1967 c. 17.	Iron and Steel Act 1967.	In section 31, in subsection (3), paragraph (*c*) and all the words following paragraph (*c*), and subsections (4)(*b*) and (6).
1967 c. 28.	Superannuation (Miscellaneous Provisions) Act 1967.	Section 9.
1968 c. 13.	National Loans Act 1968.	In Schedule 1, the paragraph relating to the Redundancy Payments Act 1965.
1969 c. 8.	Redundancy Rebates Act 1969.	The whole Act.
1969 c. 48.	Post Office Act 1969.	In Schedule 9, paragraph 34.
1970 c. 41.	Equal Pay Act 1970.	Section 2(7).
1971 c. 75.	Civil Aviation Act 1971.	In Schedule 9, paragraph 2.
1972 c. 11.	Superannuation Act 1972.	In Schedule 6, paragraphs 54 and 55.
1972 c. 53.	Contracts of Employment Act 1972.	The whole Act.
1972 c. 54.	British Library Act 1972.	In paragraph 13(2) of the Schedule, the definition of " the Act of 1963 ".
1972 c. 58.	National Health Service (Scotland) Act 1972.	In Schedule 6, paragraph 130.
1973 c. 32.	National Health Service Reorganisation Act 1973.	In Schedule 4, paragraph 106.
1973 c. 38.	Social Security Act 1973.	In Schedule 27, paragraphs 54 to 59.
1973 c. 50.	Employment and Training Act 1973.	In Schedule 2 in Part I, paragraph 15.
1974 c. 52.	Trade Union and Labour Relations Act 1974.	In section 1(2), paragraphs (*b*) and (*c*) and, in paragraph (*d*), the references to sections 146, 148, 149, 150 and 151 of the 1971 Act. In section 30(1), the definitions of " dismissal procedures agreement ", " position " and " job ".

Chapter	Short title	Extent of repeal
1974 c. 52—cont.	Trade Union and Labour Relations Act 1974—cont.	In Schedule 1, paragraphs 4 to 16, 17(1), 18, 20 to 27 and 30, in paragraph 32, sub-paragraphs (1)(*b*) and (2)(*b*) to (*e*) and, in paragraph 33, sub-paragraphs (3)(*c*) and (*d*) and (4A). In Schedule 3, paragraph 16. In Schedule 4, paragraphs 1, 3 and 6(4).
1975 c. 18.	Social Security (Consequential Provisions) Act 1975.	In Schedule 2, paragraphs 19 to 23.
1975 c. 60.	Social Security Pensions Act 1975.	Section 30(5).

1975 c. 71.	Employment Protection Act 1975.	Part II except section 40.
		Section 108(2) to (8).
		Section 109.
		Section 112.
		In section 118(2), in paragraph (*a*) the words " section 22 above or " and " section 28 or, as the case may be," and paragraphs (*b*) and (*c*).
		In section 119—
		  subsection (2);
		  in subsection (3) the figures from " 22 " to " 70 ";
		  in subsection (4) the figures from " 22 " to " 81 ";
		  in subsection (5), the figures from " 22 " to " 81 ";
		  in subsection (7) the figures " 22 " and " 29 ";
		  subsections (8) to (11);
		  in subsection (12) the figures from " 59 " to " 81 ".
		Section 120.
		In section 121—
		  in subsection (1), the reference to sections 47 and 63 to 69;
		  in subsection (5), the reference to sections 47(3) and (4) and 68(3) and (4);
		  subsection (8).
		In section 122(1), the words " Schedule 1 to the Contracts of Employment Act 1972 and Parts I and II of Schedule 1 to the 1974 Act "; and in paragraph (*d*), the words " paragraph 21(5)(*c*) of Schedule 1 to the 1974 Act and ".

Sch. 17

Chapter	Short title	Extent of repeal

1975 c. 71—*cont.*	Employment Protection Act 1975—*cont.*	In section 122, subsection (3), in subsection (4) the definition of " civil employment claim " and in subsection (5) the words from " and of the Redundancy " to " employment claim ".
		In section 123(2)(*b*) the words " 28 or ".
		In section 124, subsections (2) to (4).
		In section 126—
		  in subsection (1), the definitions of " guarantee payment " and " maternity pay ";
		  subsections (3) and (5).
		In section 127—
		  in subsection (1), paragraphs (*c*) and (*d*);
		  in subsection (3)(*g*), the words from " the following " to " also of ".
		In section 128—
		  in subsection (1), the words " or of the 1974 Act so far as it relates to unfair dismissal " and " and the 1974 Act ";
		  subsection (2);
		  in subsection (3), the words " and the relevant provisions of the 1974 Act " in both places where they occur, and the words " or the relevant provisions of the 1974 Act ".
		Section 129(2).
		Schedules 2 to 6.
		In Schedule 12—
		  in paragraph 1, the words from " and " to the end;
		  paragraphs 8 to 12.
		In Schedule 16—
		  Parts I and II;
		  in Part III, paragraphs 8 to 30 and 34;
		  in Part IV, paragraph 14.
		In Schedule 17, paragraphs 7 to 10, 16 and 17.

1976 c. 7.	Trade Union and Labour Relations (Amendment) Act 1976.	Section 1(*e*). Section 3(5) and (6).
1976 c. 68.	New Towns (Amendment) Act 1976.	In section 13(5), the words " sections 1 and 2 of ".
1976 c. 71.	Supplementary Benefits Act 1976.	In Schedule 7, paragraph 40.

Chapter	Short title	Extent of repeal
1976 c. 74.	Race Relations Act 1976.	In Schedule 3, paragraphs 1(2), (3) and (4).
1976 c. 79.	Dock Work Regulation Act 1976.	In section 14, subsections (1) to (5) and in subsection (6), paragraph (*a*) and so much of paragraph (*b*) as relates to sections 22, 29, 61, 64, 65 and 70 of the Employment Protection Act 1975. In Schedule 1, paragraph 17(2).
1977 c. 5.	Social Security (Miscellaneous Provisions) Act 1977.	Section 16.
1977 c. 22.	Redundancy Rebates Act 1977.	The whole Act.
1977 c. 38.	Administration of Justice Act 1977.	Section 6. Section 32(11).
1977 c. 48.	Housing (Homeless Persons) Act 1977.	In section 14(4)(b), the words " sections 1 and 2 of ".

Corrections

Errors appear in the first impression (August 1978) of this Act and the following corrections have been incorporated into this reprint.

Page 24, last line, after first ' of ' insert ' a '

Page 69, section 90(2)(*a*), ' section 8 ' should be ' section 88 '

PRINTED IN ENGLAND BY MIKE LYNN
Controller and Chief Executive of Her Majesty's Stationery Office and
Queen's Printer of Acts of Parliament.

1st Impression August 1978
8th Impression January 1996

Printed in the United Kingdom for HMSO
Dd 5065254 C13 1/96 56219 ON 343644

192 c. 44 *Employment Protection (Consolidation) Act 1978*